Finding Joy in the West

A Quest to Ride My Bike in All Fifty States

Joy M. Walker

Finding Joy in the West:

A Quest to Ride My Bike in All Fifty States

published by

The Spotted Feather, an imprint of Colorful Crow Publishing.

Praise for *Finding Joy in the West*

"'Let me show you my vacation pictures,' is a line that typically yields a mental groan to most bystanders. That sentiment turns to joy (pun intended) when the narrator is a master storyteller with a penchant for compelling adventures and cliff-hanging climaxes. *Finding Joy in the West* is a wild ride that will leave you experiencing a multitude of emotions as you vicariously tour this great land . . . with Joy."

Chip R. Bell
Senior partner with Chip Bell Group
Senior advisor to On3, Inc.
Author of *Inside Your Customer's Imagination*

"Many of us take pride in naming the states we've visited. But few of us can claim to have ridden our bikes in all fifty states! That's Joy M. Walker's dream—her hope! And it's more than wishful thinking—she has a plan and more than enough energy and commitment to make it happen—for this is what gives her joy! Hiking, dipping her feet into new waters, riding on rocky trails and narrow roads, making new friends, and taking chances—here is where the author discovers herself, uncovers her joy, finds God. Ride along with her on this exciting journey heading west toward California through the northern tier of states: Pike's Peak State Park, Mount Rushmore, Glacier National Park and so much more. You'll be dusting off your bicycle long before you complete this exciting adventure, travel memoir. It's a great read!"

Dr. Beverly J. Armento
Educator, Speaker, Advocate,
Author of *Seeing Eye Girl: A Memoir of Madness, Resilience, and Hope*
Life's Turning Points: A Personal Reflection Journal

Praise for *Finding Joy in the West*

"Absolutely captivating! In *Finding Joy in the West,* Joy Walker takes readers on an exhilarating journey across the United States, weaving a journey of adventure, joy, and personal fulfillment in every state she visits. Her vivid storytelling makes you feel as though you're right there beside her, experiencing each unique landscape and heartwarming encounter. This book is a must-read for anyone with a passion for travel and a thirst for adventure. By the end of this inspiring journey, you'll find your own life enriched and your spirit uplifted. Highly recommended!"

Dan Blanchard
Teacher, Youth Leader, Speaker, Best Selling Author of *A Fighting Chance: A 40-year Journey from My Birth Until My Brother's Death*

"*Finding Joy in the West* is an inspiring journey of resilience, discovery, and, most of all, joy. Joy's adventurous spirit and determination to cycle through all fifty states, despite many challenges, make this book a compelling read for anyone seeking adventure or personal growth. Her storytelling draws readers in with warmth, humor, and an openness that makes you feel like you're traveling alongside her.

Through breathtaking landscapes, encounters with strangers who become friends, and reflections on faith and perseverance, Joy reminds us that the road—no matter how winding or uncertain—leads to something meaningful. This book is a must-read for adventurers, dreamers, and anyone looking for a book that will uplift and inspire."

Patti P. Phillips, Ph.D.
Chief Executive Officer ROI Institute, Inc.
Author of *Show the Value of What You Do*

For Thomas Donaldson Walker and Helen Margaret Koenke Walker

Thanks for naming me Joy Margaret Walker
and believing in me when I did not believe in myself.
You will forever be my heroes.

Contents

Prologue

"No, no, no. It can't be broken. Not again. Please, no."

"Yes," the doctor said, with a sympathetic tone. "I hate to break it to you, but yes, you have two significant vertical fractures of your kneecap, and your ligaments are torn. We can give you a prescription for pain, a brace, and crutches."

Had she heard me tell my cousin, Ivan, on the way to the hospital that I needed drugs, an immobilizer, and crutches—and I'd be walking in six to twelve weeks?

Six years earlier, a different emergency room doctor had delivered a similar diagnosis. He pointed out three horizontal fractures on the same kneecap and suggested surgery. That time, I was home. This time, I was two thousand miles from Georgia in Spokane. As I replayed the last moments of the night before in my mind, I couldn't help but wish I had looked down before taking that final, fateful step.

Three months earlier, I had begun an RV trip from my home in Georgia to the West Coast with aspirations of riding my bicycle in twenty-five states. Completing this leg of my journey would put me over the halfway mark of my post-retirement dream of riding in all fifty.

Along the way, I planned to visit family and friends, explore state and national parks, and indulge in any unexpected adventures that might arise. After exploring the northern states, I would travel through California and return home via the southern states. Though storms and detours slowed me down, all was unfolding mostly as planned until shortly after arriving at my cousins' home in Spokane. That's when I stepped into a hole and blew out my knee, bringing my trip to a screeching halt.

But before I get to how my journey came to an end, let me take you back fifty years to where this dream began. This is my story of finding joy in riding my bike, in God's creations, in the people he placed in my path, and in the trials that led me to grow as I traveled.

CHAPTER ONE

A Teacher and a Real Author

JUNE 1969 – JUNE 2018

The summer I turned five, my dad taught me to ride my first bike, holding the seat and running alongside until I was riding on my own. As soon as I realized he was no longer holding on, my skinny, towheaded self tumbled into the grass.

"You're okay. Get back on."

I did and I have not stopped since. I love to ride, and it all started with my dad on the sidewalk in front of our house. There are six of us Walker children. I'm the youngest. Then there's Cathy, Tom, Sandi, Lynn, and Sherrie, the oldest. There's almost a twelve-year gap between the oldest and youngest. My family means the world to me, and you'll read about each of my siblings in these pages.

The summer I was nine, my brother, Tom, at fifteen, biked from Oregon to Delaware in four weeks. He made the trip sound like a blast—eighty guys touching their wheels in both oceans, stopping at root beer stands, riding across the desert, watching people gasp when he told them where they were riding to, racing to state lines and more. A year later, not to be outdone by her younger brother, my sister Sandi signed up for the same trip. Now that I was ten, I was determined to join her. I didn't want to be left out of the fun. If Tom and Sandi could ride across the country, I knew I could too. But Sandi told me all the reasons I couldn't go, as if she had anything to do with it. I wasn't eighteen. The trip required riding early every day (and no one would want to hear me gripe about that). I would have to ride in the rain, and I would be the baby on the trip. She tried her best to dissuade me, but I continued to beg.

As an early birthday present, my parents bought me a Schwinn Varsity ten-speed and Sandi took me along on her training rides. On one memorable occasion, we rode for miles down a major thoroughfare that was being re-tarred. The tar from Sandi's tire flung back in my face and into my mouth. Tar also flew up from my back tire and all over my brand-new shirt. I whined and whined about this until Sandi threatened to never let me ride with her again. Suddenly, the taste of tar and the stinking mess on my bike and shirt weren't so bad after all.

One June day, Sandi and I strapped bathing suits and towels to our handlebars, planning to ride to a lake in Warsaw, Indiana, forty miles away where we would eat at my favorite restaurant, swim, and then ride home. Other than the traffic whooshing by us without moving over, the ride to Warsaw was uneventful. However, as soon as we arrived at Arby's, I remembered I had a makeup piano lesson that afternoon at 3:30. We skipped the beach and rode home as fast as we could until unexpected rain slowed us down. The rain I could deal with. It was the spray from Sandi's wheel that made me cry. She insisted I stay close, which meant I ate road grime and cried all the way home. After the fastest bath of my childhood, she drove me across town just in time for my lesson.

That eighty miles was the longest my little ten-year-old self had ever ridden and probably my sister's longest ride too. Despite not getting to go swimming and the miserable ride home, a new dream was born. Sandi rode across the country that summer without me. I went back to bike riding with my friends, but I knew that one day I, too, would ride my bike across the country. I, too, would have the joy of saying I had ridden my bike all the way across this great country of ours.

***

In 2008, my mother died unexpectedly at the age of 79. Never had I endured such emotional pain. My mom was everything to me. She was taken from me fifteen to twenty years before I had expected. How would I—how could I—ever be happy again? I couldn't laugh for a year. In my mind, it seemed disrespectful to *go on enjoying life* when my mom was no longer with us. To move on without her seemed like forgetting her. Everything I did made me think of her. Many nights I missed her so much that I cried myself to sleep thinking maybe, somehow, I could bring her back.

As part of my grieving process and to honor my mom's memory, I opted to do something she had wanted me to do for ten years. The next year, I signed up for a weeklong bike ride called Pedal Across Lower Michigan (PALM) with her younger brother, Wil. Wil had been riding the PALM since his mid-sixties. Organizers only accepted 600 riders, so to ensure a spot, we signed up together on the first day of registration in January 2009.

In June I set off to ride my bike across Lower Michigan with my seventy-eight-year-old uncle, hoping to feel closer to my mom by developing a closer relationship with her brother. As we rode fifty miles each day, ate in cafeterias, and camped in tents on high school football fields each night, I hoped Wil would tell me stories about them growing up together.

As we were setting up my tent the first night, Wil said, "Did your mom tell you about learning to drive?"

"She always told me you taught her."

"That's right. I was fourteen and she was sixteen. No one else would teach her so she asked me since she knew I'd been driving the tractors on Uncle Harvey and Aunt Edna's farm for years."

"That's so cool."

"She was a fast learner. I don't remember the first time we got in the car, but we probably started out on the farm up there in Gladwin first, since we spent our summers there."

"Did you know Mom taught all six of us kids to drive?"

"I don't think I knew that, but it doesn't surprise me. Your mom was one special woman. Wish I would have told her that more often."

Tears welled up in my eyes. "Wish I could tell her one more time how special she was to me. I sure miss her."

I had anticipated Wil telling me stories like that all week, but it didn't play out like I had envisioned. I guess I forgot to give Uncle Wil his half of the script. People were around, and we talked more about what was happening in the moment. My uncle and I did have a memorable week, though, which led to us doing more rides together in the coming summers, but the story of him teaching Mom to drive is the only story about their childhood I remember him telling me. On a positive note, cycling with Wil and 598 others across Michigan reignited the old dream—my dream to ride my bike across the country.

That September I completed my doctoral degree—a Doctor of Education (Ed.D.) in teacher leadership. Three friends I made through the doctoral program—Amy, Lynn, and Jo—and I celebrated earning our degrees with a long weekend getaway to Florida in January 2010. That weekend I resolved to live life to the fullest. The most difficult, stressful two years of my life were 2008 and 2009. Enduring the pain of losing my mother, riding my bike across Michigan, and completing a degree while teaching elementary physical education had given me the strength and fortitude to believe I could fulfill that childhood dream.

It was time to explore and enjoy life like I had never really allowed myself to do, and 2010 would be a new start. During the winter and spring, I continued to teach full time, keep up my lawn and home, and train for a summer of long rides. I found an organization that supported people like me who wanted to ride across the country with a group. The route would traverse the country from San Francisco, California, to Portsmouth, New Hampshire, within the window of my summer break. It was the perfect match.

That summer was the best summer of my life. All I had to do was ride my bike for fifty-two days. I'm not saying it was void of all challenges, but my only responsibility each day was to get my luggage to the truck every morning by eight (a task I never did master) and ride my bike to the next motel approximately eighty miles away. I never pulled weeds, mowed my lawn, made a meal or even my bed, much less prepared lessons and taught.

Before the trip, I had seen little of our country. Except for a couple of family trips, I had never been west of Chicago and only twice had I been east of Ohio. That summer I rode with my heart and eyes wide open—taking it all in like naïve ten-year-old Joy. Every state had a magic of its own. From the barren mountains of Utah to the casinos of Nevada, the climbs of the Colorado Rockies to the exhilarating descent along the Arizona River, the rolling hills of Missouri and the cornfields of Illinois and Indiana, the steep mountains and valleys of the eastern states, every state and every day brought new adventures and new landscape. I couldn't get enough.

Not only had I not traveled much, at home I rarely rode with others. On the cross-country trip, I rarely rode alone. What a dream! The group was of one mind, whether they were eighteen, forty, or seventy-eight years of age and from California, Ohio, or New York. The group melded into one—one heart, one goal—to pedal every mile and get to the other side safely. Sometimes I rode with the fast group, sometimes with one other rider, and sometimes with people who took lots of breaks for photos and flats, but we were one cohesive group who loved to laugh and swap stories at dinner every night.

When twenty-nine of us (three had tour-ending accidents) dipped our wheels in the Atlantic at Wallis Sands State Beach in Portsmouth, New Hampshire, I pleaded with the staff to let us ride back to San Francisco just as I had begged my sister to let me ride across the country with her when I was ten.

As we stood, our feet and front bike tires still in the ocean, I smiled at Pam, the staff member I rode with the most.

"Pam, can we just turn around and go back to California? This has been the best summer of my life. I don't want it to end."

"Sorry, Joy. I know the end is actually the best and the worst. It's such an incredible feeling to have arrived, yet your body wants to keep moving. We'll be ready to go next June if you want to do it again."

"No. I want to go back now with this group. There's no way we could get everyone back next summer. Look! Everyone still has their bikes in the water. Quick, make an announcement that we are going back."

"Joy. It's not going to happen. Just enjoy the moment."

Just like that, the best summer of my life was over. It wasn't that I didn't want to teach. I just didn't want the trip, the riding, the camaraderie, or the summer fun to end.

I didn't want to say goodbye to my new forever friends. Investing fifty-two days in a group working toward a common goal changed me. This group would never be together again, but we would always share a special bond, stronger for the challenges we overcame that summer of 2010.

Now I had friends from all over the country—friends who, like me, had accomplished something most people don't even dream of. This was the dream of a lifetime, and no one could take that away from me. It gave me another level of confidence in myself. At the end of the trip, I was not only physically in the best shape of my life, but emotionally as well. I felt good about living what I taught my students, practicing what I was teaching.

In addition, as I biked across the country, I thought of ideas to make my next trip less challenging and more enjoyable. I wondered if I could do it faster or slower or if I could hit more southern states. Maybe friends could travel in a motorhome and take turns riding and driving. That last scenario stayed with me for several years. However, my imaginary cycling friends never emerged. To be fair, I don't recall asking anyone if they would want to do something like that, so I can't blame my friends. It just didn't happen like I played it out in my head.

Also, after all the years of running and cycling, the gnarled, unmatched feet I had inherited from my mom became increasingly painful. My right foot is two full sizes smaller than my left, which has caused problems since childhood. For the first forty years of my life, my larger left foot had usually hurt more, but over the last several years, the pain in my right foot had increased. Most days it hurts to walk in running shoes, so wearing tight cycling shoes almost made me scream in pain. In fact, when I rode alone, I *did* scream out loud many times.

In addition to my feet, other physical issues caused me to doubt my ability to ride across the country again. At birth, my right knee was not properly developed. My right leg is also smaller and shorter than the left, and the years of pushing myself beyond my limits began taking its toll on both legs and feet. In adolescence I'd developed scoliosis, and recurring knee injuries and arthritis developing in my hips added fuel to my doubts.

My body was falling apart. Though I had grown to love running as an adult, I quit running when I realized that running was causing more damage than good. But my desire to stay fit and my love of cycling would not let me give up cycling too. Ignoring pain had become my world for so long that I wondered if I would drive myself into an early wheelchair. In 2015, I switched my focus from long rides to short races called time trials, where competitors race by themselves against the clock. I threw everything I had into training for races no longer than twenty-five miles because I figured the race would be over before my feet and knees started screaming. Through diet and exercise, I trained my cardiovascular system into the best shape of my life. My resting heart rate was in the forties and my total cholesterol was below 150.

However, after two years of mediocre results on the podium, it became clear my dream needed more tweaking. It was time to focus on what I *could* do instead of my shortcomings. Riding my bike made me feel good. I knew in my gut that I could not give it up. Biking was my passion. It was my identity. By cutting back on the distances and the intensity, I believed I could ride for many years to come. That's when my dream of riding across the country again morphed into riding in every state.

The plan now was to buy a motorhome after retirement. Then I would drive around the country riding my bicycle along famous trails and around state and national parks. If I could hit the lower forty-eight in my motorhome, I might plan an Alaskan cruise and a flight to Hawaii for the finale. Then when I came home from Hawaii, my family and friends would throw a big party. Radio and newspaper reporters, newscasters, and magazine editors would flood the streets, welcoming me home. The world would celebrate with all the fanfare of the hometown hero winning the Tour de France. "Sixty-year-old retired teacher accomplishes feat no other single female has ever attempted," the headlines would say. Soon thereafter I would sell the motorhome and dive into a second career–a career as a writer. Of course this hasn't happened yet. For now, it remains my dream.

I had dreamed of being "a teacher and a real author," which is what I told everyone when I was a nine-year-old third grader. Writing about the things I love, like bicycling, traveling, making friends, and having fun everywhere I go, might be a way to get that second career off to a start. I would retire from teaching, explore the beautiful United States of America via motorhome and bicycle, and then write about my travels.

After teaching young children about the benefits of play and movement and a healthy lifestyle for thirty years, I had more than fulfilled my first dream of being a teacher. I loved teaching children—their hugs, smiles, funny ways of saying things, laughter, and aha moments had sustained me for many years, but it was time for a change. As I locked the gym doors for the last time, bittersweet emotions filled my soul, but I was ready for a new adventure—finding joy.

CHAPTER TWO

Getting Started

JUNE 2018 – MARCH 2019

Two days after my retirement, I made it a point to ride one of my regular twenty-five-mile loops from my home to mark Georgia as the first state I'd ridden my bike in post-retirement, which seemed fitting. It was a mid-afternoon ride, and one of the freest, most invigorating rides of my life. The sun shone on my face, and the wind nudged me along as if to say, "This is what retirement feels like, Joy. I will always have your back now." As soon as I pulled into my garage, I grabbed a red Sharpie and wrote an R (for retired) on Georgia on the United States map I had placed on the wall behind my bike—the same map I had used to mark the cross-country route I had ridden in 2010. This would mark Georgia as the official first state I rode in after retirement. Only forty-nine to go!

The day after my retirement party, my brother Tom and I shopped for motorhomes, but we didn't find one that screamed at me loud enough to bring it home. The next day, June 5, I drove my Honda CRV to Hilton Head Island where I rode my bike three days in a row with my friend Kim on the beach, making South Carolina the second state I marked off.

A bike ride on a trip to visit my brother Tom and his wife, Pam, in Asheville made North Carolina state number three. Asheville has beautiful trails and serious hills. Not long after, I drove with my sister Sherrie to close on her future retirement home in Delaware. While I was there, I rode nearly every day around her neighborhood. Sherrie and I traveled to Virginia, where she walked and I rode on a shaded, paved rails-to-trails path. When we traveled to Maryland to visit her oldest son James and his family, my Maryland ride started and ended at his house. With this one trip, I added Delaware, Virginia, and Maryland as states four, five, and six.

On my return to Georgia, I checked off West Virginia, which brought my total to seven. In less than two months, I had already ridden in seven states. It felt good, but I had envisioned riding from a motorhome, not from motels on busy streets like I did in Virginia and West Virginia. It was time to get serious about finding the right motorhome.

In August, I drove north to my home state of Indiana where my sister Cathy and I shopped for motorhomes in Elkhart, the well-known motorhome capital of the country. We went to several dealerships, checking out new and used motorhomes, trailers, and custom vans, to no avail. Back at home in Georgia, I searched the web, considering outlandish ideas such as flying to Texas to buy a motorhome and starting a trip from there or driving back to Indiana in my car, buying a motorhome, and heading west from Elkhart.

Nothing was going to keep me from the adventure and joy of biking in every state. After an exhaustive search on foot and on the internet, I bought a motorhome from a sales agent in Chattanooga that I had met at an RV show in February. The three-year-old 25-foot Class C (picture a UPS truck with windows), complete with two beds and a swivel writing chair, fit my needs perfectly. On the front bumper I mounted a plate that says: "Finding Joy." My friend Nancy made it before I started my trip. (Now I might have her add: "but don't follow me, I may be lost.")

One week after I purchased the motorhome, I camped at Fort Mountain State Park, an hour's drive from my home, for a trial run. To test the capability of having company in the small space, my sister Sandi, who lives eight miles from me, stayed one night. It was good to have her with me. When she left and I rode my bike at Fort Mountain, the reality that my dream was coming true hit me. I had finally found the right motorhome, and I was about to fulfill my dream of riding in all fifty states. I was ready for adventure.

The following week, I packed and prepared for a six-week absence. A friend moved into my house, and I took off to visit family and friends for a maiden voyage, as Sandi called it. I departed on September 15, stayed at state parks, and rode my bike in Tennessee and Kentucky, states eight and nine. Next, I stopped to visit with my friend Amy in Ohio. I rode a couple of hours on the Little Miami Scenic Trail from the Milford trailhead near her home, making Ohio an even ten states since retirement. *Ten states already! I'm one-fifth of the way to my goal!* From Amy's, I drove to my hometown of Fort Wayne, Indiana, and rode by myself and with my friend

Kathy all over the city, on the streets near my childhood home and high school, and on the twenty-six-mile Rivergreenway Trail, making my home state number eleven.

It was in Fort Wayne that my motorhome got its name when Ross, my sister Lynn's husband, asked me how I liked my rig. Immediately I thought of a kindergartner I loved named Rigdon, and the name stuck. (Later I started calling it my tiny house on wheels and then just my tiny house, but I also call it my motorhome, my RV, my rig, and Rig.) From Indiana, I drove Rigdon to Detroit to visit aunts, uncles, and cousins. (My parents and my four eldest siblings, Sherrie, Lynn, Sandi, and Tom, were born in Detroit; most of the extended family still lives in the area. Cathy and I were born in Battle Creek, Michigan, where our family lived until we moved to Fort Wayne the summer I turned three.)

As I tooled around Michigan, which became state twelve, on my road bike with its skinny tires, I realized it was getting battered by the northern potholes. I shopped for a hybrid bike in Detroit but didn't buy one.

Since Detroit is so close to Canada, a cousin and an aunt suggested I drive to Canada, just because, so through the Windsor-Detroit Tunnel I drove, camping for four days at three provincial parks. In one park, where I stayed the first week of October, most of the campers decorated their sites for Halloween. And I mean decorated! We're talking skeletons, coffins, heads with glowing eyeballs, enormous spiderwebs, and more ghosts and goblins than you'd find in any old graveyard. As I was getting ready to leave, a family began settling into my site before I pulled out and nearly trapped me with their truck, which was loaded with spooky outdoor decor. What a unique experience.

Roads and bike trails in Canada were smooth enough for my road bike, but because my dream was not to ride across Canada, I returned to Detroit via the Ambassador bridge and bought a Trek Dual Sport Three (DS3) made for rough roads and trails, and a hitch-mounted bike rack. The hybrid quickly became my go-to bike when I didn't know the terrain. By enabling me to ride on rough roads and trails, the knobby-tired bike soon brought me more joy than I thought possible.

The maiden voyage provided me with confidence that I could manage traveling in the rig on my own in unknown territory. Having this newfound self-sufficiency gave me extra comfort.

Once home, I completed a six-week nutrition course because I had recently become enamored with how what we eat drastically affects our health and fitness, then I drove my car to Fort Wayne for Christmas.

In January, I drove my tiny house to Florida and stayed through February. Riding my bike in Florida made it state thirteen. Because I was resolute about living retirement-life to the fullest, in March my sister Sandi and I enjoyed our first-ever Caribbean cruise. When we stepped off the ship, I was more determined than ever to ride my bike in all fifty states.

CHAPTER THREE

My First Big Trip
MAY 2019

By May I was itching for a big trip. Since I had traveled east the summer before, I opted to go west. In six months I could knock out half the states in the country. Given that I had already ridden my bike in thirteen states since retirement, if all went as planned, I would be close to forty states by the time I returned home. I scrambled for a couple of weeks, bubbling in anticipation while wrapping up home responsibilities: cleaning and making home repairs, mowing and weeding, finding a friend to live in my home, a friend to manage my mail, and another to take care of my yard.

The plan was to drive north and then meander west toward California along the northern states and back home across the southern states. My head filled with thoughts of meeting friends and family, visiting parks, and riding bike trails as I zigzagged my way back to Georgia. My calendar was clear until Thanksgiving or maybe even Christmas.

On May 15, I drove Rig a very long four hundred miles north to Cincinnati to visit my friend Amy, who had been my constant support through my doctoral studies. I never would have gotten my degree without our daily phone calls. Amy had dinner ready for me when I arrived, as she did every time I visited.

"This is it—you're living your dream. I am so excited for you, Joy. You're going to California this time?"

"Yeah, sometimes I can't believe it's really happening. Wish you could come with me."

"Oh, no. This is your dream, not mine. I'll stick to teaching for now. I still love it. After forty-two years, I still can't think of anything else I'd rather do."

Amy had to teach the next day but we stayed up late talking. In the morning we enjoyed a little breakfast chat. We hugged goodbye, and she went off to school and I drove off to pursue my dream.

Two hundred miles and five hours later, I arrived in Fort Wayne. My friend John had invited me to park in his driveway while I visited with family and more friends. He would make a few repairs on my rig, plus have its generator tuned up at his family-owned big-rig repair shop. John is one of those guys who can fix anything and will help anyone if he can. (Plus, he and my best friend from kindergarten had been dating a while so I got insider privileges.) John made the repairs and then I drove Rig to his shop for a generator tune-up.

The next day I drove a rental car four hours to Detroit and caught up with cousins, aunts, and uncles on both sides of my family, and returned to Fort Wayne a day later. When I got back, John said that when Evan, the technician, serviced the generator, he had re-bolted the heat shield, whatever that means. Then he told me about a potential fire hazard they'd found.

"When Evan removed the generator cover, he captured a family of four baby mice snuggled in a cozy bed of lint, leaves, and yarn. They'd caught a free ride with you from Georgia. If you had tried to charge up your generator with all that lint in the compartment, I can't imagine what kind of explosion or fire you might have encountered."

"Oh, my word, John!"

"Yeah, it could have been bad. We charged you for servicing the generator but not for relocating the little stowaways to the field behind the shop. Our tech, Evan, threw that service in for free."

"Wow. Thanks, John. And please thank Evan too."

What a blessing to have a friend like John looking out for me, ensuring my safety.

Later that night, I got another bonus. My nephew, James, who lives in Washington, DC, was on a business trip only eighty miles from Fort Wayne. I hadn't seen him since the previous summer. He slipped away from work for the evening and met ten of us at my sister Lynn's place, telling us story after story about his wife, Chris, and their two sons.

"Oh, here's another one," he said. "Chris is sitting with Christian in the kitchen helping him with his homework. He's in kindergarten so he's practicing writing his letters. Chris goes out to the living room to check on

JP, and she comes back to see Christian has hacked off his bangs! I guess he got bored with his letters, saw some scissors laying there, and cut away."

We gasped in horror. We loved Christian's long, black, curly hair.

"Oh, no. I bet Chris was horrified," my sister Cathy said.

"She was absolutely horrified. She said, 'Christian, what did you do?' And Christian said, 'It was in my face, Mommy! What was I supposed to do?'"

"That's Christian," James said. "His hair was in his eyes, so he cut it. I guess he's a problem solver."

We weren't sure if we should laugh or cry about that one.

James said, "Well guys, it's been fun, but I've got a long day tomorrow. I'd better get back."

After lots of hugs and goodbyes, the impromptu miniature Walker family reunion ended.

In the dreaming phase of having a motorhome, I had imagined traveling and seeing friends and family. But never did I dream I'd visit so many and have so much fun and laughter. With the same exhaustion and contentment as a child on December 25, I climbed into my sister Lynn's guest bed and drifted off to sleep.

Leaving Fort Wayne the next day tugged at my heart. I had stayed longer and had more fun than I expected. Bicycling to garage sales, workouts at the gym, an awards ceremony for my great-nephew, a visit to a nursing home to see a dear friend, dinners, late night talks, plus a surprise birthday party for my friend Kathy had filled my week. As I drove off, I waved goodbye to my friends and sisters, dabbing my eyes with my sleeves. What a great trip it had been already, and I was just getting started.

CHAPTER FOUR

Finally Heading West

THE WEEK BEFORE MEMORIAL DAY 2019

California is known for adventure and fun, and now my rig was finally pointed toward it. *I'm finally traveling West! Look out, California! Here I come!* But first I had to stop to see my dear friend Julie.

An hour later, I pulled into my friend Julie's driveway in Warsaw, Indiana (the town my sister and I had biked to when I was ten), forty miles west of Fort Wayne. Julie and I had been friends since fourth grade Sunday School, and we roomed together for a year in college. We don't get together often, but she is a forever friend. We talked for hours. Well, I talked for hours and she talked for minutes. Julie listens better than a therapist.

"How are you doing spiritually?" Julie asked.

I hesitated. "Well, I'm not where I want to be. I have to say I'm a long way from where I was in college and know it's time to get my life back on track."

"Really? What happened?"

"You know how you and I kind of lost touch when I moved to Georgia?"

"Yeah."

"We never said anything like, 'Let's not call each other so often.' We just got busy with our lives and quit talking so much. In a way, that's how it seemed in the beginning with God. It was like I moved away and got busy with work—started hanging out with people who didn't talk about God, quit reading my Bible, quit praying—that sort of thing."

I took a drink of water and continued. "I don't remember ever making a conscious decision to quit following him. It seemed more like two friends drifting apart because they no longer had the same interests, or didn't live in the same town anymore."

Julie listened to me reflect for a few minutes and then said, "Well, maybe you can be thinking about that on this trip. It sounds like you will have some time to think. Maybe pray about it."

"That's a good idea. I will certainly have some time to think and pray."

I paused for a second. "'Time' That's one of the things I told myself. 'When I retire, I'll have more time for God.' Sounds silly now, but that's something I truly believed. 'I've got time. I'm young. I can get my life back on track with God later.'"

Julie didn't pry or make me feel uncomfortable. She listened and encouraged me. Just by talking about God, she made me think about how I missed those days when I was close to him.

After dinner with Julie and her husband, Scott, we cleaned up the kitchen. Then she threw on a peacoat and we scurried out for a tour of my RV. Scott plugged my tiny house into a garage outlet, and I slept parked in their driveway under an electric blanket with the heater blowing full force. Although I had moved to Georgia because I couldn't stand the cold, I didn't remember Indiana ever being *that* cold in May. I woke to a magnificent view of the sun rising over familiar farmland. Scott and Julie and I enjoyed oatmeal with berries and picked up the conversation from the night before. After hugs and a quick goodbye, they wished me safe travels and headed to work.

As I thought about my travels from my home in Georgia to Ohio to Indiana to Michigan and back to Indiana, I marveled how each piece of the puzzle fit. My friends and family had made me one happy camper. This trip was fast becoming the quest to find joy that I had anticipated when I bought my motorhome.

While still parked in Julie's driveway, I called Indiana Dunes where I hoped to camp a few nights. Elizabeth, the clerk who answered the phone, suggested I register on-site. Just three months earlier, the National Park System had re-designated the Lake Michigan shoreline known as the Indiana Dunes National Lakeshore as the nation's sixty-first national park. The park is unusual because the Indiana Dunes *State* Park is within the Indiana Dunes *National* Park. The shoreline extends fifteen miles from Gary, Indiana, to Michigan City, Indiana, and encompasses 15,000 acres.

When I arrived I noticed there was no entrance gate, so I didn't get to show the national park pass a friend had gifted me. I parked in a near-empty lot and walked toward the nearest dunes. When the clouds disappeared, I went back and changed into a pair of shorts. My brother Tom called as I hiked the dunes, so I shared the experience with him, which took us back to the days when we climbed the dunes as kids. Ahh . . . nostalgia is such a wonderful thing. With sand beneath my feet, I breathed in deep, smelling the familiar fishy odor as a cool, light breeze brushed my skin. What a feeling! I find it amazing how the senses bring back fond memories.

When I arrived at the campground, Elizabeth said the park was full for Memorial Day weekend, so I booked only one night. Then she told me about a three-dune challenge. Anything with the word *challenge* stirs my soul. I backed into site #27 and threw on a tank top to climb the three highest dunes in the park, remembering that only hours earlier I had burrowed under an electric blanket at Julie's house.

The three-dune challenge posed little challenge as I traversed across the most magnificent sand dunes of Porter, Indiana. Like life, I have found that a challenge is what I make of it. Running the dunes, trying to improve my time on a second run, or completing the course in both directions might have created a bigger challenge. On that day, though, I was content to simply enjoy a walk up and down the dunes. Tom laughed when I texted him a picture of the sign at the top of Mt. Tom, a dune named for Lieutenant Tom Brady, a Civil War hero. After my hike, a beach visit lasted twelve seconds before biting flies proved too much to bear.

That evening as I enjoyed the breeze in my dining room, the campground host, Tim, knocked on my screen door and warned me of a tornado watch.

"That explains the extreme temperature changes over the past twenty-four hours," I said.

"Yeah, guess so. If the watch changes to a warning, go to the comfort station."

The dated comfort station did not appear comforting. I had ducked my head into the women's room earlier and opted instead to shower in my motorhome. Hanging out in that old brick building with a bunch of families all night would be as comforting as sleeping in a chicken coop.

"Ever had to do that before?"

"No, just figured you should know the plan, in case," Tim said.

"Okay. Appreciate you telling me."

"Sure. Good night. Hope you sleep well."

"Yeah, right. You too."

A short while later, I called my sister Cathy, who always kept me posted on the weather. She knew I didn't pay attention to the weather. Even when

I had cell coverage, I just didn't think about looking at the forecast. She said nineteen tornadoes had hit the Midwest in the past two days.

Such exciting times. This is my first night alone. Do I stay awake all night to watch the weather? Is staying awake possible? Necessary? How would I know if the watch changed to a warning? Would the host, Tim, come tell me? Does the park sound a siren? Do I wait until I hear the train coming or my tiny house tips over? Why didn't I pay attention to which rig belonged to Tim?

My mind would not shut off. I closed the door and windows and slept as well as a student the night before final exams. My tiny house rocked all night in a random, jerky, old roller coaster kind of way. Loud noises beckoned me to peer out the windows. Black night stared back, as though someone had painted my windows with black paint.

The campground remained under a tornado watch until daybreak, but the weather never compelled me to run to the comfort station. It wasn't until the sun shone in my windows that I realized my tiny house and I had survived our first storm. That was one long night.

The previous night, Julie and I had talked about my faith and there I sat twenty-four hours later, facing serious danger. The storm certainly got my attention. Howling wind rocking my motorhome had brought me to my knees. I told myself I needed a game plan for inclement weather if I planned to camp in adverse conditions. More importantly, the storm made me think seriously about my faith and death. *What if I had died?*

Despite the sleepless night, I wanted to stay another day because I relished the sunshine, the dunes, the water, and the warm memories stirred by visiting the lake. My mother had taught me that "it never hurts to ask." So I called Elizabeth, the reservation specialist, and thanks to a last-minute cancellation, I got to stay at the campground one more night.

That second day at the beach, reading by the water got sticky, so I biked around town. I planned to ride for an hour but lost my way in the metropolis of Porter, population 4,858. A quaint community called the Town of Dune Acres captured my attention, and I rode in full sun in a tank top for an additional two hours before finding the road back to the campground.

Sixty-five degrees burned like ninety-five on my skin. The afternoon sun had scorched my shoulders so badly the burns affected my sleep for the next three nights, despite the twice-a-day slathering of aloe vera gel. That night, however, a short boardwalk stroll from my campsite, I watched the most serene orange sunset over Lake Michigan. Minutes before touching the water, the sun burst through a cloud like Usain Bolt and spread its rays across the water as if to say, "Ta da!" Thankful for an extra day, the bike ride and sunset far outweighed a couple of tender shoulders.

Indiana Dunes took me back to my childhood. Every summer Mom had taken my siblings and me to Warren Dunes in Sawyer, Michigan. The dunes at Lake Michigan are mountains of fine sand the color of spots on a fawn and partly covered with trees and seagrass. As children, we enjoyed hours of climbing and running down the biggest dune, Old Baldy. We'd then dash into the freezing water to wash off the sand sticking to our sweaty arms and legs. The shore at Indiana Dunes appeared smaller, narrower than Warren Dunes, but beaches ebb and flow through the years. Multiple beaches and bike trails at the Indiana Dunes National Park—most of which I did not see—give me reason to return to the shores of my favorite lake, where I can relive the joy of feeling like a kid again.

Chapter Five

Time to Leave My Comfort Zone
Memorial Day Weekend

Despite the threat of a tornado, getting lost on my bike, and developing a wicked sunburn, I found solace in the familiar territory of Indiana Dunes National Park. Indiana and Michigan had embraced me as their long-lost child, but this westward voyage called for stepping outside my comfort zone. I think it was John A. Shedd who said, "A ship in harbor is safe, but that is not what ships are built for." The spirit of the lake I cherished pushed me to embark on my journey farther west.

As I studied an atlas, I spotted Pikes Peak State Park in northeast Iowa. *Wait. Isn't Pikes Peak in Colorado?* My friend Lisa had climbed Pikes Peak on her bike the summer before on her trip to Colorado. She'd sent me a photograph of herself holding her bike above her head in front of a sign marking the Pikes Peak Summit at 14,110 feet. So reading Pikes Peak on the Iowa map confused, yet intrigued, me. Later I learned both parks got their name from the same American explorer, Brigadier General Zebulon Pike. The connection to my friend convinced me that Pikes Peak State Park, the one in Iowa, should be my next destination.

According to my high-tech navigation tool, a.k.a. *The Rand McNally Road Atlas*, following 49 South to 30 West would keep me out of Chicago traffic, so I opted for that route. However, it took five hours to get seventy-five miles closer to my goal. Discovering that back roads are not always faster, I hit Interstate 80 West in Plainfield, Illinois, and drove to Princeton, midway across the state. Using *AllStays*, an app that provides information and directions to rest stops, truck stops, parks, campgrounds, and RV-welcoming businesses such as Walmart, Cabela's, and Cracker Barrel, I navigated to "Camp Walmart." It wasn't the oasis of Lake Michigan, but the big, quiet lot sufficed for the night.

The Saturday before Memorial Day, I took 80 West to a Planet Fitness in Moline, Illinois, where I was able to park my rig. With a search on my phone, I found the Ben Butterworth Parkway, a paved bike trail along the Mississippi River. Like a little girl without a care in the world, I had a wonderful time riding along the parkway, around large muddy sections, flooded areas, and dirt-covered patches. And the triple-decker riverboats made for great photo ops. The Ben Butterworth Parkway made Illinois the fourteenth state I'd ridden in since my retirement. *Hurray! Fourteen states down, thirty-six to go!* After my sunny afternoon ride along the Mississippi, I returned to the Planet Fitness parking lot to find my rig in the middle of a car show.

Cars and people filled the lot, and vintage sixties and seventies vehicles trapped my motorhome. People gawked at my rig as though it was part of the exhibit. The show equaled the bike ride in terms of unexpected pleasures for the day, making Illinois a memorable, enjoyable state. By 8 p.m. the cars pulled out, freeing me to get back on the road. En route to the Walmart in Davenport, Iowa, I navigated through more construction, detours, signs, and orange barrels than one might encounter in a nightmare. *Why is it so dark here? Am I driving in the right direction? Why do they make these detours so confusing?*

Fortunately, Waze, my GPS app of choice that night, had my back. Waze gave me only a moment's notice before turn suggestions, but it did get me to my next overnight destination. Being new to this exploration-style of travel, I was experimenting with GPS apps, my road atlas, and the free foldable state maps, trying to find the best way to navigate. When I arrived at my destination without incident, I considered it a win. After midnight, the winds picked up, and the rain beat down on poor Rigdon . . . again.

Haven't we had enough?

Then, with a change of perspective, I focused on the positive. I was thankful I did not have to drive through the construction in the storm and grateful that not one drop of rain fell during my bike ride along the Mississippi or during the car show.

Sunday morning, I drove to a bike path, only to find "no parking" signs upon arrival. Instead, I parked in an unoccupied lot beside a YMCA and pedaled along the most tranquil two-lane trail ever. The path wound around the suburbs of Davenport and Bettendorf, Iowa. Bright green exercise machines stationed along the route called for me to stop and exercise on each one. They added so much fun to my ride. The path ran as smooth as the road it followed and sported a yellow painted line through its center. I had never seen that before.

Though surrounded by new homes, condominiums, and apartments, I rolled along for miles, never once passing another cyclist or pedestrian. Golf course-type grass lined the path, and not one piece of trash littered the fifteen miles I rode. The return route confused me, so I used the "find parked car" feature on my phone. Apple designed that feature with me in mind. The company plans to call the updated version "find Joy." I won't get any royalties for them using my name, but that's how life works sometimes.

Later, I parked my rig at a Planet Fitness in a mall lot in Dubuque, Iowa. More heavy rain that night made sleeping difficult, but I had become comfortable camping in parking lots. Parking lots require little planning and no setup time, except for an occasional drive around to find the quietest, level parking space. Their biggest draw, however, is that they are free.

As a new retiree living on a fraction of my previous income, I endeavored to save money anywhere I could. If I stayed home, living on my retirement income posed no problem, but traveling introduced variable expenses. Gas, campground fees, entertainment, and paying people to maintain my home and yard could eat up my savings in a hurry if I wasn't careful. So for my first six-month trip, I thought it best to find free parking when I could. And here in Dubuque, I had struck gold.

It had rained every night since I left Fort Wayne, yet the days remained precipitation-free, making my trip more enjoyable. Back home, friends were having Memorial Day cookouts and parties by the pool. In contrast, contentment washed over me as I sat inside my tiny house, by myself, surrounded by acres of freshly laid asphalt and no one else around.

From Dubuque, I drove seventy-five miles to a Walmart in Prairie du Chien, Wisconsin. I arrived at dusk, and hearing the frogs and crickets croaking and singing a serenade made for a homey, park-like atmosphere. Later, for the fourth night in a row, rain startled me awake. For added drama, thunder, lightning, and wind strong enough to rock my tiny house accompanied the rain, as frightening as the night at Indiana Dunes under the tornado watch. I still lacked a plan for stormy weather, and my rig and I were prey for the wind monsters. Walmart closed at midnight. With no neighbors to keep me abreast of the storm and no comfort station to run to for safety, I enjoyed another sleepless night. That which doesn't kill you . . . and each passing storm strengthened me.

Come morning, the sun nudged itself through the clouds, the rain slowed to a drizzle, and the winds diminished to a breeze. After a quick inspection of my motorhome, I counted my blessings and thanked God for protecting me and making me stronger. I had planned to pedal into town that morning, but the drizzle kept me from venturing out. After addressing birthday cards and postcards for family and friends, I reflected on my last few days of traveling from parking lot to parking lot. Though miles away from my comfort zone, with my tiny house on wheels, I'd always be at home. My new motto: have home, have courage, will travel.

CHAPTER SIX

Pikes Peak

THE LAST WEEK OF MAY

Next to the Walmart entrance stood a familiar blue box. I dropped a stack of cards inside and drove over the Mississippi River to Pikes Peak State Park near McGregor, Iowa. After surveying the campground, I picked out a level, secluded site, checked in, and plugged my rig into the electrical socket sometimes referred to as shore power.

Because rain had followed me to the campground, I expected to sit in my motorhome all day and plan my next week. However, two minutes after arriving, silence settled over the campground. Raindrops no longer pinged off my roof. Woo hoo! I love it when things work out. *Time to ride!*

Dressed in long tights, a long-sleeved jersey, full-finger gloves, and a hat under my helmet, I ventured out on my bike to get photos of the Wisconsin and Iowa welcome signs. On the bridge that linked the states, I saw something I wasn't prepared to see. Views of the overflowing river, flooded streets, and deserted, sandbagged homes overwhelmed me and instantly dampened my mood. Blocked, flooded roads made for a challenging ride. Moments earlier I was elated that the rain had stopped so that I could ride and now all I could think about was the trauma these people were going through.

This flood brought back memories of another flood that occurred during the spring of my junior year of high school in Fort Wayne. Our superintendent had canceled school and encouraged students and teachers to help with sandbagging efforts. Seeing the sandbags stacked around so many homes brought back bittersweet memories of passing sandbags from person to person, knowing only a team effort could save those homes by the river. Because my family lived far from the three flooded rivers, I had never grasped the magnitude of the devastation those families whose homes we had attempted to save had experienced. But the way our townspeople came together instilled a belief in humanity that I carry to this day.

As I roamed the streets that afternoon, I observed no other cyclists or pedestrians, and only half a dozen cars crossed my path. An eerie feeling washed over me, and my mind flooded with questions about the families affected by the overflowing rivers. I wanted to know their stories. It was a weird feeling, but I wanted to get to know them. I wished I could help.

On my ride back to Pikes Peak, an unforeseen 1.5-mile climb at an 8 to 10% grade challenged my tired legs. Back at my tiny house, teeth chattering, I got into a hot shower and the warmth of propane. As I turned on the heat, my Georgia friends were complaining of 90+ degrees and drought. My shoulders still bore the effects of the scorching Indiana sun from four days earlier, yet I had tackled the elements to check off two more states, Iowa and Wisconsin. With my state count now at sixteen, I crawled under my electric blanket, singing a tune about the sun coming out tomorrow.

The pitter-patter of rain on the roof and a hint of daylight made for a natural morning wake-up call. I laid in bed, listening to the soft, steady beat. Though I had hoped the sun would come out, my *Weather Channel* app predicted a 60% chance of rain until late afternoon. Again I resolved to stay inside to figure out my next stop after Pikes Peak. However, as the rain slowed, the sun peeked out and enticed me to take a hike.

I called my sister Sherrie, who was walking indoors on her treadmill because of the steamy temperatures in Georgia. The previous day I had braved the freezing cold, and now I was going hiking in shorts and a long-sleeved T. I found a wooded hiking trail only yards from my site. Sherrie stayed on the line with me, so in my mind my sister and I were enjoying a great hike together. Yes, technically, she was walking nine hundred miles behind me, but I'm not one to let technicalities ruin a good hike with my sister. My earbuds had recently died, so one hand held my phone to my ear and the other waved in front of my face to keep the bugs out of my eyes and mouth.

At an overlook, I snagged photos of the rising Mississippi and followed the boardwalk-style Bridal Veil Trail to a waterfall. More stunning views. More pictures. Without warning, the trail became challenging with cliff-like drop-offs. Suddenly, the trail disappeared.

"Sherrie, I'd better head back. I'm lost."

Chatting with my sister, I had paid no attention to the trails and over-looked the trail signs. When I came to a split in the path, I questioned which way to turn.

Baseball legend Yogi Berra whispered something like "Hey Joy, when you come to a fork in the road, take it."

"You're a lot of help," I whispered back. "But which way is the shortest?"

On a sign back at the park store, I had noticed it said there were eleven miles of trails in the 1,000-acre park. An eleven-mile trek was not on my afternoon agenda.

Sherrie and I discussed the thirty-five-year-old hiker, Amanda Eller, who lost her way on a trail in Hawaii in early May. Dressed in shorts, she had planned a three-mile walk in the woods. Amanda became confused and could not find the way back to her car. She had taken no water, snacks, cell phone, or compass with her because she was not planning to be gone long and she had been in those woods before. Seventeen days later, a helicopter team rescued her miles from her car. I did not wish to be in a situation like that. I understood firsthand how easily one could lose her bearings in the woods.

I was thankful for modern technology, and Sherrie kept me company on the phone for the next forty-five minutes as we worked as a team to find my way back.

"Sherrie, do you remember that time you got lost at dusk on Arabia Mountain?"

"Of course. You were talking to me on the phone, and I wasn't paying attention to the markers on the trail. I don't think I've ever been so lost."

"And the worst part for you was that the sun was going down."

"Yes. I didn't get back to my car until it was totally dark."

"That was so scary. I felt helpless. I couldn't do anything to help you find your way except to just get quiet for a while to let you think. It seemed like forever, but I was so relieved when you finally said you could see your car."

"Yeah, pretty scary for me too. Well, Joy, let's get you back to your camper before it gets dark."

"Yes! I'm with you on that one! Do you remember us making a vow to never make that mistake again? Well, here we are making the same mistake—well, at least I'm making the same mistake. And of course, despite our vow Sherrie, I am not good at taking advantage of others' mistakes. Something in me says I have to make the mistakes myself. And I often make that mistake multiple times before I really learn my lesson."

"You're funny, Joy."

Sherrie and I kept talking as I tried to figure out where I was.

"Wait. I think I see the entrance of the trail." I walked a few more yards. "Yes. I'm home free, Sherrie! Whew! I'm back."

Lesson learned? Only time will answer that question.

I thanked Sherrie profusely for accompanying me until I made it back. My sister and I hung up, and I stopped at the park store to buy postcards. I stood outside the open window and talked to a woman named Bonnie, who was working in the store.

"Tell me your story, Bonnie. How long have you been working here at the state park?"

"This is my eleventh year. I started working in the summers while I was still teaching. I was a paraprofessional for sixteen years and then got my teaching degree at fifty. Once I got my teaching certificate, I taught seventeen years full-time and then half-time for six years before I retired."

"Wow! You must have enjoyed teaching."

"I sure did. Just love kids."

"Do you have children of your own?"

She smiled. "Yes! Two girls, two boys, and six grandchildren."

With obvious pride, she told me about each of her children and grandchildren. She also shared that sadly, her sixty-five-year-old husband had fallen off a ladder in their garage, hit his head on the ground, and died three days later.

In addition to working at the state park, Bonnie said she maintained two homes and a farm.

"How do you keep up with all that?"

"It's a lot, but I like to stay busy. I'm also an artist." Bonnie pulled up pictures on her phone. "Here are some of my paintings . . . and here's my dog . . . oh, and here's a buck I shot last fall . . . and these are my grandchildren," she said as she scrolled through the photos on her phone. "The youngest is eleven."

The seventy-six-year-old widow and I enjoyed a delightful two-hour conversation. I told her a bit of my story too, but I didn't mention getting lost in the woods. She would have laughed.

I find people fascinating and love listening to their stories. What a gem I found in Bonnie. She remains the highlight of my visit to Iowa.

The next morning I ventured outside and noticed there were eight motorhomes and trailers in the park, but not one person, not even a campground host, was outside. Then, as bugs swarmed around me like fog, "Pikes Peak campground host" fell from my potential retirement jobs list.

Since I was uncertain of my next destination, I opted to go with the flow and stay a third night. I filled out a site registration envelope, slid $16 inside, crammed the envelope into the overstuffed drop box, and walked back to Bonnie's small store.

"I've got no clue where I'm going tomorrow."

Bonnie laughed at my lack of planning. She suggested I ride on the trail in Mankato, Minnesota, and that I check out Luther College because of its beautiful old buildings and the fact that it was close to another trail. When I left Bonnie, I biked to the post office in McGregor and paid $4.50 to mail a $5 Pikes Peak T-shirt to my friend Lisa. I imagined her laughing at our shared experiences as she opened the package.

I turned onto 76 North, which ran along the Mississippi River. A sign read "No shoulder for next six miles." How comforting. A train track ran between the road and the river, and on the other side, a natural rock wall stood flush against the road.

Thankfully I remembered to turn on my DiNotte taillight. (For safety I always ride with a helmet, gloves, a rearview mirror, a headlight, and a taillight even in the daytime). When logging trucks blew by, I held my line and prayed the drivers would do the same. The draft almost swept me under the 18-wheelers as they whooshed by without giving me an extra inch. The Bettendorf bike trail had allowed more room for a logging truck to pass a cyclist than Highway 76. After six miles of hugging the jagged white line, Effigy Mounds National Monument Visitor Center and Museum on the right caught my eye. I relished the break from the tension of riding on the narrow highway.

I walked in and introduced myself. "Hi. My name is Joy. I was just riding my bike on 76 from Pikes Peak State Park and saw this place. Can you tell me about it?"

"Sure," said the woman behind the counter. "Wait. You are riding your bike on 76? That's got to be dangerous!"

"Yeah. It's got to be the narrowest road I've ever ridden on with trucks. It's been a little stressful."

"I bet. Well, to start with, you're in Harpers Ferry, Iowa. You're about ten miles from Pikes Peak State Park. So . . . about our park, effigy means mounds in the shapes of animals. Behind the building there are over two hundred mounds you can see from the trail. We've got 2,500-plus acres along the Mississippi with fourteen miles of trails and lots of overlooks where you can see the river."

"Nice! But I don't have much time. What would you recommend if I can only hike a mile or two?"

She opened a brochure and laid it on the counter. "All the trails are marked on this side. Since you don't have much time, I'd suggest you go out this door and do this little hike."

She pointed me toward a two-mile walking loop to the mounds. "You'll see five of the mounds right off the trail to your right."

"Thank you. That sounds good."

On the trail, which was lined with fresh, immaculate, reddish-brown mulch, I walked half a mile to the first overlook and turned around, wishing for more time to keep exploring. The steep grade offered a good workout even though I had only hiked one mile. I did not walk far enough to spot more than the five mounds she mentioned or enjoy any of the scenic views of the Mississippi River or the National Wildlife Refuge I saw on the brochure. As I looked at the brochure and its promise of scenic views and trails, I vowed to return one day.

When I noticed the late hour, I jumped on my bike and hustled back toward the state park. I hoped to get back in time to visit Bonnie again before she closed the store. The last three miles to the park were uphill and a little over one mile of that was a 10% grade climb. A challenge, but nothing like its namesake in Colorado.

Proud I didn't get lost, I returned to Bonnie's store by 4 p.m. I bought more Pikes Peak postcards, and Bonnie and I exchanged contact information. Bonnie is an amazing woman and now a friend. (As of this writing, she is still maintaining her farm and two homes.)

That evening I still had no clue where I would stay the following night. I admire campers who keep to an itinerary, but scheduling ahead didn't work for me. Specific dates and places to meet friends and family invite stress. The free spirit called to me. Having the freedom to stay one more hour or two more days excites me. I'd plan a day or so at a time with options for the coming weeks in mind. After Iowa, Minnesota took priority. I had never visited the North Star State, much less ridden my bike there. And according to my map, two Laura Ingalls Wilder museums claimed Minnesota as their home.

As a huge *Little House on the Prairie* fan in my elementary school days, I added the museums to my "must-see" list. My trusty atlas showed one museum near the state lines of Iowa and Minnesota and the other in Walnut Grove, at the southwest corner of Minnesota. After I visited the museums, I hoped to drive south to Nebraska and then straight up through South Dakota and into North Dakota with the possibility of driving through Anamoose, North Dakota (population 227), the birthplace of my maternal grandfather.

After a solid night's sleep, I headed toward the Pikes Peak trails. I wanted to understand why I had gotten confused the day I was talking with my sister, but once I arrived at the trails, I chose a different path so as not to let history repeat itself. In other words, I chickened out. I didn't trust myself not to get lost again, so I chose an easier loop and enjoyed a two-hour hike in the woods.

With an enjoyable, yet uneventful, trek in the woods under my belt, a one-hour drive on 76 North brought me to a Walmart in Decorah, near the Iowa/Minnesota state line. Mom always said, "Home is where you lay your head at night." Walmart was fast becoming *home*.

The next morning, I hoped to find a nearby bike trail called Trout Run Trail, which was one of the places Bonnie had recommended. After a ride, I would go to the Laura Ingalls Wilder Museum thirty minutes north of the trail. The logistics of navigating to each state, riding my bike in scenic places, and seeing the highlights of every state challenged me. Doing a little research ahead of time might have eased my stress, but I never took the time to do much of that. I more or less followed my heart or family and friends' suggestions or suggestions from people I met along the way.

Four months earlier while I was in Florida, I had reconnected with another Amy—a friend from childhood. She and her husband, Glenn, had reservations at Glacier National Park in Montana, where I planned to meet them. Navigating a meetup with them and a friend in Seattle and a cousin in California by mid-August screamed fun, yet challenge. Pikes Peak had been a great stop, but staying two extra days made me anxious about getting to Montana in time. Amy and Glenn planned to drive their RV from their home in Florida and arrive in Montana the last week of June. We hoped to camp side by side if we could work out the logistics. Getting together with my Floridian friends in Montana was fun that I did not want to miss.

CHAPTER SEVEN

The Laura Ingalls Wilder Museum

JUNE 1

June began with a bang. I parked my rig at the Trout Bend Hatchery and took my hybrid bike on the Trout Run Trail in Decorah, Iowa, as Bonnie had suggested. With saddlebags in place, I rode into town and bought fresh romaine and cucumbers at the Saturday morning farmers market. Floods had forced a detour on the bike path so, as par for the course, I promptly got lost.

Signs for Luther College (the college Bonnie had suggested touring) persuaded me to ride around the campus before finding a road back to the trail. The old redbrick buildings intrigued me but, since I'd found myself in "I'm lost again mode," I only stopped for one picture of the school sign. When I rediscovered the trail, I rode steep hills, captured photos of the trail, signs, farms, and the Upper Iowa River, and then returned to my motorhome at the hatchery. I'd recommend the well-paved, wide, and clean trail to fellow cyclists, joggers, or stroller pushers after the flood waters recede. The trail has some tricky curves around carved-out rock, along with a few steep sections, to keep it interesting.

Back in my rig, I showered and drove twenty minutes north to the Laura Ingalls Wilder Museum in Burr Oak, Iowa (population 166). A woman named Beverly captivated me with a three-hour tour of one of Laura's childhood homes. The museum, which was across the street from the visitor center and gift shop, used to be the Masters Hotel that the Ingalls family had helped manage the year Laura turned nine. The restored hotel resembled a small three-bedroom farmhouse with a welcoming front porch. Beverly said the structure was the only Laura Ingalls home still in its original location and registered on the National Register of Historical Places. She said that after experiencing financial hardships, in 1876 the

Ingalls family had moved from Walnut Grove, Minnesota, to Burr Oak. Inspired by the synopsis of Laura's life, I bought a copy of *Little House in the Big Woods* and a dozen postcards at the gift shop.

Laura Ingalls Wilder was born in Wisconsin in 1867. Her family moved a lot because her father had trouble finding work. She began teaching at fifteen and married Almanzo Wilder at eighteen. Later in life, Laura wrote articles and worked as an editor for newspapers and magazines. It was her daughter who encouraged her to write about growing up on the farms where her father worked.

Laura published her first children's book, *Little House in the Big Woods,* at sixty-five. But she didn't stop there. With her daughter's encouragement, she subsequently wrote eight more books, which became the "Little House" series that depicted her life in the pioneer days. The literary legend passed away three days after her ninetieth birthday in 1957. Wilder's books became more popular after being turned into a television series, which aired from 1974 to 1983, almost as long as her childhood. Her books and legacy live on in the hearts of many fans, over multiple generations, yet if she had retired from writing before turning sixty-five, I wouldn't know her name, much less try to emulate her. And I'm certain I'm not the only person—as a child and again as an adult—that she inspired to write.

While I was still in the gift shop, thinking about Laura's influence on my life, another tour guide and a local woman who walked into the shop gave me directions to Lanesboro, Minnesota. They said I would enjoy riding my bike on the trail there. My friend Bonnie, from Pikes Peak, had suggested riding in Lanesboro too, so off I went. Without incident, I found a park in Lanesboro (population 754). The trail, a stone's throw from the city park, offered a smooth, paved, scenic, and serene trail. The trail enticed me and the town intrigued me—both hidden gems. I rode on the charming bikeway for an hour, returned to Rig, and then drove west on Highway 16.

Road construction on Highway 16 necessitated a detour. Like a wayward first grader following her teacher's instructions to get in line, I followed the signs until they told me to turn left toward a sign that said, "No thru traffic." Once again, I sat in the middle of nowhere—lost. I conducted two middle-of-the-road U-turns (not easy maneuvers in a twenty-five-foot rig carrying two bikes on the back) to avoid dirt roads and, in time, found my way to 90 W. Two hours later, I arrived at a Walmart in Austin,

Minnesota—more exhausted from the stress of driving through confusing detours than from the busy two-trails-and-a-museum-tour day.

Getting lost every day was tiresome, but tricks to avoid getting lost eluded me. I believed I was paying close attention and reading every sign, but I am understaffed, even with my road atlas, my dashboard Garmin, and multiple GPS apps. Sometimes I think it would be nice to have someone in the passenger seat to help me navigate. I realized it was probably time to develop these skills. And quickly.

CHAPTER EIGHT

Harold

JUNE 2

When I was on the Decorah trail in Iowa, I discovered the disc brake was rubbing on my hybrid's back wheel. On my phone I searched for bike shops in nearby Austin, Minnesota, and found one that looked good. I hoped someone could fix the brake and recommend a good trail in the area. From Austin, I would head to a Planet Fitness in Mankato, Minnesota, because the women I'd met at the Laura Ingalls Wilder Museum had suggested I ride on the trails in Mankato.

En route to the bike shop, I stumbled upon the Spam Museum in Austin that my cousin Linda had told me about weeks earlier. She encouraged me to take the tour, but touring a ground meat museum did not sound appetizing to me. After parking, I sent a photo of the Spam Museum to Linda and then walked six hundred yards to the bike shop. What a gem! Antique bicycles and old cycling jerseys hung from the walls and ceiling, and a variety of bikes and accessories filled the wooden floor space of the vintage downtown building. The owners, Phil and Joanna, and a high school senior named Stephen, greeted me with smiles. The teen put my bike on the stand, spun the wheels, removed and replaced the back wheel, spun the wheel again, and said everything looked fine.

He then greased the chain, pumped up the tires, and said, "No charge, didn't do anything."

"Thanks, Stephen. That's kind of embarrassing that all you had to do was take off the wheel and put it back on. You sure it's okay?"

"Yep. Just come back after your ride if it's not."

Wow! How nice is that?

Stephen also gave me a trail map and showed me where to ride in Austin. With my wheels spinning freely, I tucked the map in my jersey pocket and headed to the trail straight from the shop. On the path, I had only gotten lost twice when I passed a white-haired gentleman on a three-speed trike, stopped at the foot of a slope.

Making a U-turn, I asked if he needed help. The man said he could not change gears. He dismounted, and I rode his bike down the hill to change into an easier gear. Then I gave him a push up the hill, which gave him momentum to keep the pedals turning. We exchanged names and "good day" and rode in opposite directions. After a quarter mile, I turned back. Sure enough, he needed another push. I jumped off my bike, laid it in the grass, and pushed him up the hill. We rode side by side with me repeating the "jump off, push my new friend Harold and jump back on pattern" three more times over the next twenty minutes. We chatted as we pedaled. Harold told me he knew Joanna, whom I had just met at the bike shop.

"This is where I live," Harold said, as we rode up to a massive three-story white brick building.

It shocked me when I read the huge sign on the lawn: "Cedars Senior Living Community, A Place to Call Home." Harold lived in an assisted living home. An employee planting flowers looked up from her work and smiled as we approached.

Harold chained up his bike in the dim garage, and we entered through an unlocked back door. He plopped into a cozy, mahogany chair in a sitting area outside the dining room, wiped his brow, and gulped a glass of water. I sat beside him, savoring the special moment with my new friend.

"Thank you, little lady. I appreciate your help. Would you stay and have dinner with me?"

I sighed. "Oh, thanks for the offer, Harold, but I can't. I need to get going. I want to ride a few more miles on the trails."

"You said on the trail that you aren't married. Is that right?"

I nodded.

"Well, I think you'd make a good catch."

I blushed.

"You know, this building we're in was originally a hotel. My wife and I stayed here on our honeymoon. It was the nicest place in town then."

"Wow, that's amazing."

"Yes. This is where we began our lives together . . . and my dear bride took her last breath here in December, a week before Christmas. We moved here last summer when I couldn't take care of her by myself anymore."

"Oh, Harold, I am so sorry to hear that."

"Yes. It's been hard, but I'm thankful I was here with her, holding her hand when she passed. I miss her, but I know she's in a better place."

Nodding, I told Harold I hated to go. We hugged, took a couple of selfies, and said goodbye.

I bet you were a good catch yourself, Harold.

His head dropped as I turned to walk away. A lump formed in my throat. I could have and should have stayed to listen to more stories—and sat and held his hand a little longer. Thankful our paths crossed, I think of Harold often. How he had gotten so far from home, I will never know, and I still wonder what he would have done had I not been riding by. I believe we found each other for a reason. My life is richer for having met such a dear, sweet man.

After leaving Harold, I rode another hour on the trails, frustrated at every turn and crossroad. Because of my tendency to get lost, I was glad Stephen had given me the map because I used it 1,001 times. It took me half an hour to deduce that the red line on the map was not a continuous asphalt path, but a loosely marked loop of trails, sidewalks, and streets. Sometimes there were arrow signs at crossroads on the trail that only confused me more. Like on many organized bike rides I've done, I kept finding myself off the red line of the map. Despite the challenges, the ride proved good enough in my book to count Minnesota as state seventeen. The brief encounter with Harold, though, made it one of my most memorable rides in the west. *Seventeen down, thirty-three to go!*

I made it back to the bike shop before they closed and seized the opportunity to talk with Joanna about Harold.

"Harold was here in the shop a week ago," she said. "Came in by himself, sweat dripping from his chin. I offered him a bottle of water and inflated his tires. Tires were so low, I don't know how he made it here. A friend of mine used to play tennis with Harold. I'll get her to check on him. You are right. That sweet man should not be out riding by himself. Too many things could happen."

Before I left the shop, Joanna said, "If you are going to Mankato, you ought to go to Minneopa State Park, which is ten miles west. Mankato and Minneopa have great bike trails.

"I've never heard of it. Would you spell it for me?"

"Sure." She grabbed a pen and notepad. "Here you go. They have bison there too."

I looked at the note, pronounced Minn-eee-ahh-puh to myself, and stuffed it into my jersey pocket.

"Bison in Minnesota? How cool. Thanks."

"Phil and I travel a lot in our 25-foot Class C. We love it. I bought a pedal-assist bike before our last trip out west. With my knees, I never would have made it up the mountains in Colorado on my old bike. I still had to work, but I kept up with Phil on the climbs. That might be a bike for you down the road if your knees and feet get worse."

"Yeah, I'm not ready to succumb to that yet, but you are the third person who has suggested I get one. Well, I'd better get going. Thanks so much, Joanna. Appreciate you taking care of me. And thanks for taking care of our friend Harold."

CHAPTER NINE

Minneopa State Park

JUNE 3

By the time I reached Planet Fitness in Mankato, it was 7:30. They closed at 8, and the lot didn't look like a place I could rest for the night.

Great. Here I am, no workout, no shower, no place to park, and the sun is setting. I hate driving in the dark, especially in unfamiliar territory.

On a side note, ever since I returned from my coast-to-coast trip in 2010 and joined a gym, lifting weights had become as important to my mental health as my physical health. Staying strong and healthy had become a priority, and I didn't feel as well emotionally when I couldn't lift at least three times a week. And although I have a perfectly functioning shower in my tiny house, sometimes I prefer to shower at the gym where the hot water is unlimited, and I don't have to take an on-and-off military-style shower. Also, sometimes it just feels awkward to take a shower in my tiny house in a parking lot.

I called the closest Walmart, and the woman who answered said they did not allow overnight parking. She directed me to an old, closed Gander Mountain store parking lot. She said she had seen a lot of trucks parked there. On my way to a gas station, I stumbled upon the abandoned Gander Mountain lot. It was closer than expected. I pulled into my new resting place and found a Hy-Vee grocery store within walking distance. It was dark when I returned to my rig with groceries. Two trucks flanked my tiny house, and a third parked across from me thirty minutes later. Feeling safer with trucks around, I slept well, despite their engines idling all night.

The next morning, I noticed two men parking travel trailers close to me.

I stepped outside. "Are you guys getting ready for a show?"

"We sure are," the older one called out.

"Should I move my rig before I leave for a bike ride?"

"Yeah, that'd probably be a good idea. Anywhere on that end should be good," the younger guy said, pointing to the opposite end of the lot.

"There's a trail a mile and a half down this Highway 22," the first guy shouted, pointing to the road ahead of us.

"Excellent. Thanks for the tips. You guys have a good day."

Feeling fortunate to now be armed with useful information, I moved my motorhome, pedaled my hybrid out of the lot, and found a path alongside Highway 22 that led to the paved trail. The forty-mile trail meandered through lush pastures, along half a dozen lakes, and dipped under overpasses embossed with its name, Sakatah Singing Hills State Trail, in gold letters. Of course I took pictures and wished my knees and feet could handle longer rides. The trail had two or three confusing jogs and a couple of gravelly areas, but it was smooth enough for me to have ridden my Trek Silque road bike. With the sunshine on my face and the wind at my back, I basked in a perfect Minnesota bike ride.

When I returned to my rig, at least thirty motorhomes and trailers nearly filled the parking lot. I waved at the guys I had talked to, grateful they had suggested moving my home to the far corner of the lot. Looking around me, I chuckled as I remembered the Memorial Day weekend adventure when I came back from a ride along the Mississippi and discovered a car show enveloping Rig.

I went back into the Hy-Vee to get more groceries and mail a package to my friend Lisa. Hy-Vee grocery stores house post offices. How convenient. How fortunate. This was my first encounter with a Hy-Vee, and the store impressed me. Also, I noticed in Iowa and Minnesota there had been a mailbox outside of each Walmart. Nice. Minor tasks like finding a post office or mailbox can be a frustration or a blessing. In this case, it was a blessing. I often have driven miles out of my way only to find the post office closed.

After a stop at the gym, I questioned my chances of arriving at the second Laura Ingalls Wilder Museum in time for a tour. I called Minneopa State Park, booked a site over the phone, and arrived at the state park thirty minutes later. Ranger Ted checked me in and suggested I drive to the waterfall first before setting up at my campsite. He also said they had thirty bison on the property, and I should ride out to see them. How exciting!

"Just to be clear, we tell people to stay in their cars, so you really shouldn't ride your bike out there," he said. "The males weigh up to 2,000 pounds and stand over six feet tall. Females weigh 1,200 pounds and are over five feet tall. They can also run thirty miles an hour if they think they need to."

"Yikes. Glad you told me that."

"The bison are usually docile, but if someone gets them riled they can be dangerous. We don't have any fencing between the dirt road and where they wander, so yeah, I wouldn't recommend you going out there on your bike."

More good advice.

In the span of ninety minutes, my plan changed from driving to a museum ninety minutes away to an afternoon of state park bliss. From the office where Ted checked me in, I drove my rig down a dirt road to encounter my first-ever bison herd. Next, I backed into my secluded, tree-lined $36 site and left the setup for later. Within minutes I was hiking along Minneopa Creek and taking short videos with my phone of two raging picturesque waterfalls close to the confluence of the Minnesota River.

What a blessing to find the park, the waterfalls, and the bison. There were even three baby bison (calves) in the herd. The calves stood out not only because of their smaller size, but because they were more the color of peanuts than their dark chocolate-colored parents. I wanted to touch them, to reach out my window and pet them. They were intriguing creatures. It was love at first sight. My heart picked up its pace as I watched them roam. The word majestic came to mind. I wanted to learn more about those amazing beings. Seeing bison for the first time in my life, and a couple of states earlier than expected, made my day, my week, my trip.

On the downside, the gnats at Minneopa were more plentiful than the black flies at Indiana Dunes and annoyed me as much as the bugs at Pikes Peak State Park in Iowa. After plugging my RV into the electric outlet, I opted for a bug-free evening and scurried back indoors. There were other people in the park, but I couldn't hear or see any campers, other than one woman who walked her dog past my campsite after dinner. Traffic rumbled in the distance, and the crickets were loud with a capital L. Other than that, the park stayed quiet. With a cool breeze blowing through my bedroom window, I fell asleep halfway through reading *Little House in the Big Woods.*

As I readied my rig the next day to leave, I reflected on how I kept stumbling upon magnificent parks, meticulously maintained trails, and delightful, helpful people. My travels were working out better than I could have expected. The waterfalls and the bison made for a special treat. And

I would not have found Minneopa State Park had Joanna at the bike shop not mentioned it, and if I had hurried along to Walnut Grove as originally planned. I was one happy camper.

CHAPTER TEN

The Storm in Minnesota

JUNE 4

As I was pulling out of the campsite at Minneopa State Park, I met a woman driving a van-style Class B motorhome who asked for help finding the park office. Understandable. The layout of the park confused me too. Two entrances created a challenge, especially since the tiny office lay in hiding a quarter mile away and across the street from the campground.

"My husband is riding his bike across the country, and I need to get set up before he gets here." She pointed out her window. "Is the office that way?"

"Yes. Right down that way on the right. How exciting! I'd love to hear details of your trip. Is it going well?"

"Yes, but I don't have time to talk now."

"Me, either. Sure wish I could stay. I would love to hear your story. I wish you the best."

Moments after I gave her directions to the office and tips on getting water and seeing the bison and waterfall, a young couple asked me for directions. Imagine that—twice in a manner of minutes—trusting souls asking me for directions. Ha! If they only knew. I shared my limited knowledge of the park layout with them, gave the woman my park map and kept moving. I drove by the bison to say goodbye. Since the herd had congregated closer to the road, I snapped close-ups. I longed to reach out and pet them as I do with the cows grazing in the pastures on my bike rides at home, but I smartly refrained and bid them good day from afar.

After a perfect start to the day, I hit another detour just two miles from the park. This was detour number ten in half as many days, and I had gotten lost on every one. Detour number ten proved to be no exception. Not only did I get lost following the detour signs, but at the height of my confusion, a charcoal sky settled over the plains as a serious storm approached. The *Weather Channel* app on my phone pegged me just below the red ball of rain, wind, and hail. When I tried to drive away from the storm, a barricade stopped me. A U-turn forced me directly toward the eye of the storm. *There's no escaping this one.*

Like a ferocious black dragon, a tornado formed in the distance. This was more adventure than I had bargained for. Frantic, I searched for a road to turn west. Confused and scared, I stopped. Studied my atlas. Asked Siri for help. No answer.

I typed in a different city on my dashboard's GPS. Nothing worked. Nothing made sense. Wanting to close my eyes, curl up, and wait for someone to get me out of the mess, I froze. My motorhome started rocking. The rain turned to hail. I prayed: *Please God, don't let me die. Not here. Not by myself. I'm not ready.*

I searched my brain for ideas, but it was a dark, empty cave. There was no shoulder, so I was forced to park my rig in the road. I squinted at the map. Maps are useless to me without a "you are here" arrow. A lack of street signs magnified my frustration. After the U-turn, the compass on the dash did not change. No matter which direction I drove, the compass read *N*.

I prayed again, turned on my flashers, and drove five miles an hour. Tears dripped on the steering wheel. I could see the tornado through the pummeling rain, but I couldn't tell if it was getting closer. The sight of it scared the bejeebers out of me. Lost cell coverage sent me into complete freak-out mode. Trembling, I inched along until I found a paved crossroad and turned left.

I still did not have a game plan for coping with a storm when parked, and the need for an escape plan if caught in a storm while driving had not been a concern . . . until now. I saw no bridges, businesses, or pull-offs where I could read a map or check my GPS. Houses sat far from the gravel roads that surrounded me. Two roads possessed two names; others had no name. I couldn't understand the reasoning. Not one road appeared on my atlas, and I didn't have a Minnesota map, much less a Redwood County map.

After ten miles of my frantic wandering, the storm dissipated. Although I was still disoriented, visibility improved, and I increased my speed. I thanked God for protection and took a deep breath in relief. He was still looking out for me in what was turning out to be one doozy of a westward journey.

CHAPTER ELEVEN

Laura Ingalls Wilder, Again

THE AFTERNOON OF JUNE 4

Within minutes, the sky looked as if nothing had happened. I stepped on the brake, pulled to the side of the road, and typed *Sleepy Eye, Minnesota*, the town where Laura's family had attended church, into my GPS. As I approached Sleepy Eye, to the east of Walnut Grove, I encountered another detour. *Another detour? Really? Am I on Candid Camera?*

Of course, I followed the detour—this time successfully—or at least that's what I thought. When I got within five miles of Walnut Grove on Highway 14, my watch said 5:30 p.m. What a relief. I still had thirty minutes to make it to the museum before it closed. At the height of the storm, I had accepted the possibility of missing the museum, but forgetting the storm I had survived moments earlier, I reverted to the goal of arriving before closing time. Surely I could drive five miles in less than thirty minutes. Maybe I wouldn't have time for a full-blown tour, but I would have time to look around and maybe buy a few things from the gift shop.

Four miles from my destination, another barricade halted my progress. *This has got to be a joke!* Dutifully, I turned right and then realized I would not make it if I had to go far out of my way. I stopped on the side of the road and called the museum. Ellen answered and suggested going through the barricade. No dice. Barricades blocked both lanes like the ones that stopped me in the storm an hour earlier. She suggested driving south. South? I had no idea which way was south. My compass still read "N." Ellen stayed on the line, navigating as I drove.

At last I found a paved road and turned as Ellen suggested. Ten miles from the museum now, the dash clock read 5:50. Certain that I would not make it before closing time, Ellen called Rita to the phone, and Rita agreed with my navigation system. I suspected that no visitors were there and that Rita and Ellen were looking forward to going home.

It took me six hours to drive to a museum that should have taken ninety minutes, and now I'm going to miss it by a few minutes? This can't be happening.

I asked Rita and Ellen to leave postcards and brochures outside and assured them I'd leave money if they'd do that for me. They agreed. At 6:10 p.m., I pulled into a bone-dry gravel parking lot. My new friends had left a note with postcards, brochures, a pencil, and a Laura Ingalls Wilder Museum sticky notepad. Ellen's note said she and Rita had paid for my postcards and memorabilia; they felt bad I'd had such trouble. She asked me not to leave any money. *More good people put in my path.*

I wrote a thank you note and took photos of a stagecoach and buildings surrounding the museum. As I affixed the note to the door, Rita slipped outside and said they were still counting money. I hugged her and took a picture of her on the museum porch. She scurried inside and returned with Ellen. We hugged as long-lost friends. Ellen struck a princess pose. She couldn't help but chuckle as I snapped a photo of her sassy self by the front door of the museum that I would not get to explore, despite my best efforts.

I needed a bright spot. And I got it. Those women brightened an otherwise scary, death-defying day. *You are saints, Rita and Ellen.*

I didn't read the brochures that Rita and Ellen had left until I stopped for the night two and a half hours later. If I had, I might have figured out that Plum Creek Campground and Plum Creek Park were a few blocks from the museum. Had I not been so upset by the storm and so determined to keep moving west, I might have been able to spend the night at the campground. I might have been able to relax and walk along the banks of Plum Creek where Laura's fourth book in the Little House series, *On the Banks of Plum Creek,* took place. Then I could have driven back the next day to visit the museum and enjoyed more time with Rita and Ellen.

Had I driven up and down a few streets, I would have seen the gift store and replicas of the chapel, grandma's house, the little red schoolhouse, jail cells, and the Ingalls' covered wagon—all memorabilia from the television series. How nostalgic it would have been to walk around the town of Walnut Grove, population 751, and visit or take pictures of Nellie's Café, the Walnut Grove Bar and Grill, churches, and more.

Hindsight tells me I should have sat in the museum parking lot, looked at the brochure, and made a new plan. That's how it goes when I travel. Most of the time my spur-of-the-moment decisions and flexible spirit work out for the best. But sometimes they don't. All I could think about after I met Rita and Ellen was moving on. This was not my first missed opportunity, nor my last, but it ranks among the top five disappointments of my trip west. However, now I have a good reason to go back to Walnut Grove—if I can find it again, of course.

Chapter Twelve

Lost Again

Evening of June 4

Dear sweet Rita from the Laura Ingalls Wilder Museum had given me directions before I pulled out of the parking lot, steering me away from the next blocked off section of Highway 14. Having just stared down a tornado on top of all the detours, I was not about to trust any of the navigation apps on my phone or the Garmin I kept on the dashboard.

Rita's instructions were to "Get on 14 about ten miles down CR 20. Then take 14 West to 23 South all the way to 90 West."

That sounded easy, right? I drove ten miles and then got confused. The roads didn't look like what Rita had described. I stopped at an intersection and pulled out my atlas, which held a batting average of .000. A man a few years my senior in an oversized black pickup turned on the street where I had pulled over.

He backed up, rolled down his window, and said, "Need help?"

Wow! What would I do without all these people willing to help me find my way?

"I'm totally lost!"

He parked behind me, walked to my window, and asked where I wanted to go. Five minutes later, I was back on course. The kind soul directed me to 14, then 23 South to 90, as Rita had said. It all made sense when he explained it and showed me on my map.

When I saw the ramp to get on 90 W before the South Dakota state line, guess what happened? Yes, you guessed it. Another road-closed sign stood before me, blocking the on ramp.

This cannot be happening!

I followed the detour signs again. And again, they let me down. What was I thinking? I did an 8.5-mile loop and arrived at the same ramp and the same stinking detour sign. Ignoring the sign the second time, I found my way to 90 E to go west.

Before the next exit, I pulled into the Minnesota Welcome Center. Since I had come into the state on a small country road, I had not gotten a picture of a Minnesota state sign. This sign was small and unremarkable, but I took a photo anyway. At the end of this journey, I hope to have pictures of all fifty state signs, preferably with me or me on my bike in front, but I knew that was not always possible. This pitiful little sign at the welcome center would have to do for Minnesota.

There was just one car in the lot. A man lowered the American flag as the sun colored the western sky a striking red-orange. I snapped a picture of the amazing sunset with my rig in the foreground.

I approached as he folded the flag. "Hi. Can I stay the night here?"

"Yes. Officially, we have a four-hour limit, but I leave at 10:30, and no other workers come back until morning. The building will be open all night and trucks will roll in soon. You are more than welcome to stay."

"Yay! Thank you so much. You made my day. It has been one stressful afternoon."

He nodded and returned his focus to folding the stars and stripes.

Earlier, while on the detour, I drove past flooded farmlands. Acres and acres of flooded, unplantable land. The devastation brought tears to my eyes. But throughout Illinois, Iowa, and Minnesota, I saw lush, rolling farmland. It amazed me that the farmers could grow any crops on those hills with the rain they had gotten. The soil looked so black, so fertile, yet it seemed as though farmers had planted little of the land. I know one could offer many reasons why so few fields had crops growing in June, but as I drove past miles of marsh, I surmised the floods had made the fields too wet to plow and plant. If that was the case, it made me sad for those farmers. Yet as I drove along, I noticed there were still areas where tiny green plants lay in perfect rows, defying the odds and reaching toward the sky as if to say, "We've got this."

Minnesotans had their fair share of flooding due to excessive rainfall that year. Too much rain had to be the reason for the road closures. What I don't understand is why the signs had to be so confusing. Why was I constantly led to barricades? The closed roads and poorly marked detours were taking hours from my days, in addition to costing me more money on gas. And the toll the dead ends were taking on my psyche could not be measured. My frustration level rose with each wasted minute as I felt I was dropped in the heart of a corn maze with no escape route. My biggest question is still why the road crews couldn't have posted a sign that said, "90 W ramp is closed, take 90 E instead"? How hard would that have been?

Though the storm and detours frustrated me, they ignited my will to persist, just like the green crops growing in the fields. And I'm convinced the storms also nudged me closer to God. I was thankful to be alive. Being lost in that storm was one of the scariest times of my life. I feared I might die. That night I did some thinking. Some soul searching. I still hadn't figured out how to avoid storms or what to do when I got caught in one. But I did try to focus on the positive and look for the good in it all. I was thankful to be alive.

The day had started well with the bison, and it ended well with a kind attendant allowing me to stay at the rest area. In the storm, God had protected me and my motorhome from devastation. Then the women at the museum and the man in the truck helped me find my way. As I reflect on that day now, the phrases *what if* and *thank you* come to mind. The magnitude of what was happening wasn't yet clear to me, but now I can tell you something special was taking shape in my mind and my heart.

CHAPTER THIRTEEN

Sioux Falls, South Dakota

JUNE 5

My mother used to say, "What a difference a day makes." The next day was 80 degrees, tranquil, and sunny. From the Minnesota welcome center, I drove 5.5 miles east to the next open exit. When I finally started driving west on Interstate 90, I expected to find a South Dakota welcome center. No such luck. Workers were either remodeling the rest area or they were building a new one. Either way, South Dakota did not welcome me with maps and brochures as I had hoped. There were miles and miles of road construction on 90 W, but I didn't have to get off the highway. I got gas in Brandon, South Dakota, so naturally I had to text my nephew Brandon to tell him I was thinking of him. At the Falls Park exit, the city greeted me with more road construction but no detours.

Thanks to GPS, I found Falls Park in Sioux Falls, South Dakota, without a glitch. At 123 acres, the park was more expansive than I had expected. I parked my motorhome in a large farmers market lot across the street (open Saturday mornings from May through October) and rode my bike to the falls. The falls completely captivated me. I took pictures and videos, knowing it was impossible to capture the splendor of 7,400 gallons of water dropping one hundred feet every second over the falls. It was simply amazing! The falls reminded me of a mini-Niagara but on a stretch of river so calm I could easily walk onto the rocks for panoramic views. Concrete walking paths flanked the Big Sioux River. The original Sioux Falls Light and Power Company building that had opened in 1908 had been converted into the Falls Overlook Café, and its outdoor patio claimed the best view of the raging latte-colored water. And there I stood, appreciating the wonders of nature, the beauty of the day.

After walking around, I jumped back on my bike, rode on the street to downtown Sioux Falls, and twenty minutes later found a way back to the path. The path was smooth enough for my road bike with its skinny tires, but not knowing the terrain, I had opted for my hybrid bike with knobby tires. The path appeared well-marked, but the signs and multiple paths confused me so much that I botched my plan to ride the loop.

It almost felt like a comedy show about how dozens of signs still couldn't keep me out of trouble. Fifteen miles into my trek, I completed a loop around a bridge and ended up right back where I started. Honestly, I couldn't decide if it was funny or downright sad that I got lost on trails that on maps looked like a high school track. In the end, I chose to laugh at myself.

Plus, it was a beautiful day with summer approaching, and the shorts and sleeveless jersey I'd chosen to wear were perfect attire for this ride around the falls. Despite my difficulty in following the signs, it was clear that the trail planners had designed the path to make a 26-mile loop connecting at least a dozen little parks throughout the city. Every park had a map sign, nearly the size of a billboard, each erected with two solid brown posts and "Greenway Trail System" printed in huge letters above the map. Many sections of the trail had been flooded recently, as the path and uncut grass were gray with sediment. One of the ten-foot-high signs was muddy to the top. Thankfully, when I was there, only one short spur off the main trail remained underwater.

While at Falls Park I learned the Big Sioux River is a tributary of the Missouri River and flows over three hundred miles, through South Dakota and into Iowa, before the confluence of the two bodies of water. I wondered how the falls looked in each season. Do the waters get low in autumn? Does it get cold enough for the falls to freeze in the winter? The park would certainly be spectacular under a blanket of snow with Christmas lights in the trees and around the café. It seems I always had questions running through my mind when I visited such enchanting places.

The missed opportunities here were the visitor information center, the gift and memorabilia shop, and the five-story observation tower I did not learn existed until after I had left. With Sioux Falls being the third place where I knew I had missed key attractions; I told myself to relax and enjoy what I did get to see. No one could see it all. I made a mental note to return to the places I could when the opportunities arose, but I also understood that if I hiked one more trail, stayed another day, or visited one more attraction, I would miss something else. Traveling, like life, is a series of trade-offs.

I would have many more opportunities to ride in South Dakota, but I considered the twenty-eight miles in Sioux Falls sufficient to make South Dakota state eighteen. Joy washed over me when I realized I was one-third of the way to completing my fifty-state goal.

I then drove three and a half miles to a Planet Fitness, intending to finish by six, but it was 7:30 p.m. when I completed my workout.

Of course 90 percent of my goals or deadlines were self-imposed. That morning I had hoped to drive between one to two hundred miles west, but at 7:30, reality hit, and groceries topped the priority list. I noticed a grocery store at the corner of the Planet Fitness shopping center. Perfect!

After shopping, I took off in the wrong direction. I could clearly see the sun behind me. *Go west, Joy … as in drive toward the sunset!* I turned around in a parking lot and chased the orange sky.

CHAPTER FOURTEEN

Welcome to South Dakota

JUNE 5 – JUNE 6

With the blazing orange sunset ahead of me, I drove forty miles on the perfectly paved Interstate 90 and stopped at a welcome center where I planned to get a South Dakota map and then keep driving west. My sister Cathy called as I tugged on the center's door. Locked. No map.

Who needs maps? They never include the "you are here" arrows for me anyway.

After talking with my sister, I decided to stay at the rest area. The rest area the night before had worked. Seeing a dozen trucks in the lot, I concluded that overnight parking was allowed. I was excited to be in South Dakota, and it looked like a safe place to stay until sunrise. The parking area was closer to the road than in Minnesota, which meant loud traffic noise, but that wouldn't keep me from sleeping. As the sun disappeared beyond the horizon, I considered myself at home.

At daybreak, I found that staff members had not yet unlocked the welcome center doors. Still with no map, I returned to 90 W. My only task: drive west. I had two hundred miles before I'd need navigation help. The road was as smooth as an indoor roller rink. It was as though my rig and all its contents had been bubble wrapped because nothing rattled. The speed limit shot up to 80 mph. Seriously? Never in my life had I seen an 80-mph speed limit sign. No way would I drive my motorhome that fast. I set the cruise at 65 and let the other drivers have all the fun of zipping past me. I had ten hours to drive to Valentine, Nebraska, 250 miles away.

A few days earlier, as I was looking at a map, I realized I could dip down into Nebraska to add another state to my trek. The name "Valentine" caught my attention. It sounded like a fun city to visit merely because I liked the name. That's how much thought went into my decision to visit Valentine.

The smooth road and light traffic made driving along I-90 W effortless. Occasionally, the four-lane narrowed to two because of construction, but I did not get caught up in even one detour. What a great drive!

I could get used to this.

Hoping this was not the calm before a storm, I relaxed and enjoyed myself. A roadside sign showed another Laura Ingalls Wilder Museum at yet another childhood home, this one in De Smet, South Dakota. Intrigued, I quickly took the exit. Life had handed me a second chance! I'd swing by the museum, take photos, walk around, and buy postcards or another book. When I pulled off the exit, though, the sign read: "De Smet: 25 miles."

As a Laura Ingalls Wilder fan, I wanted to see another home, especially since seeing the inside of the Walnut Grove Museum didn't work out. However, twenty-five miles out and twenty-five more miles back seemed like a long way. The need to keep moving west overtook my wish to see another Wilder home. Driving away from the opportunity, I questioned whether I should have taken the time, even though it would have added three hours to my trip. I supposed I would always wrestle with those decisions.

At the next rest area, I studied the map on the wall.

The attendant on duty said, "Where ya heading?"

"I'm planning to take 90 W to Murdo and get on 83 S to Valentine—also planning to visit the Badlands, Mount Rushmore, and Custer."

"That's the safest way to Valentine. There's construction on this road," he said, running his index finger along a black line, "so it'd be best to go the way you're planning. Highway 83 is a good road. After Valentine, I'd say you should take 20 W through Nebraska. It's a smooth ride, not much traffic. Take it all the way to Chadron here, get on 385 N, and you'll run right into Custer," he said, tapping the word "Custer" on the map.

"Okay, thanks. I'm Joy, by the way."

"Ah, my name's Jerry. Is that your motorhome?"

I nodded.

"Looks like a good size. I'm sixty-seven, waiting for the missus to retire so we can travel. She's younger than me and still likes her work." He adjusted his cap and said, "This is my retirement job. I like it, but I'd also like to travel before I get too old."

"Some people buy a motorhome a few years before they retire," I said. "They go on shorter trips to see if they like it."

"Hmm. That's an idea. Who knows? Maybe we can do something like that."

"Thanks for the help with directions. Hope you get to travel soon."

One hundred fifty miles later, since the welcome center at the state line was under renovation, I stopped at the rest area in Chamberlain, South Dakota, which proved superior to all others. The greeter, Diane, handed me a pen and asked me to sign a guest book with my name and home state, as though I were attending a wedding. I had never seen such a big rest area. Maps and brochures filled the counter like in other states, but the Chamberlain Welcome Center included a miniature museum with information about the explorers Lewis and Clark and a display of native taxidermy. A host behind the counter introduced himself as a travel counselor and offered me maps and brochures and advice on what to see in South Dakota. I had to drive 150 miles past the state line to get the royal treatment, but Chamberlain knows how to welcome guests.

I walked through the museum and then stepped outside, which looked like a city park, sporting an iconic metal sculpture, several paths and picnic tables, some covered with awnings, and trails that led to views of the Missouri River.

I hiked on the trails, which were swarming with other visitors taking pictures of the Missouri River a thousand feet below. Then I snapped a couple of pictures of the magnificent fifty-foot-high stainless-steel sculpture depicting a Native American woman with her arms outstretched and her back to the Missouri River. The sculpture is called *Dignity* or *Dignity: of Earth and Sky*. Complete with braids, mukluks, and a buckskin-type dress, the silver structure with striking blue accents honors the culture of the Lakota and Dakota people.

An hour after signing the guest book at the welcome center, I moved on. At the exit for Highway 83 S, I zipped into the Flying J to fill my rig with unleaded. The truck stop offered an exclusive fueling island for motorhomes, complete with a propane tank to refill onboard propane tanks like Rig's. Because it was convenient, I inquired about getting propane. The woman behind the counter sent a guy to fill my RV, but after three tries, he said their tank was not working. He told me there was a place to get propane ten miles south on 83 called the Co-op. I thanked him for his efforts and pulled onto 83 south.

One hundred yards later, I realized that Highway 83 was not as good a road as I thought Jerry at the rest stop had told me. He must not have known about their road repair project. Workers were apparently resurfacing the road and had dug up a section of both sides, leaving only sand for vehicles to drive on.

Flaggers made one lane of traffic stop for the other, challenging my off-roading skills through eight hundred yards of soft sand. After easing down a twelve-inch drop-off from asphalt to sand, it felt like my rig was going to fall apart and end up in a heap. Slowly but steadily, I drove my rig through the sandy patch. As I hurdled the second jagged twelve-inch lip, the tires slid on treacherous mud.

After maybe a quarter mile, the mud gave way to rough asphalt again, and I could not have been happier that my rig pulled through. I cheered as I picked up my sunglasses and water bottle from the floorboard. *Whew! Made it!* The mystery of how my house on wheels bounced over the next ten miles of torturous pavement without blowing a tire will remain unsolved.

At the Co-op, I met another man named Jerry, and he and Curt filled my propane tank. People often have trouble getting the propane hose *on* my rig's tank, but these guys needed a monkey wrench to get their hose *off* my tank after they filled it. (I don't know why it's always so difficult, but I'm always thankful when the process is complete. It's a job that requires certification, and I'm glad I don't have to do it myself. Every tank is a little different, so it requires some experience too.) Jerry, the older fella, told me to pay Curt, so I followed Curt inside.

Curt, another young local named Kevin, and I talked about where I planned to go. They recommended a park and hiking trails, but from the description, I knew my feet couldn't handle the terrain. Jerry came inside and joined our conversation, unfolding a map and highlighting a route for me.

Clearly I had misunderstood rest stop Jerry because I thought he had said to drive west through northern Nebraska and then straight to Custer State Park on 385 in Custer, South Dakota.

Had I followed those instructions, I'd have missed the Badlands. Not looking closely at a map has gotten me into trouble too many times. Fortunately, because the truck stop had no propane, I crossed paths with Curt, Kevin, and Jerry #2, who got me back on track to Valentine and beyond with a highlighted map in hand. It always felt good to get directions from locals as my GPS apps had not always proven reliable. And, as a baby boomer, I still prefer to see "the real map" sometimes.

When I thought about it, the last truck stop not having propane proved to be a blessing in disguise. As bizarre as my trip was playing out, I felt God was looking out for me. The mishaps led me to great people who added to my adventure—people who were adding to my belief in humanity.

The skies remained clear all day. Little did I know though that a storm of a different kind was brewing as I made my trek to Valentine.

CHAPTER FIFTEEN

Valentine, Nebraska

JUNE 7 – 8

Thanks to my *AllStays* app I found a cozy, tree-lined, forty-acre city park in Valentine with several dry (no hookups) camping spots to pitch a tent or park a camper. I wouldn't need power or water for just one night because I carry plenty of water, and my rig stores enough battery power to last twenty-four hours. Sometimes all I want is a safe, pleasant place to park my rig. After driving around the quarter-mile dirt loop, I happily paid the suggested fee of a whopping $5 a night. But when I settled in by a picnic table next to Minnechaduza Creek, I discovered my rig's house batteries were dead—D-E-A-D—dead.

What? How could they be dead? I drove 250 miles today. The batteries are supposed to recharge while I drive.

The batteries were so drained that the house lights would not turn on, and the generator would not start. I tried the emergency start button trick that Cody, my sales guy, had taught me when I bought my rig. Nothing. As I always do when I have a problem, I called my brother. Troubleshooting with Tom brought no answers. I racked my brain. Nothing there either.

Out of ideas, I called an RV technical support line. They had closed an hour earlier. Note to self—do not have technical support issues after hours. Thankfully, I was able to use the battery-powered lights Tom had gifted me when I bought my rig, and I planned to call the technical support hotline again in the morning. It's good to have backups. When the smoke detector started chirping, presumably due to the dead house batteries, I took it down and pulled out the 9-volt battery so I could sleep. Then I prayed the carbon monoxide detector wouldn't start chirping. If it did, I'd be awake the rest of the night because I had no clue how to dismantle that one.

I woke to chirping. No, it was not the birds chattering in the burr oaks along the creek. It was the carbon monoxide detector, and the chirping is probably a safety feature to let me know the batteries were dead—as if I didn't know that already. I called a technical support hotline and told the support tech, Fred, that this was the third time this had happened. His only suggestion was to find a repair shop to see if someone could figure out why the batteries were not recharging while I drove.

Gee, thanks Fred.

An electrical outlet on the back side of the park bathhouse looked like it might be my savior. There was a cell phone plugged into one outlet. Its apparent owner, looking nervous, scurried over from his tent site nearby.

"What's up?"

"I was just looking for a place to plug in my motorhome. The batteries are dead. Hi, I'm Joy. I noticed you when I pulled in last night. Where are you heading?"

"Anthony . . . Seattle."

"Whoa . . . Seattle? You by yourself?"

"Yeah. I left Iowa City the last week of May. Aim to get to a friend's place by mid-July and fly home in time for graduate school in August."

"Impressive. That's got to be over 2,000 miles!"

"Yeah, That's about right. I've ridden about 600 miles since Iowa City, and I have about 1,400 to go."

"Wow. Kudos to you. I'm heading to Seattle too, but I'm going in that motorhome parked down there." I pointed to my rig at the opposite end of the campground. "I've never done a self-contained trip on my bike. How's it going?"

"I've had a few rough days, but overall, it's been good. I'm not riding today. The winds are going to be 20 mph with gusts of 30 to 40 mph. I've got a route mapped out with places I know I can stay every night. Don't think I could make it to Cody with such strong headwinds. With all this gear, I'm averaging forty to fifty miles a day. Did sixty yesterday and that was too much."

"Wow! I'd like to hear more. Be right back."

I drove my rig to the front of the bathhouse, pulled out my extension cord and plugged it into the other outlet, noting the six inches of cord left to spare.

"Looks like I'm going to need to find a repair shop."

Yeah, right, an RV repair shop in Valentine, Nebraska. Don't hold your breath, Joy.

Anthony immediately pulled out his phone.

"Hey, looks like there's an RV dealership with a service center in Rapid City," he said.

"Rapid City? That might work. Thanks. So, how do you track the weather? Do you know when it's going to storm?"

Settling in for a comfortable chat, Anthony and I sat on top of the picnic table by his tent.

"You've got a nice spot here under the tree," I said. "That's why I noticed you last night. You've got the best site here at the entrance and you can't miss that orange tent."

"Yes. I got here early yesterday."

"Do you ride in the rain? How did you know it was going to be so windy today?"

"Not if I can help it. I've got a couple of good apps."

Anthony showed me two weather apps on his phone.

"I like that one," I said, pointing to his screen. "It looks more detailed than the ones I have."

He then downloaded *Dark Sky* on my phone and showed me how to use the features he relied on, such as wind speed and chance of rain, which were tracked by the hour up to ten days ahead. From that day on it was my go-to app until *Dark Sky* merged with *Weather* on January 1, 2023, and shut down the app I had grown to love.

As we looked at our phones, I noticed my phone said I had not backed it up in two weeks. That happens if it isn't connected to Wi-Fi for a while.

"Do you know where I might get an internet connection? I need to do a backup on my phone."

"Sure. On my way here yesterday, I rode past a coffee shop. Bet they would have it. If not, there's a library down the street from the shop."

"Nice. How about a trail? Are there any bike trails close by?"

"Yes. There's a really nice one called the Cowboy Trail. If you want to ride into town together, I can point it out to you on the way to the coffee shop. Then you'll know where to go after you get your phone updated. The trail is that crushed granite stuff. Do you have a bike for that?"

"Oh, that would be perfect, Anthony. You're like the Valentine tour guide. And yes, I've got a hybrid I bought just for those types of trails. And for the bad roads in Indiana and Michigan."

Anthony set his phone on the table and leaned back on his hands. "I mapped out my whole trip to Seattle before I left Iowa City. So I know a little about each place before I camp. Then I also try to pay attention to things when I get to towns so I know what's out there."

"That makes sense. Especially since you are on your bike. I know I should do that, but I don't do a lot of planning. Gets me in trouble sometimes but that's just how I roll."

"How 'bout we leave here in thirty minutes? Would that work for you?"

"Sure. I'll leave my rig plugged in here while we're gone. Maybe it will be charged when we get back."

Anthony and I biked into town together. He took me by the Cowboy Trail trailhead and then we rode a few blocks and parked our bikes outside a coffee shop called Paula's Gift and Coffee Shop on Main Street. It was a charming place with an elaborate coffee counter in the back. I got my first-ever vanilla coffee shake made with almond milk, comparable to a Frappuccino from Starbucks. Yum. We chatted with Donna as she made our drinks. She and her daughter, Jennifer, own the place.

Donna told us about life in Nebraska. She said her family had lived on a cattle ranch about seventy-five miles south of Valentine until Jennifer was in high school. Then she and her four daughters moved to Cody, Wyoming, so Jennifer wouldn't have to drive fifty-six miles to the school, which was in Cody. Donna's husband stayed on the ranch, coming when he could for ball games and special events. They had lived that way for twelve years, until their youngest graduated. Donna said people had to do that or what her friend Paula had done, which was find a family to "board" their children while they went to school.

I told Donna that her experience was a little different from mine. "I lived five miles from my elementary, junior high, and high schools."

"Cherry County is larger than Connecticut," Donna said. "We have family and friends who live in Connecticut. They did not believe me until they came out here and saw the area for themselves."

Fascinated, I asked her to jot down some of those stats. She wrote: Cherry County, 6,000 square miles, population 5,770. Valentine, population 2,600. Connecticut, 5,000 square miles, population 3,600,000. If all those numbers were accurate, I calculated that Cherry County had roughly one person per square mile, and Connecticut had one person per 0.0014 square miles. Then I speculated that most Nebraskans would never wish to live in Connecticut and vice versa.

Paula's Gift & Coffee Shop provided no public restrooms or Wi-Fi, so Anthony suggested we venture to the library, a block away. Never had I gone to a library to use the internet. What a find! I sat in a cozy reading nook furnished with comfortable family room-style reading chairs. I couldn't seem to get my phone to back up, so I texted friends, zeroed out my email, posted pictures on Instagram, and organized photos on my phone. Anthony settled into the computer corner.

An hour or so later, Anthony and I walked outside together. He rode back to the park, and I saddled up for the Cowboy Trail. On my way, I encountered a campground and stopped in to inquire if they knew a mechanic in town who could check out my house battery issue. A woman named Mary pointed me in the direction of an auto repair shop. When I got there, Stan said his shop was about to close, and it would not be open Saturday. However, he thought plugging into an outlet would not give the batteries a full charge. He loaned me a long, super-duty extension cord and suggested I use my battery charger in addition to plugging in my rig. The battery charger is a complicated contraption I bought in Michigan on my first motorhome trip. About the size of a car battery, it's designed to "jump" the truck or house batteries if they went dead and other methods didn't work. The battery charger connects to the house batteries like jumper cables connect to vehicle batteries. To plug in the battery charger, I would need his extension cord to reach the back of the bathhouse. I told him I was about to ride the trail, so he offered to stop by the park and drop off the cord at my motorhome.

Cornhuskers sure are friendly people. I got the sense that residents rely on each other (friends or not) in the rural parts of the state because resources can be miles and miles away.

I jumped back on my bike and a few blocks from Stan's shop, I found the trail Anthony had told me about.

The Cowboy Trail is a crushed gravel rails-to-trails phenomenon. Near the trailhead, a wooden and metal bridge spanned one-quarter mile twenty stories above the Niobrara River, a tributary of the Missouri River. When I got to the middle of the bridge, I stopped for pictures. Seeing the river from high above and thinking about the challenge of building such an expansive bridge made the ride a memorable one. The trail was one of the longest rails-to-trails in the country, stretching nearly two hundred miles from Valentine to Norfolk, Nebraska, with parks, cities, camping areas, and trailheads every ten to twenty miles. Trail planners hope to expand the trail to traverse the entire state. I hope they succeed. The completed trail could blaze the way to lots of nice rides for lots of cyclists.

I rode thirty minutes on the Cowboy Trail and zipped back on Highway 83. On my ride away from the campground, the wind was so strong I struggled to ride ten mph. The return ride on smooth pavement with the wind at my back was a lot more fun. I averaged thirty mph, an impressive clip for me on my hybrid. I hoped to ride more in Nebraska, but this special stint on the Cowboy Trail would suffice for checking off the state, which brought my total to nineteen. Nineteen! Sometimes I marveled at how quickly I was headed toward reaching my goal.

On my trek back to the city park, I stopped in at the library, chatted with the librarians, and snapped pictures of the homey haven for memory's sake.

When I got back to my RV, I said hello to Anthony, asked when he planned to head out, and we agreed to talk in the morning. Stan's extension cord was right beside my front door. The batteries showed a full charge, so I didn't need to use the cord Stan had dropped off. I unplugged and drove to the same alcove by the creek where I had lodged the night before.

While recharging my rig at the bathhouse in the morning, I helped Anthony get ready for the next leg of his trip. We used my floor pump to fill his bike tires to 80 psi. (He only had a hand pump, and no one can pump enough air into a tire with one of those little things.) We cleaned and greased the chain, washed out water bottles and filled them with cold, filtered water. As he packed and rolled his tent, we talked.

"I just don't want the typical life of feeling trapped in a job I don't like so I can have stuff I don't need," he said.

"I hear ya. So what led you to riding your bike by yourself all the way to Seattle?"

"I want to be a writer, but I haven't had any experiences worth writing about. I've kind of lived a boring, sheltered life—raised in the suburbs, went to college, worked in corporate jobs—nothing exciting."

"And?"

"I wanted to change that. I got accepted into a creative writing master's program at the University of Iowa, but when I got there, I had little to say."

"Then what happened?"

"Well, I've been intrigued by books about radical individuals pushing themselves to their limits. After my first year in the writing program, I received a $5,000 grant to pursue a writing project of my choice."

"How cool!"

"I know, right? So, with the grant, I decided to ride my bike across the country. Maybe then I would have something to write about. I chose to ride because of a guy I used to work with in Manhattan who rode his bike to work. From my perspective he was the only one in the office who had a soul. Everyone else seemed robotic, but something inside him was real. I picked Seattle as the destination because I have a good friend who lives there. When he said he didn't think I would do it, the bet was on."

"So you're doing it! That's so impressive."

"I guess so. That job in Manhattan was my first job after college and I hated it. I fantasized about quitting, getting on a bike, and riding with no end in sight."

"Well, with a story like that, we will have to keep in touch. I want to read your book when you finish it. Who knows, maybe I'll write about meeting you. I've been keeping a journal because I want to write too."

We agreed to keep in touch. I unplugged and prepared my rig for travel. Anthony and I took pictures, exchanged phone numbers, and connected on Instagram.

"I'm driving to the library. Couldn't get my phone to update yesterday. Maybe I'll catch you down the road. You're riding to Cody, right?"

"If this storm holds off."

"I should pass you on my way. I'll let you finish packing."

I drove to Donna and Jennifer's place for another vanilla coffee shake and to get the facts straight about the ranch. (It's a good thing I don't live in Valentine. Those coffee shakes are to die for. I fear I'd become a coffee shakeaholic!)

"Yeah, I drive forty-five miles into Valentine six days a week because I don't want to live in a city," Jennifer said. "Valentine's got like 2,600 people. That's too crowded for me. I like to look out my door and see nothing but rolling sand hills. Mom drives thirty miles from outside Cody every day for the same reason. We are used to it."

"That's mind-boggling, but I'm sure more people drive long distances than I would ever know."

"Everyone here drives a lot. We put on too many miles each year for folks to lease, so we just buy new cars more often. That's what people do when they live in the country."

I nodded, encouraging her to continue.

"The ranch where we lived when I was in elementary school sits forty-five miles south of a place called Nenzel, thirty miles west of Valentine. We had 1,200 head of cattle, but we didn't own the ranch. Daddy just worked on it." She grabbed a wet rag and wiped off the counter. "Where are you going from here?"

"Badlands National Park. Well, the KOA outside of Badlands."

"If you're going to the Badlands, don't take 44. The White River flooded, so you'd have to take a detour way out of the way."

"Oh . . . I don't like detours."

Jennifer pulled out a pen and piece of paper. "Take 20 to 61 N till you get to Martin. Then take 18 E to 73 N to 90 W. I'd take 90 W to exit 131 to go to Badlands. Here, take these directions in case you get mixed up."

"Thanks for saving me from another detour, Jennifer."

I said goodbye to Jennifer and headed to the library, but it was closed when I pulled up at 12:05. I sat on the top step of the library stairs and tried to connect to the Wi-Fi. No such luck. As the wind picked up and the clouds rolled in, Anthony rode by.

"ANTHONY!"

He turned toward me and waved. "I'm going for it!"

After giving up on the phone update, I slipped into my tiny house parked on the street across from the library, made a sandwich for myself and wrapped another to give Anthony if I met him along the way. I then drove to the auto repair shop and left the extension cord and a thank-you note for Stan. Five minutes from Stan's repair shop, I stopped at a McDonald's to tackle the phone update again. Backups, updates, navigation, and connectivity can be petty annoyances when traveling. Technology is never perfect. It's helpful when I travel but it's exasperating when it doesn't work.

Fortunately, McDonald's Wi-Fi worked. While my phone updated, I finished addressing the remaining postcards from the Laura Ingalls Wilder Museum. Mailing cards from the Valentine post office ensured a fun postmark for the recipients. Twenty miles later, as I was heading west on Highway 20, I spotted Anthony. I passed him and parked on the shoulder. I jumped out and motioned for him to stop and handed him a sandwich. Anthony thanked me for the PB&J, and as we talked, a policeman stopped beside us.

"Do I need to move my rig, officer?"

"No, I just wanted to make sure everything was okay."

Anthony told him we were fine, and the officer pulled away.

"The temp is dropping," Anthony said. "I need to keep moving or I'm going to get too cold."

"The wind is picking up too. I'm wearing a sweatshirt and I'm cold. Get moving and text me when you get to Cody."

Nodding, Anthony rode off.

As he disappeared in the rearview mirror, I felt like such a cheater. However, like the tortoise and the hare, I predicted Anthony would reach Seattle by bicycle before I arrived in my motorhome.

After my visit to the city of love, I realized I had missed the Valentine visitor center and the Fort Niobrara National Wildlife Refuge five miles outside of town where I likely would have seen bison, elk, prairie dogs, and who knows what else. I probably could have stopped at the visitor center on my way out of town, but I was distracted by my house battery troubles and the need for a phone update. I will never see all there is to see in this country, but narrowly missing an attraction I would have loved still disappoints me. Sometimes I didn't want to take the time to look things up, sometimes I just didn't think about it, and sometimes the lack of cell coverage kept me from looking ahead. After meeting Anthony I made a note to self—*when possible, research before you travel or at least when you get somewhere. Preparation just might lead to more joy.* Unfortunately, I promptly lost that little "note to self."

When I stopped for gas at the intersection of 73 N and 90 W in South Dakota, I noticed a text from Anthony. "Made it to Cody. No problems!"

I responded: "Yay! Thanks to Jennifer's directions and advice to avoid a detour, I made it to my destination without a glitch too. Hope to see you in Seattle!"

A Subway restaurant and a motel with a football field-sized parking lot flanked the intersection. Katrina at the motel desk said I could park anywhere in the back. Three abandoned-looking semitrucks bordered the back lot. I cozied up with them. Trucks pulled in and out, but I was the only one to stay the night. The wind picked up after I parked, but I saw no signs of a storm.

As my tiny home wobbled in the wind, a teenager revved a muscle car in the parking lot for over an hour. I thought the kid was keeping everyone in the motel awake too and wanted someone from the motel to address it. Too exhausted and not brave enough to go out in the dark myself, I pulled a pillow over my head, but I still heard the rumble. What was the deal? My watch read 1:10. Unable to sleep, I peeked out each window only to discover there was no one in the lot. There wasn't even a car in sight, save for the half dozen parked alongside the motel. The wind whooshing between the abandoned trucks was making the rumbling sound. Laughing at myself for thinking the wind was an annoying teen gunning his engine, eventually I fell asleep. But the noise of the wind made for one long night under the pillow.

The sun was shining high in the east when I heard tires crunching over gravel, unnerving me each time a vehicle pulled in. Peering out my bedroom window, I noticed truckers were merely parking and walking into Subway or the gas station. I turned over and looked at my phone: 9:35. It was time to get my butt out of bed and head to the Badlands.

That's right! I'm going to Badlands National Park. Let's go, Joy!

CHAPTER SIXTEEN

The Goodlands

JUNE 9 – 14

Check-in at Badlands/White River KOA Holiday outside Badlands National Park was at 1 p.m., and the campground was no more than an hour's drive. When I made a phone reservation for two nights a few days earlier, Kim instructed me not to arrive early so I hung around the motel parking lot and got on I 90 around 11 a.m. Kim had told me to travel through the national park to the campground. She did *not* tell me to allow time to stop at the overlooks, visit the welcome center, shop at the store, hike the trails, or ride my bike. She hadn't prepared me for what I would see.

Badlands is one hundred square miles of mountains and canyons that resemble humongous sandcastles and inverted sandcastles. It's breathtaking! The landscape reminded me of stalactites and stalagmites I'd seen in caves, but in mountain-like forms with magnificent cinnamon- and chocolate-colored striations throughout mostly fawn-colored formations. The endless views from the overlooks were remarkable. I had never seen a landscape as unique as the Badlands.

The Badlands are bad.

When I'd spoken with her, Kim had implied I would drive through the park—no big deal. Yeah, right. Did she expect me to encounter those inconceivable views and drive straight through to the campground? Not a chance. Curious to know if it was legal to bike on the main road, I paused at the Ben Reifel Visitor Center. In the front lot, a couple of guys stood next to a dozen high-end bicycles leaning against a trailer and a portable bike rack. I asked one of the guys if they were renting bikes and if it was ok to bike on the main road.

"No, we're a touring company. We've got twelve people on a six-day tour through the Badlands, with stops at Custer State Park, Crazy Horse, and Mount Rushmore."

"Oh, that sounds fun. Where are the riders?"

"They're inside checking out the visitor center."

Andrew and Peter were the guides, so they had designated themselves as the official bike protectors. Andrew, a rugged mountain bike type with a friendly smile, talked to me about Wilderness Voyageurs Biking Vacations and gave me a brochure in case I might like to join them one day. He said they do similar rides all over the country and then he answered my second question.

"Absolutely. Everyone's allowed to ride on any of the park roads." He pointed up the road. "Our group is going to ride that way when they finish their visit inside."

"Thanks for the information. Who knows, maybe I will join you for a ride one day."

Inside, after I bought gifts for friends, I asked the employees what park roads they recommended for biking. The man behind the counter pulled out a map and highlighted the route to ride to the highest point on Highway 240, turn around, and ride back to the visitor center, a ten-mile trip. Another option was to ride up 240 a few miles, turn left and ride on a gravel road to the town of Interior, and loop back to the visitor center. Not confident in my ability to find the return road, I opted for the more direct, less-chance-to-get-lost trek up Highway 240 to the summit.

What a splendid choice. The beauty of the striated sandy-looking landscape stretched farther in every direction than I could imagine. A smile remained on my face for the rest of the afternoon.

Overlook parking areas along the route allowed for safe photo ops. Of course I took pictures while telling myself pictures on my phone could not do the views justice. I envisioned being at the Grand Canyon (which I planned to visit on my trek home) and knew my photos would not capture the magnificence of the canyon any more than the landscape I admired that afternoon.

In every direction I saw gorgeous, calcified, dune-like mountains and canyons surrounded by grass resembling uncut fescue. I can still picture those views when I think about the Badlands. They were just that stunning! What I described as sandcastles, the park employees called buttes. Badlands National Park is one of roughly 420 areas of the national park system, but it's unique in that the US co-manages half the park with the Oglala Lakota Nation, one of the largest Native American Reservations in the United States. As I understand it, our National Park Service splits the park fees with the Oglala Lakota Nation.

When I was in the gift shop, an employee told me over one million travelers visit the park every year. But at every overlook on Badlands Loop Road, I saw the same people, three families who complimented me for riding my bike up the mountain, each saying they were only strong enough to ascend by car. On a bike with gears, climbing isn't too hard until the sustained climb is 8% or more—or if a rider is trying to go fast. Because I wasn't in any hurry, I rode my hybrid slowly. The mountain grade was about 6 to 7% most of the way, so climbing that mountain was not an enormous challenge for me. I had summited hundreds of steeper climbs in the past thirty years. However, getting encouragement along the way inspired me to keep going. A little extra encouragement never hurts.

I rode to what I thought was the highest point in the park, asking fellow tourists to take pictures and returning the favor. When the road turned downward at Bigfoot Pass, I turned around. Days later, when I left the park, I realized Bigfoot Pass was nowhere close to the highest point of the climb. I had ridden ten miles, and I understood the man at the gift shop to say it would be a ten-mile ride, but Pinnacles Overlook was still miles up the road. It was best that I didn't know how far from the top I turned around because not only was it getting late, I doubted my feet and knees could have handled much more.

Once I got to the bottom of the mountain, I rode back to the visitor center and then hiked up the buttes near the amphitheater to capture more panoramic views. Although they are made of rock, the buttes mimicked endless sand dunes and that made me think of the dunes at Lake Michigan. My first day in the Badlands provided warm, homey memories.

I arrived at the Badlands/White River KOA Holiday around 6-7 p.m. It offered all the amenities: a pool, remodeled showers and restrooms, Wi-Fi, cable, water, electric, breakfast, a store, a laundry room, miniature golf, playground equipment, rental bikes, cabins, and tent sites. I shy away from fancy private parks like the KOAs because they have to charge more for all the amenities I don't usually need, but when I had checked my *AllStays* app a few days earlier, the campground at the national park did not have any sites available.

Upon my arrival, it was clearly dinner time in South Dakota as evidenced by the mosquitoes eating me alive while I hooked up to the water and electricity. When I biked through the Badlands, I didn't notice any bugs, yet when I stepped outside at the KOA the word "relentless" came to mind. The campground is on the White River, and my site was a few feet from the water, which created the perfect habitat for millions of mosquitoes and gnats. I presumed I was interrupting an annual bug convention; hence, I hid indoors that Sunday night.

Monday was laundry day. I was camping in one of the most stunning areas of the country, and I spent a good part of the day doing laundry, but laundry is part of traveling. You fit laundry in when you can, when your laundry bag overflows, or when you run out of socks, whichever comes first. As I did my laundry, I chatted with a woman from Blairsville, Georgia, and a woman from Missouri named Lynn. After the laundry was done, I made phone calls and spoke with Cory at Dakota Battery in Rapid City, South Dakota, who agreed to inspect my rig on Friday. That meant I would need to stay in the area for a few more days. I reserved a third night at the KOA and secured two sites at Cedar Pass Campground in the Badlands: a non-electric site for Wednesday and an electric site for Thursday.

After dinner, my new friend Lynn, her husband, Jim, their red coonhound, Buddy, and I sat at their picnic table. The mosquitoes feasted on everyone except Buddy. In two minutes' time, those pesky little varmints made my legs look like I had caught a case of chickenpox. Jim suggested we talk inside, so we moved into their luxurious 37-foot fifth wheel and continued talking until sunset about my battery troubles, traveling, family, Wall Drug (a huge drug store my brother had recommended I visit), and their health.

"How long have you two been together?"

"We've been married twenty-seven years," Lynn said.

"Wow, that's a long time. Do you travel a lot?"

"Not a whole lot, but we try to get out when we can. It's good for both of us to get away. A while back, Jim was diagnosed with a rare disease called Schnitzler's that attacks his skeletal muscles. He's been going through chemo-like treatments for five years. He's in constant pain, but he never complains."

"Oh, my word. Jim, that's awful."

"The worst part for me was having to sell my cattle farm and furniture business. Just couldn't keep up with those and with all the treatments and pain."

"But we were able to sell the furniture business to a young guy who's like our adopted son," Lynn said. "We love him and his wife and children like they are our own."

"Do you have other children?"

"Jim's oldest daughter was killed in a car accident three years ago. Thank God her three-year-old was not in the back seat. She's precious—almost seven now."

"My youngest is twenty-nine," Jim added as he stood up to stretch. "She's not doing well. She seems to have trouble with relationships, and it's tough for her to keep a job. We will leave it at that."

"How 'bout you, Joy?"

I told them about being the youngest of six, that I retired from teaching elementary physical education, about my dream to ride my bike in fifty states, my tiny house battery issue, and about my bad knees and feet.

When I said I had seen lots of specialists about my feet, Lynn said, "I had foot surgery a year ago that didn't go so well. Don't let them talk you into surgery unless you just can't stand the pain anymore. Surgery isn't always better."

We talked more about our feet, Lynn's current battle with sciatica, Jim's condition, and other fun stuff. Lynn told me they had to go home the next weekend because she was seeing a new therapist for her sciatica and Jim had another treatment. Our conversation might sound depressing, but despite their tragedies, they were positive and encouraging. (We did talk about fun things like traveling and the Badlands too.)

When we said good night, Lynn said she'd stop by my place the next day. As I walked back to my site, I thought about their ongoing medical issues and family tragedies. I wondered how they were able to keep functioning, yet they were at the Badlands living life to the fullest. Kudos to them. What an amazing couple.

The next morning, eager to ride into the town of Interior, South Dakota, I donned my trusty black windbreaker, threw the hood over my head, and leaped over puddles to the camp store to verify directions. Kim gave me directions and quick tips about the town. She said the camp store was stocked better than the ones in Interior and added that the stores in town were old and smelled bad. I thought she was exaggerating and anticipated seeing the town myself. Still wearing my windbreaker to ward off the drizzle, I grabbed my hybrid, added the saddlebags in case I found a trinket or souvenir I couldn't live without, and headed for town. The asphalt road to Interior rode as smooth as a bowling alley—a cyclist's dream. And the rain stopped ten minutes into my ride—another plus for the day.

Kim had not exaggerated. Upon arrival it was clear the town had turned the calendar back fifty years. Interior, South Dakota, was as old and small as Kim had said. I rode around and snapped pictures of a school, two churches, and a jailhouse.

The school, painted bright white with red trim, was the largest building in town by far, but it was extremely small compared to schools in other small towns. Fire-engine red paint spelled out INTERIOR SCHOOL 1939. The building seemed to be in good condition and included a fenced-in playground in the rear. Room air conditioners jutted out above various windows. After a nostalgic moment at the school, I rode on over to the jail.

It appeared that nobody had been in that jail for a long time, if ever. It was about the size of a single-car garage. I questioned its functionality. Did Interior even need a sheriff? Does one sheriff work the entire county? Questions led to more questions. Interior measured smaller than the fictional town of Mayberry, immortalized in the *Andy Griffith Show* in the 1960s.

Sheriff Andy and Deputy Barney would have gotten a good laugh at Interior's jailhouse. CITY JAIL was hand-painted on the building between two small windows. In contrast with the old buildings, the jail stood out due to its new dark-green tin roof, fresh coat of whiter-than-snow paint, and pine tree-green door and trim. There was no driveway or parking lot. Was the jail merely for looks? I would have to investigate.

A stone's throw across the road from the jail, the post office and a convenience store shared a building. I had never seen such a setup—a tiny store connected to a tiny post office. The two women working there walked between the buildings through an interior archway; however, the building was too small for customers to do the same. Instead, customers had to walk out of the post office (or store) onto the front porch that spanned the length of the two buildings, and then walk into the store (and vice versa).

After buying stamps, I chatted with the women.

"How many would you say live in Interior?"

In unison, they said, "Sixty-nine or seventy."

"We know all of them," the taller woman said.

"We've both lived here all our lives, well, except for when we were in high school," the other woman said, "Yeah, we like it here."

"We went to that school across the way up till the ninth grade. That's when we had to move because the high school was too far away."

"Wow, I cannot even imagine."

"We didn't know any different. That's what everyone does here."

"Now eighty children attend the elementary school," the shorter woman said. Most of them are bused in from the surrounding ranches and reservations."

As we were talking, a man wearing a blue "Air Force veteran" hat breezed into the store, saying he'd seen my bike outside, and shared a story with me.

"I ride a recumbent bike because I hurt my back jumping out of an airplane and can't ride a regular bike anymore."

"That's awful. Vietnam?"

"Yes."

"How many times did you jump?" I asked.

"Seventy-four."

"Wow. I'm guessing it was jump seventy-four when you hurt your back?"

"No. It was jump six."

When he saw my eyes widen, he explained.

"My sixth jump didn't go as planned, and I was in tremendous pain, so I visited the Air Force doctor. The doctor said, 'There's nothing wrong with you. Keep jumping.' He wouldn't even listen to me. I jumped for two more years before I got a second opinion. The civilian doctor said the X-rays showed a piece of my tailbone had broken off. After that I quit jumping. I've lived with that pain forty-plus years. Can't do anything about it now, but I still get angry when I think about that military doctor telling me the pain was all in my head."

"That's awful! I don't even know what to say to that, other than thank you for your service."

"Yeah. That's just life sometimes. Hey, I'm Bruce. Are you in the area for a while?" he said as he reached out his hand.

I gladly shook his hand. "Joy. Yes. Actually, I just made reservations to stay until Friday morning."

"Joy? That's my wife's name."

I nodded and smiled. "She must be a wonderful woman."

"She most certainly is. I tell everyone she's the joy of my life. Oh, if you get a chance, check out the Night Sky program at the amphitheater."

"Okay. Thanks. So nice to meet you."

Bruce set a bottle of water on the counter and pulled out his wallet. I said goodbye to him and the women, mounted my bike and rode toward a rustic log cabin with a lighted OPEN sign in the window.

Two minutes later, I parked my bike next to the little building. Noticing the small gravel lot was empty, I inched inside and surveyed the merchandise. No one came out to greet me. Jewelry, blankets, moccasins, leather boots, and handsewn clothing filled the one-room gift and specialty shop. With no one around, it felt eerie. I felt like a trespasser. Too nervous to take pictures, I gawked at the high-quality merchandise for a good five minutes. Nobody showed up. I stepped outside and glanced left and right. Still no one. Feeling uncomfortable standing there alone, I guessed the clerk or owner had gotten called away so I left.

Next I rode to a store called Cowboy Corner, adorned with old-fashioned gas pumps in front. One step inside took me back in time and not in a good way. Seventy-five-year-old decor screamed "old," not "charming." Like the store attached to the post office, the candy and other snacks and toiletries wore a thin layer of dust. And Kim was right. There was a definite unpleasant odor. Old fryer grease, maybe. Unlike the three other townspeople I'd met, a man behind the counter avoided eye contact, and none of the local girls eating burgers at a side table glanced up. Hundreds of questions about the town rattled in my brain.

It didn't occur to me until days later that I forgot to get the story about the jail. The women at the post office probably could have answered my many questions, and I regret that missed opportunity. Also, I realized it was peak tourist season, and it saddened me that I was the only shopper around. Interior looked like a forgotten little community. I hoped I was wrong about my speculations because I viewed the town as a charming, hidden gold mine.

When I returned to the KOA store to tell Kim how well she had described Interior, she wasn't available. Thankful for their well-stocked store, I bought a loaf of whole wheat bread and a gallon of water. My new friend Lynn stopped by my site as I got my bike back on the rack. I invited her inside because getting bitten by mosquitoes spoils the fun. Both of us felt as though we were long-lost cousins. We connected on Instagram and swapped phone numbers. I love how technology makes it so easy to connect with new friends. Lynn and I talked for an hour and then another hour the next day before I left the KOA. There is something special about campers and cyclists. The immediate camaraderie we shared told me Lynn and I would keep in touch. We are friends to this day.

At noon on Wednesday, I arrived at Cedar Pass Campground within Badlands National Park. State and national parks are my favorites. It didn't seem right to be at a national park and not stay in the park, plus the national park was about half the price of the KOA. I also love the old, rustic feel of years gone by that I get when I stay at national and state parks. Two more big pluses—Cedar Pass was the first campground that wasn't swarming with bugs, and the weather could not have been more perfect: 75 to 80 degrees and sunny with a gentle breeze. The campground, void of trees, offered a picturesque view of the Badlands.

Just like laundry consumed my day on Monday, simple bike maintenance kept me at my site for the better part of the afternoon because my road bike had needed a new saddle and tires since I left Georgia. The maintenance turned out to be yet another situation where I did not learn my lesson.

Note to self—don't take something apart before taking a photo of it, even if it means pausing a phone conversation and even if it is a simple task like swapping saddles.

In hindsight, though, if I needed to put on new tires and a saddle, what better place to do that than Cedar Pass Campground on a perfect sunny day.

With new tires and saddle, I hopped on my bike and headed for that silky smooth road. I took Highway 44 E past the town of Interior and past the Badlands KOA. Dressed in shorts and a sleeveless jersey, the sun warmed my skin. I had the trail-like road to myself. Climbing hills on my road bike invigorated me. Steep hills beckoned me to push myself to aerobic exhaustion, something I enjoy doing once in a while. It makes me feel good to push myself until I can't go any more. The freedom I experienced that afternoon sparked the joy that riding brings me. My bikes take me to places physically and emotionally I could never experience on foot or by car or RV. For a moment, I was in seventh heaven.

At fifteen miles in, however, my feet started screaming at me, and I was glad I had turned around at the ten-mile mark. I winced with every pedal revolution. The last five miles were excruciating. It felt as though someone had tied a tourniquet around both ankles but still expected me to pedal. If I dismiss the moments I contemplated a double foot replacement, though, it was a perfect ride: perfect roads, perfect weather, perfect scenery, and zero traffic. I can't explain it, but the joy I get from riding has always outweighed the pain it causes.

A few years earlier my feet had forced me to quit running. They would hurt so badly after about three miles that I would limp home and not be able to run or ride the next day because of the pain. The pain of riding usually subsides by the next day, so I continue to ride—just not as hard or as far as I used to.

Thursday I moved my rig to the non-electric site I booked when I was at the KOA. Then I rode on those perfectly paved roads again, but in a different direction and not so fast. Around 4 p.m., I stopped for pictures at a sign that read: *Buffalo Gap, National Grasslands area*. At the sign, I turned around to keep from getting lost and to avoid the foot pain I'd experienced from riding hard the day before. It turned out to be another perfect day. Those mid-June days in the Badlands blessed me with warm, fresh air, with a pleasant breeze. The sky, with its light blue backdrop for the wispy white clouds, added an artistic effect, and the gray, rust, and beige buttes created a stark contrast to the vibrant green vegetation.

What a serene oasis. I could get used to this.

Because I found joy in the Badlands, I resolved to call them the Good-lands.

After that exhilarating bike ride in the Buffalo Gap area, I rushed to take part in the Night Sky program by 8:15, only to find out the show did not start until 9. I don't know how I got mixed up on the time, but it turned out to be a good thing. When I got to the amphitheater, I noticed Bruce, the Air Force veteran I had met in Interior. At the store, he had mentioned that he sometimes directed the show, but he wasn't leading another session until Friday. When I told him I hadn't expected to see him, he explained they had asked him to fill in for someone at the last minute. His night sky program would take place after the ranger's program about bison that started at nine.

Since I arrived early, Bruce introduced me to his wife, Joy, who said she had retired after teaching for forty years. And for twenty-seven of those years, she had taught all over the world, having followed her husband in the Air Force. What a story! The stark differences in Joy's career versus mine intrigued me. If another visitor hadn't interrupted our chat, I would have listened to Joy for a long, long time. I enjoyed this lively couple's stories.

Moments later it was time for the ranger program to begin. Bruce said he would follow the ranger with his night sky lesson.

A park ranger named Conner presented a fascinating forty-five-minute program on bison. He said that up until 1850, United States citizens had called them buffalo and explained that bison was the correct scientific name. In 1800, the buffalo population was estimated at thirty to fifty million. They were almost wiped out by the late 1800s, when fewer than five hundred remained. Drought, famine, harsh winters, and disease contributed to the bison's demise, but Conner said the primary reason for the massive decline was the people who came from England in droves, killing the animals ten times faster than they reproduced. Conner explained that when the Native Americans killed a buffalo, they used every part of the animal, so nothing got wasted. When the explorers killed them, they killed them for their tongues and their hides.

After Conner concluded his presentation, Bruce began the night sky talk about the moon, planets, and stars. At 10, he invited attendees to peer through his telescope at the moon, which moments earlier was covered by clouds. Joy stood by the telescope and instructed us to search for a "rebound" inside a crater. Despite my untrained eye, I spotted a significant dot that I presumed was the rebound. Although I understood little of what Bruce and Joy were saying, I deemed the evening a fabulous finale to a fantastic *Goodlands* visit. Meeting Joy truly made the evening special. I could not have asked for anything more.

CHAPTER SEVENTEEN

Rapid City, South Dakota

JUNE 14

Early Friday morning, I hit Highway 240, Badlands Loop Road, the same road where I had ridden my bike the day I arrived. I drove twenty-three jaw-dropping miles, stopping one hundred times for pictures, each stop vying to be a better view than the last. I wish I could describe the buttes and the overlook views better, but trying to describe the beauty of the Badlands is nearly impossible. You might just have to go there yourself one day.

My desire to visit the famous Wall Drug Store and my appointment with Dakota Battery forced me to rush through those twenty-three miles from the campground to the exit. I would like to return to Badlands, not only because I didn't get to hike the many trails or see much of the wildlife or the sunrises and sunsets, but also because what I did see was unique. It is one of the most amazing national parks I have explored.

In a couple of blinks, I found Wall Drug at the junction of 240 and 90 at exit 110, not far from the Pinnacles entrance to the Badlands.

Let me say that out loud. I found my way to Wall Drug. I couldn't believe I didn't get lost!

Thanks to the hundreds of signs advertising Wall Drug, I drove directly there without one wrong turn or detour. The city of Wall even marked their parking lots clearly, so I slipped into a lot across from Main Street and filled two free parking spaces. The town of Wall is home to 811 year-round residents, but because of time pressures, I did not drive around the residential area to visit with any of them—something I would have loved to do if I had the time.

Wall Drug Store was established in 1931 and struggled to stay in business during the Great Depression. Using huge signs along the road, the owners advertised free ice water for travelers, and business flourished. The now

76,000 square foot establishment spans one entire city block. Ice water is still free, but a cup of joe will set coffee drinkers back five cents. Yes, that's right: free water and five-cent coffee. Who does that? Besides a pharmacy, the store includes multiple cafés, an art gallery, and room after room of snacks, candy, drinks, clothing, and souvenirs. It's like a miniature mall and welcomes more visitors every year than Badlands National Park.

Opposite Wall Drug on Main Street is a block of touristy stores and eating establishments, along with the city's administration building and the chamber of commerce. Although I could have shopped all afternoon, I bought souvenirs for friends, took pictures of the nostalgic strip, and headed out within the hour.

After driving sixty miles west on I 90, I found a place to park on the back side of Dakota Battery in Rapid City. Since I had an appointment, a mechanic named Bob met me as I approached the office. He drove my motorhome to the front of the building by the open garage doors, asked me to describe the problem, and began an investigation. In less than an hour, Bob discovered the problem, changed a fuse, and replaced the solenoid.

"You should be good to go, ma'am."

"Seriously? This has been a problem since I bought this baby, and you fixed it that fast? Thank you, Bob. You're outstanding." I slipped him a $20.

Inside, Lester swiped my credit card for the hundred-dollar repair while I talked to Todd, the owner, and thanked the guys repeatedly. As I walked out, a woman traveling solo in a motorhome stopped in for help, and we talked for a minute. By 2:30 I pulled out, once again a happy camper.

I was hungry and low on groceries, so I navigated to the nearest Walmart. The woman I had met at Dakota Battery, Judy, pulled up beside me in the Walmart parking lot. After giving me a quick tour of her camper and introducing me to her little dog, a papillon named Harper, she said she needed to get going. She wrote her name and phone number on a piece of scrap paper and said to call if I needed anything. As I walked from Judy's RV to mine, a man with a dog on a leash approached his Class C, which was parked beside mine.

"Nice rig," I said.

Noticing that our motorhomes were identical, he laughed and came over to meet me.

"Hi, I'm Joy," I said, stretching out my hand.

"Tony," he said, giving me a firm handshake and a genuine smile.

Tony's motorhome appeared newer, and he had a shiny BMW Adventure bike on the back, plus a white Geo Tracker as his tow-behind.

"What's hiding under the cover?" he asked.

"A road bike and a mountain bike. Unlike your bike, I have to use these," I said, slapping my quads, "to make them go. What's your dog's name?"

"Miles."

"Will he let me pet him?"

"Absolutely, if you've got an hour. He'll get mad when you quit."

"Sounds like my brother's basset. What breed is Miles? He looks like a mix."

"Yeah, he's a mix of a Labrador and a dachshund. A dachsador."

"I have never heard of a dox-a-door?" I said, questioning my pronunciation. "He seems sweet."

"He's the best."

We talked a few minutes, asking each other the usual questions. Some people call it the "four-minute what's-your-story" conversation. Tony said he had retired, sold his home, and had been living in his motorhome full time since he bought it new in January. I told him my story and then told him I had just gotten my house battery issue resolved.

"You might want to look into getting solar for your rig. Solar would keep them charged all the time. And I think you can get a monitor for your batteries that is more precise than the one that comes with the rig. It shows exactly, by percentage, how much battery power you have at all times."

"Oh, that would be nice. I have always hated that my indicator only shows that my batteries are full, one-third low, two-thirds low, or fully drained. That's clearly not good enough. I've been told if they go below 50 percent, it damages the batteries."

"That's right," Tony said.

With the flashlight on his phone, he showed me how to check the water in the house batteries. I didn't even know that was something I needed to do. Then he told me about places to boondock (camp for free with no hookups), gave me his number, and said to call if he could do anything for me. What a great day: Badlands, Wall Drug, Dakota Battery, and meeting two full-time RVers willing to help a newbie. Campers and full-timers are kindhearted souls, willing to share their knowledge and experience, and Judy and Tony were the epitome. I looked forward to keeping in touch with them.

I overnighted at the Rapid City Walmart along with more RVers than you'd find at a rally. Groups of young guys and older men by themselves strolled through the lot. Uneasy, I locked the doors, but slept well. Sleep is usually my strong point. Awakened by the whirring and rumbling of a weed eater and a lawn mower in the nearby grassy area, I rose quickly in case Tony wanted to visit before he left. As my oatmeal cooked on the stove, Tony knocked. He and Miles came inside and I kept cooking. We talked through my fixing, eating, and cleaning up my breakfast. I offered to share but he declined. After an hour, Tony and I agreed to cut our conversation short and double-checked our phone numbers. He and Miles, who had fallen asleep on my front passenger seat, stepped out and pulled away in their look-alike tiny house on wheels.

Within minutes, I was on the road again headed toward a longtime bucket list destination, and full of anticipation. By my calculations I was less than forty-five minutes away. What joy would come my way today?

CHAPTER EIGHTEEN

Mount Rushmore

JUNE 15

When I spotted the iconic National Park Service sign and an overlook large enough for me to stop and take in the view, my stomach turned cartwheels of joy. I had dreamed of seeing this park for twenty-five years: Mount Rushmore National Memorial. Chills ran up my spine as I read the sign.

The moment I arrived, I fell into tourist-mode. I snapped a picture of the sign, jumped back into the driver's seat, drove around a bend and BAM! There it was. Straight in front of me towered one of the most majestic mountains in the United States of America. Awestruck, I pulled over to the side of the two-lane road and snapped a picture right there. I took pictures for the next four hours, but the one from the road is the one that became the screensaver on my phone.

Parking and walking to the memorial could not have been easier. They gave me the royal treatment—allowing me to park in a special section designated for motorhomes. Everyone receives a parking ticket when they drive in and pay at the park kiosks. I walked inside the park and paid $10 at the kiosk, which covered parking and admission for one whole year. Ingenious! Somebody figured out how to be efficient since the park welcomes over 3,000,000 visitors each year—no more waiting in a line of vehicles at the entranceway.

As I walked toward the entrance, I thought the walkway, made of different shades and sizes of smooth gray pavers, looked fancy enough to be inside a museum or a state capital building. A huge multi-arched entrance welcomed visitors in style. When I walked through the state flags tunnel, I smiled. All fifty states and a few territories were represented, their flags flying at the top of more than a dozen twenty-foot-high pillars spaced out over maybe two hundred yards. Each state and the date of its entry into the union was engraved in the marble pillars, similar to the names and dates on tombstones. I took pictures from far away and then several close-ups of the state engravings, noting I had never studied much about the states and the particulars about them joining the union. The far end of the tunnel made for a perfect view of the monument. Glorious! Surreal, even. Again, I could not believe I was really there—standing face-to-face with four of the most recognized presidents of our nation.

Concrete, rock, or wood stairs and walkways throughout the entire park make it easy to navigate. In fact, from the entrance, through the flag tunnel, and all the way to a large deck where people can take pictures with and marvel at the faces of Presidents Washington, Jefferson, Roosevelt, and Lincoln, is all wheelchair accessible.

After taking a selfie and two shots of a young family of four with the dad's phone, I walked to the left of the monument and noticed the amphitheater was closed for remodeling. Though I couldn't see it, a couple from South Dakota told me that on the back side of the huge rectangular building where we stood were football stadium-style bleachers. They said at night the park conducts a ranger program and then shows a film about the monument.

"At the end of the show they light up the presidents' faces," the woman told me. "It's spectacular. You'll have to come back when it's open and see it lit up at night."

"Yes, I will definitely need to come back. I always love those park films, and seeing the faces all lit up at night would make another visit even more special."

To my right as I faced the monument, I took pictures of the huge gift shop and massive food court which are also wheelchair accessible. From there I strolled down a 0.6-mile all-paved sloping pathway to the sculptor's studio where a park ranger spoke about the monument every thirty minutes. The path continued in a loop, allowing visitors to get closer to the presidents, but never as high as their faces, so the view is always looking up at our presidents as small children look up at adults.

As a park ranger spoke of the connection between the carving here and at Stone Mountain, Georgia, I scribbled notes, fascinated by the history. The same sculptor, Gutzon Borglum, began both projects. However, a dispute early in the Stone Mountain project prompted Borglum to take his toys and go home, well, to find a new home in South Dakota, anyway. He was born in Idaho and bounced around the country working on various statues and sculpting projects, living in Kansas, Texas, Nebraska, the East Coast, and Georgia before moving to the black hills. If he could pull it off, Mount Rushmore would be his biggest accomplishment yet.

It took fourteen years for three hundred workers to complete Mount Rushmore, not only because of the enormity of the job, but because a lack of funding constantly slowed progress. The ranger told us the Borglum family had said the mountain carvings could have and should have been completed in five years.

The project began as a ploy to draw visitors to the Black Hills of South Dakota in 1927. Many setbacks, including the rock being too soft to carve Jefferson on Washington's right, a sculptor and project manager quitting, and even the Great Depression, threatened the completion of Borglum's vision. Still, he remained focused and determined to see it through. The ranger told our small group about the enormous amounts of dynamite that workers used to blast away the rock. Then jackhammers, hammers, and chisels (in that order) were employed to carve the granite rock mountain into the distinguished faces of four former US presidents.

Workers blasted and chiseled away approximately 450,000 tons of rock. The blasted chunks have never been touched or removed. From a distance, it looks as though dump trucks dropped them at the top, and they tumbled down the side of the mountain to add a natural touch.

As he pointed to the model behind him, the ranger told us the original plan included Washington's complete bust, but funding, focus, and time ran out because of WWII. Gutzon Borglum died in March 1941, before his crew finished the carvings. Borglum's son, Lincoln, who had supervised much of the work for years, saw the project to its completion. A dedication took place on October 31, 1941, six months after its designer's death. Despite the dangerous conditions for the workers, not one crew member died while working on the project. Unbeknownst to me, I would later get to meet one of those workers.

The park and the monument were so fascinating and visitor friendly I wanted to stay. Because a man I had met on the way to the park and the couple I had met earlier had told me the carving was more majestic when highlighted with lights, I contemplated staying until dark. However, that idea did not make practical sense. First, I wasn't even sure if they were going to turn on the lights because of the renovation project. Second, I had no campground reservation for the night. And finally, I would have to wait four hours until the show and then drive to an unknown destination in the darkness of the Black Hills.

I slipped into the food court, bought a latte, and sat down to reserve a site at Custer State Park, just a few miles south. Success! Over the phone, I booked site #29 at Blue Bell Campground for three nights for $81 plus a $20 state park fee to be paid upon arrival. To give some perspective on the size of Custer, there are nine campgrounds within the park. Blue Bell provided thirty-one sites, and I landed the second to the last site in all of Custer. Reluctant to leave Mount Rushmore, yet excited to experience Custer State Park, I followed the directions on my phone, hoping Siri would direct me there without losing a signal in the mountains and without getting me lost.

CHAPTER NINETEEN

Custer State Park

JUNE 15 – 19

Siri and I didn't lose our connection, but she didn't make my drive to the campground easy. The drive to Custer took me forty-five minutes longer than Siri originally promised, but she did get me there, and for that, I was thankful. At dusk, Blue Bell Campground hosts Paul and Jan met me at the entrance to tell me I was not the only one who booked site #29.

Paul said, "It happens occasionally when someone books online within minutes of someone else booking on-site."

My hosts led me to another site where I could stay for the night and said I could move to #29 the next day. It was now dark, so they guided me into the overflow site and told me to come see them in the morning for suggestions on what to do and see. The site was not level. Some RVs have automatic levelers that raise or lower each wheel with the push of a button. My rig doesn't have that, so I have a couple of sets of ten plastic interlocking blocks I call Legos to put under the lower wheels. It requires a bit of time to determine which corners need to be raised and then to stack the blocks into a ramp formation and park the rig precisely on the top of those ramps. I was too exhausted to play with my Legos in the dark, so I ate dinner and called it a night.

Sunday morning, not sure of cell coverage, I called my sister Lynn and rejoiced when she answered. I loved talking to her because she encouraged me and showed a genuine interest in my travels. We talked about the weather. Unusually cool and rainy weather had kept her from enjoying her pool in northern Indiana. Even though it had been open for over a month, the water felt too cold, even with the heater running. I told her my weather had been close to perfect. Temperatures stayed in the high fifties at night, perfect for sleeping with the windows open, and mid to upper seventies during the day, perfect for hiking and biking. I said I had not seen heavy rain since the day I drove in the storm on my way to the Laura Ingalls Wilder Museum. Fortunately, since surviving that storm, it either rained at night or intermittently during the day.

Paul and Jan stopped by around noon. Jan plotted a bike route from the campground and left to help another camper. Paul told me how to get to site #29 and said he would meet me there in a few minutes. He walked up the hill to #29, arriving just in time to guide me into the site and then help me level my rig with my Legos.

"A paving crew recently re-graded the sites here and didn't make them level. I do not understand why they would go through the trouble and expense of regrading, yet not make the sites level."

"Yeah, makes no sense to me either."

It started sprinkling, and Paul said, "You might need to hold off on your ride."

I looked up at the sky and told him he'd better run. Paul took off jogging toward their place. The wind picked up as I frantically plugged my rig into the electricity and got back inside in the nick of time. As people say in Georgia "the bottom fell out," and being inside protected me from a monsoon. I hoped Paul and Jan made it back to their camper in time. According to the forecast on *Dark Sky*, Custer State Park inhabitants would receive a whole day of rain.

Serves me right for bragging to Lynn about my perfect weather.

It had not rained an entire day since I started my trip six weeks earlier, but a rainy day offered me an opportunity to get inside tasks completed. I needed to write postcards, read, write in my journal, prepare packages to mail to friends, and cook a meal. Not once had I opened any of the three recipe books I brought along.

Well, I don't want to say I wasted my day, but I did nothing on my list except make a meal. After dinner, I contacted my childhood friend Amy about meeting up in Montana. She told me that she and her husband, Glenn, had a disastrous houseboat trip, and their story was aired on the local news.

"What? Tell me what happened!"

"Glenn and I and our puppies, Samson and Delilah, were on a trip in the Gulf in our houseboat—the boat we took you on in February. Well, we were thirty miles offshore, and Glenn said something wasn't right. He thought it was something electrical, like with the generator. He thought it had overheated, but nothing he tried to cool it down worked. Flames took over in like two minutes. He says, 'Amy, I think this is it. I don't know what else to do. We're going to have to get off.' He busts out the kitchen window, grabs a gallon of water and a couple of boxes of cereal and tells me to get the puppies while he lowers the dinghy. Everything happened so fast, but we were both calm about the whole thing. We got in the lifeboat expecting to be stranded for days."

"Oh, my word, Amy. Did you have time to get anything else?"

"No. I didn't even have my cell phone. We were 'home,' so Glenn didn't have his wallet in his pocket, and I certainly didn't have my purse on me. Joy, it was unreal. We were only in the dinghy for a few minutes when our houseboat exploded. It just EX—PLOOOODED, like in a movie. We got off just in time. Glenn said the flames and smoke probably shot up twenty feet in the air. It was heartbreaking to watch our boat burn. We got married on that boat. But we were thankful we got off in time."

As Amy told me what had happened only days earlier, she was calm.

"How can you be so calm? This just happened on Thursday last week? You sound as though it happened years ago to someone else."

"I don't know. Glenn and I both had a calm about us. Neither of us was anxious. We felt we would either get rescued or we would die together and go to heaven. Nothing we said or did would change those two options. Our lives were in God's hands, and we were at peace with whatever the outcome. You know that verse, I think it's Philippians 1:21, where Paul says, 'For to me to live is Christ, and to die is gain.'? Well, we prayed. Neither of us ever envisioned we would die that way, but we were ready to meet Jesus. And if we lived, we would have a good story to tell—a story to share our faith."

"Wow. This is unbelievable. Okay, so you are in your little lifeboat and then what?"

"We were only in the boat for a few hours when we saw a cruise ship. I will tell you more details later, but yeah, we got rescued by a cruise ship. We figured a bunch of the passengers saw our boat burning from far away. They told the captain and he came back to rescue us. When we climbed on board, everyone was cheering and hugging us and telling us they were praying so hard that they would get to us in time. The puppies got spoiled. Everyone wanted to hold them. It was unbelievable."

"Unbelievable is right, Amy. Wow! You've got to tell me the complete story again when we get together. Speaking of . . . that's why I called. We need to figure out how we can connect. Are you and Glenn still planning to go to Glacier?"

Amy assured me they still planned to go. They were at home in Florida, trying to get new driver's licenses and file insurance claims and whatever else a couple would need to do after their houseboat blew up in the middle of the Gulf. We talked over several scenarios and agreed to talk again when they got on the road.

Hearing Amy's story highlighted the fact that I was not where I wanted to be in my faith. That calm Amy talked about? Yeah, I didn't have that. I had joy, but I knew I didn't have the peace Amy and Glenn had in the middle of the ocean.

Finally, the rain stopped, and I rushed out to hear the ranger program about bison, my new favorite animals. The ranger focused her talk on the six people instrumental in repopulating the herds after the Europeans had nearly caused them to go extinct. Thanks to their work and the work of many others since around 1890, extinction is no longer a threat for the American bison.

The next morning, I woke to a steady pitter-patter on my roof. Another day of rain offered me a second opportunity to knock out my to-do list. I am a successful task-avoider. I'm proud to say, though, I did take a two-hour walk in the drizzle as I chatted with my new friend Lynn, who was already back home and into her routine in Kansas City, Missouri. Since the rain had kept me from seeing Custer State Park, I checked with Paul and Jan to see if I could stay another day. Once again, not planning had its pros and cons. Someone else had reserved site 29 for the rest of the week. I could stay if I was willing to change sites again.

Tuesday morning I moved to a third campsite. Using every leveling block I owned still didn't get me level, but I was happy to stay another day. I ate breakfast and then pedaled my hybrid a mile down the gravel roadway before the rain came down—again. I *really* should have kept my mouth shut about the perfect weather.

A couple I met on the road provided me with directions to the Centennial Trail and cautioned that a storm was coming. Centennial is a multi-use trail within the state park, meaning it's for hikers, horses, and mountain bikers. About a half mile from the trailhead, I came upon a steep, muddy, treacherous section. Not being a mountain biker, but rather a road biker who owns a hybrid bike for riding on poorly paved roads and gravel bike paths, I reluctantly turned around. Along the gravel roadway I rode through French Creek Horse Camp, a campground specifically designed for campers with horses, to the Blue Bell Lodge and cabins on Highway 87 and then back to my site. Another torrential downpour began minutes after I secured my bike to its rack.

When the rain subsided, I walked around and stopped for a visit with Paul, who was sitting under the awning of their fifth wheel.

"I passed by your place last night. I love those little white lights everywhere. It looks like Christmas."

"Yeah. We like the way they look too, but the ones around the bottom are supposed to help deter mice and squirrels."

"Hmm, never heard of that."

"Supposedly they don't like light, so they won't set up camp with us when we are in one place for a long time."

"Interesting. How long have you been hosts here?"

"This is our seventh year at Blue Bell. We're retired, so we host six months out of the year and travel in the southern states during the winter. They tell us they can't find people willing to host, so we keep coming back."

We talked a couple more minutes and then Paul got back to work. That evening, Jan and Paul stopped by on a golf cart to collect my fee for the night. Paying them in cash made life easy. I stood beside their cart, and we talked about the pros and cons of hosting, plus some of their experiences and my travels. I said I wasn't ready to take on the responsibility of hosting, but it sure sounded like something I might want to do one day. Twenty minutes into our conversation, Jan said something had awakened her early that morning.

"Oh? Tell me what happened."

"Well, you know living in a campground—basically a field—brings you up close to nature, sometimes too close. I fell asleep last night watching TV, and the glow of the television cast a little light into my dark bedroom. In my groggy state, I felt a light touch on my forehead and brushed away what I thought was a stray hair. Then I opened my eyes and in the glow the TV provided, I saw a mouse scampering down my arm!"

"Oh, no! What did you do? Oh, how creepy!"

"Did you not hear me scream? I screamed so loud I was certain I woke everyone in the camp. Paul was sleeping in a recliner in the living room. He came rushing in to see what was wrong. We turned on all the lights. He set a trap. No more sleeping for me. And you know the crazy part? Our dog, Annie, paid no attention to the commotion. She slept through it all. About an hour later, I heard the trap snap, but I could not go back to sleep. Luckily Mickey did not bring friends or family with him. We would have hated to kill Minnie too."

"Oh, my word, Jan! That would ruin me for life! It makes me shudder to think about that little fella running across your face. And then down your arm? Yuck! I've heard mice get into people's campers, but I've never heard of any trying to sneak into bed with them. I would have freaked out! Wait. Paul, didn't you tell me the lights under your camper are to help deter mice?"

"Yeah, *help* being the operative word," Paul said. "The lights are probably the reason Mickey didn't bring his whole family with him. We are keeping the lights."

After her terrifying mouse story, Jan gave me directions to Wildlife Loop Road and told me where to look for burros and bison before I would drive on to the memorial in Crazy Horse, South Dakota, the next morning.

"The Crazy Horse film is better than the one at Rushmore," Jan said.

"Really?"

"Yeah, but the amphitheater and the museum under the amphitheater are being remodeled. That's where they show the film. You can find it on YouTube, though."

"A couple I met by the amphitheater told me they show a film there. I'll try to find it on YouTube, then. Thanks for telling me. And can you tell me a little about Crazy Horse? I only know my brother told me to go see it if possible."

"Oh, it's a crazy story all right. It's a sculpture in the rock like Mount Rushmore, except it's a chief on his charging horse. It's still under construction, but his face is finished. Eventually he will be sitting on a horse with his arm stretched out in front of him. Like he's pointing toward something. There's a model of the chief on the grounds there. They offer a tour where you can walk out on his arm, and they tell you more about the sculpting process."

"Whoa. That sounds like something I'd like to do."

"Yeah, check it out if you can."

"I will have to do that. Now . . . I have been here since Saturday night and I still haven't really gotten to see Custer. Can you tell me where I should go tomorrow to see a little of the park? I know there's lots more to the park than Blue Bell Campground."

"Yes. Of course. I'm guessing it's twenty miles through the park. Oh, I need to tell you, there are three parts of Custer you won't get to see because there are low, narrow bridges that motorhomes can't fit through."

"Thanks so much, Jan. My brother told me about the bridges, but I had forgotten. I'm here because he said how much he and his wife loved Custer. They said it feels more like a national park than a state park."

"Yes, it's one of the largest state parks in the country. The entire park is over one hundred square miles. If you turn right out of here, you will see the main road that will take you through the park. That's where you will see the bison and burros."

"Okay. Thanks. I'm going to scoot. I need to wash my bike and get to the ranger program. Oh, and thanks for telling me that mouse story. I'm sure I'll sleep well tonight. I'll be pulling the covers over my face for the rest of my life, thanks to you and Mickey."

Jan laughed. "Glad we could help. Yeah, we'd better get going too. We've got to catch up with two more campers tonight."

"We wish you the best," Paul said. "Will you be leaving early tomorrow?"

"No, I never leave early unless I have to."

"Well, swing by and say goodbye in the morning if you can," Jan said as they drove off in their golf cart.

I turned and looked at my hybrid. Thanks to the gravel and rain, it was filthier than I had ever seen it. I washed it and secured it on the rack in time for the 9 p.m. program about the wildlife in Custer. Park rangers conducted programs every night. They talked about dinosaurs, edible plants, bison, and the other animals that live in Custer, including deer, elk, burros, bighorn sheep, bison, prairie dogs, mountain goats, coyotes, and turkeys.

Cindy, the ranger who taught the program on my final night, did a marvelous job. Before she began her presentation, she told us the park had had more rain the past three weeks than they could handle. It had rained constantly. And three weeks before, they got twenty-two inches of snow. She said it was awful. People tried to leave and got stuck. Many visitors got stranded in their vehicles overnight. The park had no power for two days. After the snow, it rained twelve inches in one day. I cannot imagine that much snow and that much rain, in May and June especially. Cindy kept the group engaged for an hour by asking us questions and then answering them if we didn't know the answers.

Wednesday won the blue ribbon for best day! Before leaving Blue Bell, I found Paul and Jan by the cabins. They had finished cleaning the last of eight cabins moments earlier because the employees who cleaned them needed help. Jan allowed me to look inside the last one—a clean, simple log cabin with two twin beds, no water. She then reviewed my route through the park and told me I could use the dump station at the other end of Custer. As I hugged my new friends and gave Annie, their bichon frise, a scratch under the chin, I asked Jan for her contact information. I love making new friends. It was difficult to leave, but it was time to explore the rest of the park. I jumped in my rig, excited to see Custer State Park.

At the visitor center, I watched a fifteen-minute IMAX movie about the bison at Custer. When the herd thundered across the plains, they stampeded toward me. The movie reminded me of *Dances with Wolves*, and the narrator sounded like Kevin Costner, so it was an easy listen. As the credits scrolled, the name *Kevin Costner* flashed across the screen.

Ok then, I guess that's why the narrator sounded like Kevin Costner.

Afterward, I drove through a serene state park with rolling hills, lush grass, brilliant wildflowers, and dark green pines against enormous charcoal-colored rocks. Even if I had seen no wildlife, it would still have been worth the drive. About ten miles into the loop, the traffic slowed. Eight burros socializing in the road and a pull-off area had caused the slowdown. When I saw one man feeding an off-white burro a stack of saltines one at a time from his driver's side window, I cringed. I joined the dozen or so people petting—and feeding—the precious burros and stroked one of the two brown burros on the back as a white-haired couple enticed him with carrots.

Is this what a petting zoo looks like?

Who knew I could be so happy in the middle of a traffic jam?

I knew we should not feed the wild animals, and I was certain that salty processed foods like saltines should not be part of their diet. But apparently such feeding practices are common because Ranger Cindy had told us about the "begging burros" that we would likely see as we drove around the park loop. Cindy warned that if people insisted on feeding the burros, they should keep their hands flat with fingers down because the burros can't distinguish between a finger and a carrot. Discovering how matted and snarled their fur felt against my fingers surprised me. But now that I think about it, they have never had a bath, and no one has washed, conditioned, or combed their fur. What was I expecting? It was long and tangled and felt like fleece.

I noticed how gently the burros took food from people's hands and how they allowed us to pet them, put our arms around them, and pose with them for pictures. Of course, I exchanged picture-taking duties with a woman enjoying the moment with her family. Young children, older adults, and everyone in between remained intrigued with the burros and approached them with kindness. The white jenny (female burro) who agreed to have her picture taken with me stood a little shorter, and her fur felt softer than the brown jack (male burro) nearby. Two burros, oblivious to the excitement going on ten yards away, stayed in the field and continued to eat the grass on the other side of the road. Memories of those gentle souls hold a special place in my heart now and forever.

Across from the visitor center, I found the dirt road where Jan had told me I might find bison. However, one woman I spoke with at the "burro petting zoo" had said there was a herd ahead on the paved loop road. Sure enough, in a couple of miles, I got caught in another traffic jam as a herd of bison roamed with no regard for spectators. Some walked across the road, so cars stopped. Rangers had advised us not to get out of our vehicles, but it was so tempting. The herd seemed mellow. I had an overwhelming desire to jump out and pet them like we had done with the burros, but I refrained.

There was no place to pull over, so when the cars in front of me moved, I followed. I took several pictures of the herd and of a bull crossing, but I wanted more close-ups and more videos. A guy on a motorcycle in front of me seemed antsy, like he was late for work and annoyed. He revved his engine, which I thought might agitate the bison, but they remained unfazed.

Cindy had told us how to tell the males (bulls) from the females (cows). The males grow to be a foot taller and can weigh twice as much as the females. They all stay together, and the mommas and other members of the family are protective of their babies. I like that parental/family instinct to protect and care for their young. After the bison crossed the road, I drove on to the dump station. Driving through Custer took four hours, and I had only allotted ninety minutes to drive the twenty-mile loop. I did not realize the speed limit in the park was 25 to 35 mph, and I did not expect to spend so much time with the burros and bison, but I would not have changed a thing. The park lived up to its reputation. As I have said so many times, I did not want to leave. Staying another day or another week at Custer would have been enjoyable, especially because I had connected with hosts Paul and Jan, but I needed to keep moving. My goal was to get to Glacier to meet up with Amy and Glenn, but I had much to see in the meantime.

CHAPTER TWENTY

Crazy Horse

JUNE 19

Crazy Horse was a Lakota leader who took part in the Battle of Little Bighorn, also known as Custer's Last Stand, and was chosen as a symbolic representative to ensure his people would not be forgotten. The Crazy Horse Memorial is said to be the largest mountain sculpture in progress in the world. It all began shortly after WWII with a handshake between dreamer Chief Henry Standing Bear and sculptor Korczak Ziolkowski. The mission of the project is to honor the heritage of the Native Americans and to educate the public through on-site museums, tours, programs, and a university. A medical school is in the planning stage.

Although I can get lost in an elevator, I had no trouble finding Crazy Horse. Using the directions from Jan, my map, and the plentiful road signs, I found the entrance as easily as I found Wall Drug. My success was certainly due to the road signs rather than my improved map-reading skills, but it still made me feel good to find the place without any trouble. The parking lot was as large as three Walmart lots and as accommodating to big rigs as Mount Rushmore.

The entry fee to Crazy Horse Memorial cost $12, and the park was worth far more. It included three museums, a gift shop, a restaurant, a snack bar, memorabilia from sculptor Korczak Ziolkowski's home, multiple live shows, and more.

Upon entering the park, I watched the informational film—a first-rate introduction to how the sculpture of Crazy Horse began. According to the film, Korczak Ziolkowski considered the project for seven years before agreeing to take on the task of creating a sculpture of a Chief on a horse, similar to the carvings of the faces of Washington, Jefferson, Roosevelt, and Lincoln depicted on Mount Rushmore. In 1948, after forming a

300:1 scale model of Crazy Horse sitting on a charging horse with his arm outstretched and finger pointing forward, Ziolkowski began the project by himself. Later he solicited help, and now each of his ten children has worked on the mountain. When he died in 1982, his wife, Ruth, took over as the supervisor.

Currently, three Ziolkowski children and three grandchildren are working on the project. They hope to have it completed, along with a medical college at the base of the mountain for Native Americans in another seventy years. Ruth lived to see the face completed, which was dedicated and opened to the public for viewing in 1998. Originally, Korczak hoped they would finish the project in thirty years, but the tedious work, the brittle rock, and the slow private donations have all contributed to the extended completion time. Although it might speed up the progress, the Ziolkowski family has vowed not to accept any government funding due to the belief that the government would take over control of the project.

After watching the film, I explored the museum. A few artisans positioned outside the gift shop sold their crafts. Intrigued by a large display of handcrafted jewelry, I stopped to admire a woman's intricate work. The woman put down the bracelet she was beading and told me about her jewelry.

"These materials are strong," she said. "The sterling silver bracelets can handle almost anything but chlorine, and a pair of wire cutters, of course. You won't be disappointed."

She spoke the truth, as I am still wearing the sterling silver bracelet I bought for myself. This confident, soft-spoken woman said every year she works at her booth for the six-month tourist season, and she does not pay overhead because of her Lakota ancestry. She said she and her husband go back to their home near Chamberlain in the off season where their children and grandchildren live.

Next, I toured the museum and noticed a ticket booth for a bus tour. I bought a $4 ticket and jumped on board. As the bus traveled to the bottom of the mountain, we saw Crazy Horse's face, completed on both sides, which the driver said is called "sculpture in the round." As he drove, he explained that even though 98 percent of the people who visit the mountain will never see the other side, Ziolkowski wanted his masterpiece to be completed all the way around.

"Unwilling to relinquish control to the government, the family has turned down two $10,000,000 government grants. Instead of government money, the family relies on visitors and private donors to support the project," the driver said.

I could not wrap my head around working on a project that will take several generations to complete. Seventy years of work behind them with plans for another seventy to complete the project? What dedication! What a labor of love!

Our tour guide-bus driver stopped at the bottom of the mountain where passengers could take pictures of the side of Crazy Horse that most of the world would never see. We re-boarded the bus ten minutes later, and he drove us back up to the starting point. As I made my final rounds of the park, I saw the model of the memorial Jan had told me about. Then I found a bin of rocks that workers had blasted and gathered from the mountain for visitors to take as souvenirs in return for a small donation. Visitors can keep a piece of history, the family receives donations, and the rubble is carried away. A win-win-win for sure.

Without hesitation, I dropped a donation in the box and selected a three-pound chunk of multicolored granite, which doubles as a Crazy Horse keepsake and a doorstop for my tiny house's bathroom door. As I walked toward the exit, I noticed the ticket booth for the tour to walk on Crazy Horse's extended arm that Jan and Paul had told me about. The booth was closed.

As the sun dropped below the horizon, I left Crazy Horse. I should have left earlier, but I was enjoying my visit and did not think I had far to drive. Siri told me that a Walmart in Spearfish, South Dakota, was only an hour away. Well, maybe the crow could make it in an hour, but it took me two. The first thirty minutes went smoothly. Then it turned dark and became nearly impossible to drive in the Black Hills as the hills became pitch black—as in train tunnel black. Even my high beams couldn't touch the darkness. By 9:30, the drive was as dark as the inside of a cave and then rain, gusty winds, thunder, and lightning nearly scared me to death. For miles I looked for a place to stop but could find nowhere safe *and* legal. Forced to keep driving outside my comfort zone, I was never so happy to see that familiar blue and gray building. When I pulled into the parking lot at 10 p.m., it was raining *bison and burros,* and the wind nearly rocked my camper off its wheels. Boy, was I grateful to be parked at a Walmart. Home sweet home.

Thank you, God, for your protection . . . again.

CHAPTER TWENTY-ONE

Déjà vu, Mount Rushmore Again

JUNE 20-23

In Spearfish I woke to dry pavement and a gentle breeze brushing over my camper. One would never have known I had endured a terrifying night in gale force winds. That morning I had planned to drive to North Dakota to Theodore Roosevelt National Park, about two hundred miles due north. Oh, how plans can change with the wind.

While still in the Walmart parking lot, I got a text from my friend Amy, saying she and Glenn would be in Rapid City, South Dakota, that evening. (Rapid City was fifty miles southeast of where I was in Spearfish.)

Even though she had initially told me that she and her husband were going to be in Montana for the last week of June, I thought the houseboat fire had bought me more time. (I was trying to hurry to North Dakota so I could meet up with them in Montana sometime in July.) I also thought she had said she would call me when they left their home in Florida. Amy and Glenn were sticking to their plan to camp at Glacier National Park at the end of June, and Glacier sits on the west side of the state, 650 miles from Spearfish if I drove straight there.

In my head I always think I can make everything work. How I thought I would get to Teddy Roosevelt National Park, Yellowstone National Park, The Grand Tetons, and Glacier National Park—probably over a thousand miles—in a week, I will never know. That's not how I travel.

I realized there was no way I could meet them in Montana. There were too many places to visit, and I travel too slowly to make it to Glacier in a week. After five and a half seconds of contemplating my options, I texted Amy that I'd drive an hour east to Rapid City to meet them there, instead of Montana. Amy responded with a thumbs-up emoji.

Gifted with a whole day to make a one-hour drive, I prepared several packages, birthday cards, and postcards for mailing—all projects I had intended to complete at Custer. I also shopped at Walmart and the Dollar Tree across the street, drove to the nearby Sturgis post office to mail packages and cards, and navigated to Planet Fitness in Rapid City, where I had worked out a week earlier.

Later that day, Amy texted a message I interpreted as saying she and Glenn would not make it to Rapid that evening. She wrote they were stopping two hundred miles away. Happy with their decision, I relaxed, knowing they would not drive exhausted. We would connect whenever they arrived the next day. After my usual Planet Fitness weightlifting and shower routine, I drove to Cabela's in Rapid City to spend the night. The parking lot was the size of a small farm, and though several campers had settled in for the night, they left plenty of room for me to snuggle in.

Once I got settled, I noticed Amy had sent me another text asking me where I was and that she and Glenn were looking for me at the Rapid City Walmart—the same Walmart where I had met Tony and Judy a week earlier. Oh, my word, what a misunderstanding! I thought she had stopped two hundred miles away and here she was, three miles away. Since it was late, we agreed to meet at Walmart in the morning.

The next morning as I left to meet Amy and Glenn, I realized it was the summer solstice, the longest day of the year. I parked next to their 40-foot Class A motorhome, with a crimson Toyota CX-5 hitched behind it. We had finally connected. I stepped out of my rig and knocked on their door.

Their six-month-old Shih Tzu-terrier mix puppy, Samson, a bundle of black fur and excitement, greeted me at the door. Amy invited me in. We hugged and sat down to talk. I waited for Samson's sister to appear, but Amy told me they had to find a new home for Delilah after the whole rescued-from-the-ocean miracle. She was too hyper, barked incessantly, and resisted training, including potty training. They simply could not have her with them on the road. Samson relaxed a few minutes after I arrived, and his little puppy maturity and mellow demeanor amazed me.

We left both motorhomes at Walmart and set off together in their Toyota to Mount Rushmore, where I had visited six days earlier.

It was so perfect and a little miraculous that Amy and Glenn and I were able to meet up, and I couldn't believe we were going to see Mount Rushmore together. Four months earlier, Amy and I had reconnected after not seeing each other for thirty-five years, and now we were together in South Dakota after she and her husband had nearly died the week before.

We toured the park for a couple of hours, taking pictures, walking on the Presidential Pathway, and listening to the same live ranger program about the sculpting of the mountain I had heard the week before. I don't usually remember things when I hear them just once, so I appreciated getting to hear everything again.

Later, as we checked out the gift shop, Glenn pointed out an elderly man at a table. Upon further investigation, we discovered he was conducting a book signing, accompanied by his wife. The gentleman turned out to be ninety-seven-year-old Donald "Nick" Clifford, the last living driller of Mount Rushmore. Of course, I bought a signed copy of his book, *Mount Rushmore Q&A*, and posed with him as Glenn took a photo. (In December 2019, I heard on the news that Nick had died in November, at age 98, four months after I met him.) I will forever treasure his autographed book, the picture of us together, and the memory of the moment I crossed paths with a Mount Rushmore worker at the place of his proudest achievement.

On this second visit to Rushmore, I noticed features I did not remember seeing on my first visit. Glenn drew my eye to details like the striations in the pink, shiny, quartz-like rock along the path, the intricacy of the presidents' eyes, and the fallen trees on the mountain. I marveled at little details and big ones too. One phenomenon that amazed me was that the Ponderosa pines thrived on the rocky mountain, yet I could find no weeds growing there. It baffled me that trees could grow in rock—not rocky soil—but r-o-c-k rock!

Exploring Mount Rushmore again was such a treat. I kept pinching myself. It amazed me how everything fell in place. Six days earlier, I had said I would love to visit again, but I certainly didn't think it would happen so soon. Amy and Glenn were patient when I wanted more time to take in the views or find gifts at the bookstore, which I appreciated.

Back at the Walmart parking lot, I made a reservation at the RV Park in Rapid City where Amy and Glenn already had a spot reserved. We drove our respective motorhomes ten miles to the park, checked in, and set up. Though packed with campers, the grounds had not seen a lawnmower, weed eater, or maintenance worker in years. And I'd had ten times more space between me and the next camper the night before at Cabela's "campground." Amy and Glenn barely had enough room to extend their slides that expand a segment of living space by two feet when the camper is parked. It's all about location: In Rapid City, South Dakota, campground owners could charge $55 for a parking space because of the proximity to Rushmore, Crazy Horse, Custer, and more.

We walked around the half-acre campground with Samson. The Wi-Fi was not strong enough to watch a video or send pictures, and the pool held more algae than the Okefenokee Swamp. Glenn pointed out the beams of the buildings and said they would soon give way because they were in such disrepair. My priority was to enjoy time with Amy and Glenn, but it killed me to pay so much for so little. It was by far the worst place I had ever stayed, yet the most expensive campground to date. Today it seems trivial, but at the time I was tracking every dollar.

That afternoon, we were having such a good time Amy suggested we spend more time together and, despite the crummy accommodations, stay another night. I agreed. It was all about friendship, and I was tickled to be with my friends. We planned to leave the next morning by 7:30 to drive through Custer State Park and possibly visit Crazy Horse. Seeing the burros, bison, and the majestic black hills a second time would be a special treat.

The next morning, I texted my new friend, Jan, the host at Blue Bell Campground in Custer, from the back seat of Amy and Glenn's Toyota. I told Jan I was coming back with friends to visit the park. Blue Bell was about thirty minutes away from our campground. Jan said to stop by their place first so she could give us a bag of carrots for the begging burros. Unfortunately, we turned the wrong way and ended up bypassing Blue Bell. We quickly ended up on Wildlife Loop Road where I had seen the burros and bison the week before.

Glenn saw a herd in the distance and said, "Is there more than one herd in the park?"

"I think there's just one herd at Custer, but I'm not sure about that," I said.

Glenn pointed out a pronghorn antelope, and I wondered why the antelope traveled alone. Deer ran across the road and glided over the barbed wire fence with ease. Wildlife running free made me happy. In the same place I saw the burros on my first visit, we spotted a few of the magnificent beasts beside the road. Glenn parked and I could not get to them fast enough. They seemed to enjoy our love and attention, even though we did not come with Jan's carrots.

We got a few fun pictures with the burros. I got one with Amy and Glenn posing on either side of a chocolate brown fella, and Amy took a picture of me as I stood on a boulder beside a brownish-gray burro, pretending to throw my leg over his back for a ride. I snapped a picture of Glenn holding a banana for a brown jenny. She ate it and then tasted part of the peel. Not sure if the peel would be good for her, I threw it away when she turned her head. As I stroked two or three of the burros, I noted their matted hair as I had on my last visit. Leaning into the chocolate one's shoulder, I took in a deep sniff of his coat but smelled nothing. I thought he might smell bad, musty even, but he did not smell at all.

As Glenn drove through the park, the rolling hills amazed us. Satisfied we had seen enough animals already, I said it would be fine if we did not get to see any more. But then, a hundred yards down a dirt side road, Glenn spotted another herd of bison standing on both sides of the road, right at the edge. Two cars pulled away, so we were the only ones there.

Glenn drove slowly, stopped for pictures, and drove some more. He repeated that pattern of driving and stopping over and over. Amy and I got hundreds of pictures and videos of the bison that were only a yard or two from Glenn and Amy's Toyota. We were so close we could see they were losing their coats.

"Usually they've lost their winter coats by now," Glenn said. "It's weird how it kind of falls off. Then they get a new lightweight summer coat that's more like hair than fleece or fur."

"Must be nice to get a new winter coat every year," I said.

Amy kept calling to them in a gentle voice, trying to get them to look at her for a picture. She made me smile. I could not have been happier to be wrong about the number of herds in the park. Clearly, at least two herds roamed the hills of Custer, and we were fortunate to be right there in the middle of one of them.

One bull walked straight to Glenn's car, turned, and then walked across the road only inches from Glenn's back bumper. I videoed the bull, and Amy got an excellent picture of him before he turned to walk behind us. We watched a bull poop and a calf pee and then laughed at how excited we were. I gawked like a child. Two calves tried to nurse as their mommas walked away, and another calf slept through the excitement. We took pictures and videos for so long that one bull got up and walked away, which prompted a calf to follow him. Then the sleeping calf woke and walked away, as did a couple more.

"We must be too close," Glenn said. "Let's not disturb them anymore. Most of them are in the grass now. I'm going to drive, and I can get by them if I keep going slow."

"Good idea, Glenn. I got caught up in the moment. Thank you so much. I never would have gotten to see them that close in my motorhome or on my bike. I feel blessed to have had so much time in their presence. And Amy, you got some great shots, especially the one of that bull looking right at you."

When I think about that time, I realize we were being stupid. We hung around for too long. For five minutes, we were trapped because the herd stood in front of us and on both sides of the road, but we could have scooted by sooner than we did. We were fortunate we got so many photos and that they did not get startled and ram into Glenn and Amy's car.

The bison are so intriguing, so enticing, so seemingly docile, that people get close, and closer still. Tourists want pictures. They lose their minds, and before they know it, they are ten feet in the air. We could have been a statistic. We were fortunate the bison didn't make examples out of us.

Two miles down the road, Amy pointed out three bison by themselves. Because they were grazing a good five hundred yards off the road, we did not take pictures. Besides, between the three of us, we already had 10,000 close-ups from when the herd held us hostage. We pondered if people who live in the area ever lose their appreciation for the burros, the bison, and the wildlife in general.

At the visitor center, we watched the same movie I had viewed the week before. I certainly did not mind listening to Kevin Costner's soothing voice again. The movie also showed the bison running en masse as cowboys cracked whips beside them. Someone told me that every year at Custer State Park, they organize a bison roundup, and cowboys come from all around to corral the herd in front of thousands of spectators. She said it's the park rangers' way of keeping the bison population in check.

After the movie, my friends and I stopped at the Game Lodge, which offered a delicious buffet. We ate, perused the gift shop, and drove to Blue Bell Campground to visit with Jan and Paul and their bundle of white fur, Annie. During our brief stay, Jan gave us more pointers for visiting Crazy Horse, and I asked her what she knew about the bison.

"The herds are primarily matriarchal. When the male calves get to be two or three years old, the females kick them out. There are three young bachelors out there in the park by themselves."

Amy and I smiled at each other, realizing Jan must have been talking about the three bison we noticed. Now I wished we had taken a picture of the young bulls, even though they were far away.

"How interesting that the young males get kicked out of the family by the mommas. Is it that one herd can only handle so much testosterone?"

"Funny, Joy. They come back to the herd during mating season," Jan said. "The females' scents are so strong that the males can smell them from far away, and they come into the fold to mate. However, the males wait until they are older to mate."

One day I would like to study bison behavior. Their relationships and interactions with one another are as interesting to me as their physical qualities, such as how big they get, how fast they can run, and how high they can jump. There is so much to learn about the psychology, habits, and dynamics of every species.

When we left Jan and Paul, Glenn and Amy said they'd like to go back to the campground, rather than the Crazy Horse Memorial. We took winding Highway 16A, with its sharp hairpin turns and a couple of pigtails (super curvy roads that wind around and around like a pig's tail) adding excitement to the drive. Glenn handled the switchbacks just fine, but neither of us could have driven our motorhomes down that road, even without its low-clearance tunnels. At the edge of one tunnel we had a perfect view of Mount Rushmore, but pausing on a narrow, zigzaggy road for pictures would have caused a problem. We had no time for an accident. And a puppy waited for our return, so Glenn drove "straight" back to our campground.

Little Samson took Amy and me for a walk. After that, Glenn said Samson could hang out with him, so Amy and I drove to nearby Ambassador Park for a hike. We stumbled upon tents and people covering the lawn. A band played on a portable stage while a man shouted unintelligible announcements. My fit friend planned to walk six or seven miles. Knowing the limitations of my feet, I agreed to walk a mile and turn around.

Amy started at a brisk pace, and my right foot cramped within the first quarter mile, so I told her to go ahead without me. I would walk a mile out and back at a much slower pace and wait for her at a bench. However, once I slowed down, my foot allowed me to keep going, so I hiked toward the top of a hill, looking for a view. Oncoming hikers told me the summit was around the bend. Just then, Amy phoned me. She had gone shopping and would wait for me in the parking lot. I turned around, regretting that

Amy had to wait thirty minutes for me to descend. Near the bottom of the mountain, I heard a racket behind me.

A guy on a bike screamed in a harsh voice. "There's a bike race going on!"

Without looking back, I dove into the weeds to avoid getting run over by two racers. Despite all the happenings in the park, a bike race never crossed my mind. I had thought little of the cardboard signs with arrows at every Y on the trail, other than appreciating someone not wanting me to get lost. Had I reached the summit, I would have been diving out of the way of mountain bike racers on a single-track trail for thirty minutes. "Woman Gets Killed by Mountain Bikers" may have enticed readers to pick up the newspaper the next day, but I fancied staying out of the news.

According to my Garmin watch, I had walked 7.5 miles and tallied over 20,000 steps for the day. Of course, my feet were killing me on the way down the hill, but completing such a distance exhilarated me. I never asked Amy how far she had hiked, but she said she saw the city from the summit. We concluded that there must have been multiple routes to the peak because we never saw each other after parting ways.

Back at the campground, after another walk with Samson, we agreed to say goodbye in the morning. They wanted to get out early, as they were looking at an 800-mile drive and wanted to get to Glacier National Park in two days. In contrast, I never planned to get out early *or* put in a lot of miles in one day.

There's no right or wrong way to travel in a motorhome. I found it interesting how some fellow travelers like to keep a schedule and plan their entire trip before leaving home and how others wing it like me. One never knows how life will play out, but before I bought my tiny house on wheels, I envisioned driving 100 to 200 miles a day, and mostly, that vision had played out. There was too much country to see to drive long distances between stopping points. I found joy in taking my time, taking it all in, and savoring the beauty of every mile.

CHAPTER TWENTY-TWO

Ambassador Park and the George S. Mickelson Trail

JUNE 23 – 24

The next morning's weather report forecasted freezing rain at Glacier Park. Yikes! Glenn and Amy discussed alternative plans as we strolled around the campground with sweet little Samson one last time. They opted to continue with their plan and keep an eye on the weather as they got closer to Glacier. We hugged goodbye, and I marveled at the ease with which Glenn hooked up their CX-5 to their motorhome. At 7:30, my friends drove away. I thought it was a great two-day visit and hoped my friends agreed.

After checking out of the RV park, I returned to Ambassador Park in Rapid City and pulled into the empty overflow lot. No evidence of the bike race from the previous day remained. There had been a little obstacle course for children where three- and four-year-old boys and girls riding tiny balance bikes with no pedals traversed the zigzag course. The little speed demons were adorable. Also, unicycles had covered a large area, and there was no sign of those, either. Not one cone or hint of the previous day's events remained.

I knew the festival, or race, would be over, but now the park seemed so calm and deserted that it felt like a totally different park. I rode my bike on a paved path that wound its way along the raging waters of Rapid Creek, and I made the connection that the creek was the inspiration for the town's name. Curves and turns in the path confused me, but somehow, after ninety minutes of exploration, I returned to my starting point. Woo-hoo! Not getting lost is always cause for celebration.

On the ride back to my motorhome, I stopped at a coffee shop for an iced coffee. As I sat outside chatting with an employee, a loud clap of thunder jolted me to my feet. With a quick goodbye, I grabbed my coffee with one hand and rode my bike with the other, being careful not to spill what remained of my liquid treat as I eased my way back to my rig. Drizzle began as I lifted my bike onto the rack, becoming rain after I pulled the bike cover over both bikes. The rain turned into a downpour before I could snap the buckles. Leaving the straps for later, I zipped inside Rig seconds before getting drenched. Thirty minutes later, I buckled the straps on the bike cover and drove to Planet Fitness. This marked my third visit to the Rapid City Planet Fitness. If I checked in again, I feared corporate would require me to claim Rapid City as my home gym.

After my usual routine at the gym, I landed at Cabela's, where I had camped the night Amy and Glenn arrived. Once settled, I scrolled through Custer and Mt. Rushmore pictures on my phone and added to my journal. I read, edited, and typed for four hours, trying to capture all the experiences. After that, I did an online search for a nearby bike shop because my road bike was now pedaling as rough as a rusted-out kid's bike.

The next morning, I spoke with my friend Anthony, who was still en route to Seattle. He told me a spoke in his back wheel had broken, and he had hitched a ride to Black Hills Bicycles across from Ambassador Park. They had fixed his wheel in ten minutes on the same day I met up with Amy and Glenn. Anthony recommended the shop, so back to Ambassador Park I drove, discovering the bike shop was a stone's throw from where Amy and I had hiked, and where I had parked my motorhome to ride my bike along the creek. I had just missed meeting up with Anthony, but I was glad he could direct me to Black Hills Bicycles.

At the bike shop, a mechanic named Randall forced the bent derailleur back into place, tweaked the gears, and said I would need a new chain, cassette, and crank in about five hundred miles. He charged me only $10. Immediately as I pedaled across the lot, I felt how much smoother the gears shifted. Yay! It felt like I got a new bike for ten bucks. What a deal! I was a happy camper again. Once I secured both bikes on the rack, I asked Siri to help me get to a rails-to-trails bike trail that Randall had mentioned.

With Siri's help, I arrived at the George S. Mickelson Trailhead in Deadwood, South Dakota, an hour after leaving the bike shop in Rapid City. However, a downpour stifled my enthusiasm, so I called my friend Lisa to chat. Hail beat against Rigdon's windshield and hood as I looked on helplessly. When the precipitation slowed to a light rain, I discovered they charged a $4 day-use fee for 109 miles of crushed gravel bike and hiking trails. I dropped four singles into the drop box and took off. After thirty minutes, the sun poked out and, as the sun always does, lifted my spirits. Forty-five minutes up the trail, I came to a crossroads of sorts and turned around. An hour and a half would be a long enough ride.

However, unbeknownst to me, I had been climbing a 2 to 3% grade, so I returned in a mere eighteen minutes. One hundred yards before the trailhead sign, two deer sauntered down the street past some old cars and into a yard near the trailhead. By now, you know me well enough to figure out that I did not miss the opportunity to catch that rare moment on my phone. As I snapped a photo, the deer looked at me as though they wanted to say hello. Sweet! Though I returned dirtier than a kid after a BMX race, I enjoyed a perfect ending to a ride—sunny, secluded, downhill, and deer-laden.

At dusk I ended up back at the Walmart in Spearfish, South Dakota, where I had endured that dark, stormy night after Custer and Crazy Horse a week earlier. Once nestled into a couple of parking spaces at the rear of the parking lot, I talked to Tom. We had not talked in a week because he and my sister-in-law, Pam, had just bought a house and driven everything they owned from Memphis, Tennessee, to Asheville, North Carolina.

As I talked to my brother, someone pulled up beside me in a little gray Hyundai sedan and yelled my name. It was Judy, the woman I'd met at Dakota Battery and then again at Walmart in Rapid City. I talked with her for a minute and got her phone number again. If I hadn't gone back to meet with Amy and Glenn, I might never have seen Judy again. It was as if she knew I had misplaced her number. How funny is that? What are the odds of her finding me at two Walmarts in two cities, ten days apart? It still makes me smile when I think about the way we connected. She said she planned to visit Theodore Roosevelt National Park (TRNP), the park I had planned to go to before my change of plans with Amy and Glenn. We both hoped we could connect there. This time, to make sure I didn't lose it, I typed Judy's name into my phone before she pulled away. I remember thinking that this was kismet—our meeting was meant to be. I hoped so, anyway.

After Judy left, I noticed a text from Amy. "Made it to Glacier. Scary. Glenn hit a couple of icy spots, but we made it before dark. Will stay put for the rest of the week." After responding with a clapping emoji and the blue teeth chattering face, I texted, "So glad you made it safely!!! It was good to see you. Hope you enjoy Glacier."

I called my brother back. He was happy to hear my visit with Amy went well and laughed when I told him how Judy and I kept crossing paths. My brother was the one who had suggested I go to Teddy Roosevelt National Park, so he told me to make sure I visited the south and the north units and to let him know when I got there. Despite our twenty-minute phone call, I still didn't get the details about him and his wife each driving a moving truck, both larger than my motorhome, five hundred miles to their new home high on a steep hill overlooking the city of Asheville. That would be a story for another day.

CHAPTER TWENTY-THREE

Bowman, North Dakota

JUNE 25 – 26

The lush green rolling terrain on scenic route 85 N made for a refreshing drive. I stopped for gas in Buffalo, South Dakota, not because the tank was empty, but because I'd heard gas stations in the west were few and far between. I paid $2.99 a gallon for gas I thought was $2.67. Who knew if I had pushed the wrong pump, if someone hadn't updated the sign, or if $2.67 was a cash price? I chalked it up as a disappointing $10 oversight, not worth going back to investigate. I tried to be careful about spending and saving money, but I told myself to let minor mistakes go. Still, situations like that kept happening. Spending more than I planned was becoming almost as common as getting lost and, like getting lost, I seemed incapable of stopping the cycle. Being new to the fixed income retirement gig, I was cautious with my money. I knew I had enough money to live on if I stayed home, but travel expenses were an unknown.

I talked to my sister Lynn (she kept tabs on my whereabouts, and I appreciated that) until I hit the North Dakota state line twenty-five miles later. At the North and South Dakota welcome signs, the design team had included a circular drive to pull off and take pictures of each. Grateful for their foresight, I took advantage of that perk.

Another twenty to thirty miles of driving brought me to Bowman, North Dakota, where I found a little ten-site park maintained by the Bowman Lions Club, complete with fancy picnic tables painted purple and yellow, restrooms, and a clean, accessible dump station with fresh water. (Typically, I dump and refill my tanks about every five days. If campers are frugal with their water they may be able to stretch that to ten days, but if they try to go much longer than two weeks the black tank, toilet sewage, becomes offensive.) Finding the park vacant and inviting, I backed

Rig into the first spot and made myself at home. The clean, open grounds provided a lockbox like the park in Valentine, Nebraska, asking for a $12 donation and a three-night maximum stay. The park offered no hookups, but I found the grassy cove off the highway cozier than a parking lot, and the honor system appealed to me.

What a gem. Some parks and truck stops charged $12 for dumping, so to stay a night for that price was a steal. The find fell into the positive column in terms of travel expenses. After sliding cash into the box, I washed the George S. Mickelson grime off my bike at the dump and water station. A young couple drove through on a motorcycle, drove across the street, and returned minutes later. They asked me for the time and left again to find food. After dinner, I walked around the little park and noticed the motorcycle couple all set up with a tent at the other end of the park. After dark, a motorcycle or pickup truck thundered through the campground, but I didn't investigate. Except for the chirping crickets serenading me through my open windows, I enjoyed a quiet night.

I woke up to text messages from friends wishing me a happy birthday. My friend Sherry called, and while we talked, I noticed an older navy-colored van several sites away and determined that the van must have been the late-night motorcycle or truck I heard. After Sherry and I hung up, I strolled around the circle and met a thirty-something couple living out of the van. Unkempt, but attractive, the two ate at the picnic table next to their van as I waved good morning. They walked out to the circle to meet me and wasted no time with small talk. The petite woman, attired in a white T-shirt and cut-offs, spoke first.

"Hi, I'm Faith. This is my husband, Daniel. We sold our house and we're living very frugally."

"Wow. I'm Joy. I'm not brave enough to sell my house. That sounds scary to me."

"It really wasn't a big deal. It was time for us to make a change," Daniel said.

"Kids?"

"Yeah. We've got seven between us—four from previous marriages and three together," Faith said.

"Oh, my. You don't look old enough to be empty nesters. Where are your children?"

"Daniel's two live in Vancouver with their mom. They're fifteen and seventeen. My daughter lives near Rapid with my ex. She's a daddy's girl.

My son thinks he's a man. He's eighteen, living with friends near his dad. My daughter comes to visit when school's out sometimes, but we haven't seen Daniel's kids or my son for a couple of years now. The youngest three, an eleven-year-old and six-year-old twins are staying with Daniel's mom."

"Why didn't the youngest three come with you?"

"I told them we needed some mommy and daddy time," Faith said, snuffing out her cigarette butt with a twist of her foot.

"And they like being with my mom," Daniel said, somewhat contradicting his wife's answer. "They didn't want to miss soccer, and they wanted to be with their friends since school's out."

"Hm. Okay."

Daniel's all-black tattoos on his right forearm caught my eye, but I couldn't determine what the arrows and letters or symbols might mean.

"Yeah. It's nice not having the responsibility of the house. The van needs a little work and some organizing, but it's working for now," Faith said. She pointed to the open end of the van, which revealed a mattress on the left side of the floor and crates and boxes crammed next to the bed on the right.

"We've only been living in the van since spring. Might have to figure out something different when it gets cold again, but we like it," Faith said.

Daniel and Faith were friendly and showed an interest in me, but these were not typical campers. Their demeanor gave me the impression of a couple running *away* from life rather than running *toward* fresh adventures.

"We've been here a lot," Faith said. "Tell us if we can help you with anything. Oh, the $12 fee is just a suggestion. We never pay nothin' and no one says anything to us. I talked to the guy who drives through here sometimes, and he said it's fine, long as we don't stay too long."

Daniel said, "We was here a few days last week, so we'll probably stay just a couple more nights. We're going to stop by Mom's place to see the kids and get some food because we're running low on cash. I'm going to need to get some work pretty soon, but that won't be no problem, because I can fix most anything. A guy gave me twenty bucks here last week just for changing his back tire."

We chatted a little more, and I politely excused myself.

"Well, nice to meet you. Wish you the best and safe travels. I'm pulling out in a few minutes."

As I walked away, I thought about how the world is full of people from all walks of life, all with stories different from my own. Not knowing how much of Daniel and Faith's story to believe, my heart hurt for them, their children, and Daniel's mother, too. As I write this, I wonder how they are.

CHAPTER TWENTY-FOUR

My Birthday

JUNE 26

As I left Bowman Park, I dropped a thank-you note for the Lions Club along with a few more dollars into the drop box. I drove around the town of Bowman, North Dakota (population 1,500), and noticed a small park and a tiny strip of stores across the street. Remembering that I had turned right to get to the campground, I turned left to head back to 85 N. My sister Sandi called me right then. I should not have answered until I knew for sure I was on the correct road. But since I cannot learn from my mistakes, I answered and then drove an additional fifteen miles talking to my sister before a 12 W road sign confirmed my suspicions. I had missed 85 N in Bowman.

Aaugh! I did not have time to drive thirty miles in the wrong direction, and my brain felt the need to dwell on how much driving out of my way was costing me: eight miles to the gallon times thirty miles equals about four gallons at three bucks a gallon . . . and on and on the thinking went as I beat myself up for making such a mistake. As I drove through Bowman again, undistracted by a phone call and this time having no trouble seeing the 85 N sign, I also noticed that gas in Bowman was $2.54 as opposed to the $2.99 I had paid in Buffalo, South Dakota, just forty-five miles south. Bam, another stab in the pocketbook.

Gotta let it go.

Can't let it go, the other half of my brain retorted.

I drove one hundred miles to the intersection of 85 and 94 and stopped again for gas, this time paying the stated price of $2.69. Then prompted by an email for a free birthday coffee from Starbucks that I could not cash in on (since the closest Starbucks was seventy-five miles away), I googled "coffee shops near me" and found a tiny coffee hut called Gypsy Java in an empty gas station parking lot a half mile away. (Later, I noticed that little coffee huts were quite common in the west, but this was a first for me.) As I slurped on a sweet and cold vanilla coffee shake, I talked with Lana. She and her sister Laurie owned the place. I'd gotten hooked on these sugary frozen delights, thanks to Jennifer at Paula's in Valentine, Nebraska. Lana explained the differences between her coffee and those of Starbucks and segued to differences in the south and north Roosevelt parks. She told me the north park was more remote and didn't see as many visitors per year. A reservation specialist the day before had confused me by telling me the south and north were two loops within the same park. However, a sign I spotted between the gas station and Lana's coffee hut stated the south park was fifteen miles west and the north park was fifty miles north. That's one big campground.

During my initial online search for a campsite, I had only seen Cottonwood Campground (the south park) on the *AllStays* app. After I read the sign on the road and Lana explained the differences, I looked at the app again and found the north park. Theodore Roosevelt was essentially two national parks separated by about sixty miles.

As she was fixing a second coffee shake for me—on the house because it was my birthday (that beats a Starbucks coupon any day), Lana told me I'd likely see bison walking through the south park and possibly prairie dogs and wild horses. Life was looking up. At the smaller, more primitive north park, I was apt to see bighorn sheep. Lana lived so close she said she had never camped at the park but drove through when family and friends visited. That prompted me to contemplate how many of us don't visit attractions close to home yet drive or fly across the country to explore what locals take for granted. It saddened me when I pondered how many of us might miss the beauty in our own backyards. I determined to change that, at least for myself when I got home, and I planned to encourage others to do the same.

Earlier, when I called from Bowman City, the national park reservation specialist said the reservable sites were booked and recommended I get to the south park early to secure a walk-up site. I had intended to do just that, but chatting with Faith and Daniel, driving thirty miles out of my way, getting gas, stopping for a coffee (well, two), and a visit with the proprietor of Gypsy Java thwarted my early morning plan. After verifying directions, I took pictures of Lana in her adorable pink and green coffee hut and thanked her for my birthday drink as I pulled away and headed to the south park.

A few miles from Lana's place, I toured the welcome center, bought postcards, and chatted with Janet from Fargo, North Dakota, who was traveling with her friend Harry. They were heading to Montana but were going to stay that night in Medora, outside the Theodore Roosevelt National Park, South Unit. Because I love to hear people's stories, I wished we could have talked longer, but the woman who rang up my postcards told me there were four RV sites left. With an urgency in her delivery, she advised me to secure a campsite first and explore Medora later.

I drove through the touristy town of Medora and found the park entrance on the right. The woman at the gate told me I had better go straight to the campground to get a site. The spectacular green buttes made my jaw drop, but I did not dare stop at any overlooks for fear of not getting a campsite. I stopped at Cottonwood Campground, and Tim, the host with soft blue eyes and a delightful disposition, gave me three choices. Phew! Made it.

Tim recommended sites #2 or #4. I backed into #2, grateful that I had jumped out twice to double-check. I backed so close to a post the first time that the passenger side might have peeled off like the top on a can of sardines. The second time, I nearly backed over a boulder the size of a coffee table, which would have obliterated my black tank, a.k.a. poop tank. Either accident would have put a damper on an otherwise delightful birthday. Tim rode his bike over to check on me and arrived as I was finishing my professional backing maneuver. A tree branch had harpooned my bikes.

Half joking, I said, "If I had thought to bring my loppers, I could just cut off this branch and all would be fine."

Tim grinned and said, "Yeah, but that would be illegal."

"Well, if you're going to put it that way, how 'bout I pull forward a foot?"

"I think that would be a better idea," Tim said.

I had no desire to get arrested for cutting a tree branch—on my birthday, no less. Tim watched as I eased forward and signaled me to stop inches before the front bumper met the road.

"You can use your credit card number and pay for as many nights as you want. If you decide to stay longer, all you need to do is fill out another envelope and pay before noon."

"At $14 a night, I will absolutely stay at least through the weekend. I'll start with that."

Tim smiled.

When he told me the park offered no hookups or dump station, I wished I had taken advantage of the dump and fill station at Bowman. To stay past Monday, I'd need to find a place to dump and refill, but I would tackle that problem when needed. Sometimes my brain wanted to figure out every feasible solution for every potential problem before the problem even existed. For once, I focused on enjoying myself in the here and now. And for the moment, all was good.

Eager to ride in the park, yet inundated with text messages, I felt compelled to respond before the time got away from me. Because my brother had suggested I visit Teddy Roosevelt, I took pictures of my RV tucked into the tree-lined landscape and sent them with a caption that read, "Look where I have to spend my birthday." Then I had fun exchanging multiple texts with half a dozen "happy birthday wishers" for an additional forty-five minutes. At 4 p.m., I mounted my knobby-tired bike and took off without a map and without asking Tim to suggest a route. Not smart. Hindsight said the next few hours might have gone smoother with instructions from Tim.

A few miles into my birthday ride, one lone bull plodded toward me on the road. I slipped behind two cars that were facing the oncoming 2,000-pound beast, and my heart nearly imploded. The driver of the second car hung out his window, pointing his phone at the bison. Feeling vulnerable on my bike, I decided hiding between two cars was a safer bet and asked the guy if I could get between him and the car in front. Without a glance in my direction, the fella filming the scene on his phone agreed to allow me in front of him.

"Stay over to the right so you're not in my way," he barked at me.

The bison walked along the yellow line of the road, half a football field in front of us. Following orders to stay out of the way, I snapped one pitiful picture of the bison's back end as he walked into a ravine and disappeared into the brush. It killed me to stand so close to my new favorite mammal on my birthday, yet not get one decent picture. The cars moved on and I followed. At least I stayed safe. (It had never occurred to me to ask a ranger about protocol for riding my bike around bison. If there is a book about biking with bison, I have yet to come across it.)

At the coffee hut, Lana had told me that part of Scenic Loop Drive had closed a month earlier, so people could not drive the entire loop. I rode a mile and stopped at a road closed sign. Limbo-ing myself and my bike under the gate, I pedaled a few hundred yards past the sign, took pictures of barking prairie dogs, which sounded more like birds than dogs, turned around and ducked under the gate again. I biked six more miles to another sign that said "Road closed in twelve miles." At the next overlook, I met two white-bearded brothers in a shiny red Ford pickup who said if I got to the "road closed" sign and couldn't ride through, they would see me on their way back and would check with me to find out if I needed a ride. They offered to throw my bike in their truck and drive me to the campground if I needed their help. Now I had a plan B. I always like a plan B. Thank you, Leonard and Lawrence.

Four miles later, I was breezing down a hill and saw a herd of bison on the right side of the road. One bull strolled across the pavement and the others followed. Wishing to remain undetected, I stopped mid-descent a soccer field away, keenly aware of the power and speed of agitated bison. Even if I waited for them to cross, I was not inclined to find out what they would think of me if I bicycled past. Having learned from multiple sources that bison can run faster than I can pedal knobby tires on a downhill, not one bone in my newly turned fifty-five-year-old body wanted to challenge that information. I pulled my phone out of my jersey pocket and took pictures and video of the herd crossing at a distance too far for my phone to depict the gravity of the situation.

Minutes later, a sharp-dressed, middle-aged couple in a charcoal Suburban drove up behind me and said I could follow them. I coasted behind, riding my brakes, as they did the same. My heart was pounding. The husband stopped and took pictures of the last bull to cross the road. Apparently, he filmed too close for too long, and the bison got ticked off and took off at a full sprint, encouraging his relatives to do the same. Whew, was I thankful the bull ran *away* from the car (and me). Seeing the herd run like that kind of freaked me out, and the Tatanka stampede scene from the film at Custer came to mind.

Though probably not as close a call as it seemed to me, it was scary enough to make me need a restroom. Unfortunately for me national parks don't have Porta-Potties. Being out there on my hybrid bike rather than in Glenn's car or in my rig made me feel way more vulnerable. Having even less desire to be attacked by bison on my birthday than arrested for cutting off a tree limb, I wished to have a peaceful birthday in a spectacular national park. And so . . . I did.

When I reached the barricade eighteen miles into the loop, my water bottles were as dry as a desert. If I could get through the roadblock, my trek back would measure nine miles rather than the eighteen it would require if I turned around. At a nearby overlook I asked a family if they thought I could get through the closed road, and one man said he'd heard the road was washed out. He knew they could not get through in their truck, but I "most likely could, even if I had to carry my bike for a short stretch." I asked if they had any water, and he offered me a Gatorade bottle someone had drunk out of already. Being more concerned about running out of water than a stranger's germs, I accepted his offer with a big "thank you."

A family with a Wisconsin license plate drove up, gave the same answer to my question about the washed-out road, and offered me half a bottle of water. I could not recall ever drinking from a stranger's cup, but there I was accepting drinks from anyone who offered. It's not like I had better options. I was eighteen miles from the visitor center that may or may not even sell bottled water. There are no vending machines, or roadside markets in the middle of a national park. I graciously accepted the water. Thanking both families again for their encouragement, I squeezed the brake levers and eased down a slope toward the orange mesh barricade across the road, comforted by the idea that two families supported my decision to take the shortest route. They knew no more than I did about the barricaded road, but since I had little water, my feet were hurting, and my plan B (the two brothers in the truck) was uncertain, I opted to follow the families' advice.

Three orange plastic barriers stretched across the road well in front of what I saw next. On the other side of the barrier, there was no road. The road was just gone. A cavernous hole wider than a football field and deeper than an Olympic pool replaced what used to be a national park scenic byway. Beyond the hole, the asphalt lay broken into massive chunks, and the understructure had sunk enough to prevent vehicle travel for another three hundred yards.

One barrel-sized drainage pipe lay exposed under the rubble. On the far side of the broken pavement loomed another drop-off of maybe forty stories. I didn't get close enough to that edge to measure. It looked like I would fall forever if I stepped too close. Somehow, I balance-beamed my way through the barricades on the side away from the drop-off, then eased back to take pictures. The vastness of the problem shocked me, and I wondered how anyone would be capable of rebuilding the road. I also pondered how long it might take engineers and a road construction crew to make the road safe for tourists to drive around the loop again if it was even possible to rebuild.

Edging my way along the mountainside looked challenging, but doable. I decided to go for it. With me on the mountainside and my bike on the cliffside, I walked along a ledge barely wider than a balance beam, guiding my bike ever-so-slowly. At the halfway point, I stopped to reconsider my options. I looked in front of me. I looked behind me. What lay ahead looked precarious but not much worse than what I had just inched my way through. I weighed my options. Going back would be eighteen miles with little water plus more strain on my already hurting knees and feet. If I could make it across this stretch, I could be back at my site in seven miles. Then, it took me a full minute to realize the most important fact. There was no way I would be able to turn my bike around on that ledge with the rock wall of a mountain on one side of me and a bottomless pit on the other.

I looked over the edge into the hollow abyss, once again, my mind reeling with questions about how this road could have just disappeared. And of course, the "what was I thinking" question consumed my thoughts too. Staying there was not an option. I had to make a decision. Given the fact that there was not enough room for me to turn my bike around, I realized I had no choice but to continue on.

Two minutes later, I was safe on the other side. *Whew!* I stood there for a minute, giving myself time to regroup. When I re-mounted on the back side of the chasm, I was hypervigilant in my search for bison. I was riding alone on two wheels in an area no one had been for a long time. No cars would come up behind me, offering me protection from a charging bison herd on this part of the loop. Leonard and Lawrence wouldn't be coming along to save me. They didn't even know I was there. What if I encountered a herd again? How would I get past them? Trying not to dwell on the seriousness of the circumstances I had gotten myself into on this forsaken trek, I thought it best to focus on the positive and keep moving.

The road was rough in three or four places, and a few stretches were so sandy I had to descend more cautiously, but no obstacle proved too problematic. I passed one bison on a downhill but did not slow down. At the overlooks, I snapped pictures of grass-covered buttes but never stopped to take any pictures of wildlife.

As I took my last swig of Gatorade, the loop dumped me off at the prairie dog town at the closed gate. The entire expedition, from barricade to gate, had left me spooked. I made it back to civilization unscathed, but any number of scenarios could have landed me on the five o'clock news or caused a rescue team to risk their lives saving a woman who should have had better judgment.

Before ducking under the gate again, I took pictures and videos of the active prairie dogs. It surprised me to see how small prairie dogs are and to hear their calls. Perhaps they possess multiple distinct barks and calls, but every call I heard sounded like a bird chirping. They probably weighed only a few pounds, so I don't know why I was perplexed that they didn't have baritone barks.

One dog's entire chest rose with each bark, like he had to take a deep, lung-filling breath to produce such a sound. With so many cute little varmints barking and running in and out of their holes, it wore me out to watch them. Of course I wouldn't think they were so cute if all their tunnels and mounds filled my backyard, but I sure enjoyed watching them in Teddy Roosevelt's backyard. Though I didn't understand what they were barking about, I marveled at their quick movements and loud utterances.

Rangers ask tourists not to get too close to the animals, but these little fellas wouldn't let me get close even if I tried to sneak up on them. Twice I parked my bike and walked toward one. They scrambled into a hole faster than I could snap a picture.

When I returned to Cottonwood Campground, Tim greeted me at the entrance, so I told him about my ride. (I may have skipped the part about the likely illegal stretch beyond the barricade.) "Sounds like you had quite the adventure, Joy," he said.

"It was an adventure, all right. You're fortunate to live in this paradise. What's your story?"

"Yes. We are very fortunate to be here, but we are only hosting until mid-July. It's beautiful but we don't want to stay in one place too long. Donna and I sold our home in October and have been living in our van since then. We put 13,000 miles on our brand-new van between October and the first of May when we pulled in here. We hope we'll see our kids and grandkids more often now that we are mobile. They live all over the country so we can park in their driveways for a week here and there and spend time with the little ones. In July, we plan to spend some time with our son and his kids in Wyoming before the children start school."

"That's great. I hope that works out for you."

I said goodbye to Tim and headed back to my RV. Earlier in the day, I had planned to fix a special birthday dinner, but I returned after generator hours. A lot of parks have restrictions on generators because they are loud, like a diesel truck engine. TRNP allowed generators to be run from 8:00 in the morning until 8:00 at night. I settled for a sandwich and called my friend Lisa and then my sister Sandi, who had called me when I was leaving Bowman.

When we hung up, I journaled about my day until after midnight. I never would have remembered the details for this book had I not written in my journal most nights. Before my retirement, I told friends, family, coworkers, and students that I planned to travel and write about my travels. I enjoy writing for writing's sake, but my deeper desire was always to write and publish books about my travels.

This was certainly a birthday to remember. Little did I know, though, that I would pay for my birthday choices the next day.

CHAPTER TWENTY-FIVE

Theodore Roosevelt State Park, South Unit

JUNE 27 – 29

Having slacked off on a recent vow to cut caffeine, soda, and sugar from my diet, I determined that the day after my birthday would be a good day to renew my vow. No more caffeine. No more sugar. It was time for a clean break. By mid-morning, however, I had a headache and horrible body aches—clear signs of caffeine withdrawal. I was regretting drinking not one, but two sugary, caffeinated, coffee-flavored shakes to celebrate my fifty-five years of life. The summer sun was turning my tiny house into a sauna, so I added a dose of ibuprofen to my oatmeal-with-blueberries breakfast and biked into town.

Weak and lethargic, I lacked all ambition to ride hard up *or* down the hills but made it to the post office in the little town of Medora, North Dakota, to mail a stack of cards. I would have more opportunities to ride in North Dakota, but this excursion, along with my birthday ride on the wild side, allowed me to claim North Dakota as state #20. Twenty states! I was cranking them out. Twenty down. Thirty to go!

I tooled around town hoping to find Wi-Fi, settling for a bench outside a coffee shop where I could talk and text . . . and inhale the aroma of the now-forbidden brew. When I attempted to upload a video of bison crossing the road on Instagram, I discovered that videos must run less than one minute to post. That served as useful but disheartening information for a fledgling Instagram user. I had never tried to edit a video, noted I'd like to learn, vowed to take shorter videos in the future, and settled for posting bison pictures on my account.

As I mounted my bike again, a gentleman told me he and his wife had passed me on their way into town and asked if I had ridden from the campground. That I would tackle such a ride impressed them and he complimented me on my gumption. That made me feel good. How nice of him to encourage me. He didn't know I was feeling down, and his smile and words made me feel better.

It's wonderful how a kind word and a smile from a stranger brightened my outlook and made me feel better. Joy really isn't that hard to find. We can find joy in something as simple as a smile from a fellow tourist. We can find joy anywhere, if we just look. I hope I will remember that feeling when I encounter others who might need kind words and a smile to lift their spirits. I wouldn't recognize that man if I saw him again, but his smile and kind words and the way he made me feel—that I will remember for a long time. Our conversation reminded me of a quote: "I've learned that people will forget what you said, people will forget what you did, but people will never forget how you made them feel." I believe it was Maya Angelou who first spoke those words.

On the five-mile stretch from Medora to the campground, my bike rolled along as smoothly as skates on an indoor roller rink. As harsh as the winters are in the north, and as short as their road repair season is, I found the roads to be silky smooth through the plains and in the Dakotas. Good roads are important to me in the motorhome and on the bike. When I drive my motorhome on bad roads, everything bangs and clangs, and when I ride either of my bikes, my body takes the brunt of the bumpy pavement. Neither is enjoyable. I found myself especially grateful for the smooth roads in the Dakotas.

As I drew close to the campground, a woman with a wide-angle lens camera was taking pictures of wild horses on a crest. I introduced myself and stopped and took pictures too. She told me her name was Linda, and she was from the area. For over an hour, she stood at the foot of the butte taking a picture every time a colt stepped into view, or when the horses seemed to pose for her camera. For twenty minutes, she eyed one horse grazing by himself and captured him on video running to the others. I did not have my phone ready to shoot the video as she did. I admired her patience. I am not a photographer and gained a new appreciation for their patience to get an animal at the right angle or the sun rising or setting at the right moment. She let me watch her video of the horse running to the others. There is a big difference between one who takes pictures and one who is a photographer.

As I said goodbye to the photographer and rode toward the campground, my mind wandered. Those horses were intriguing. Was that my first encounter with wild horses? Are they in other national parks? What about the national park system in general? I realized I knew so little about our national parks and the evolution of their existence. Theodore Roosevelt, I had heard, was instrumental in campaigning for the national parks, but I had much to learn.

The history and geography involved in travel struck me as a bonus. Pioneers and early settlers intrigued me as much as the never-ending landscapes and wildlife. As a child and young adult, I would not have appreciated the museums and movies and probably not the hikes either. When I observed families in national parks, I wondered how much the children absorbed and whether they appreciated the sights, the sounds, the wonders. Certainly some soaked it all in while others whined and asked to go home. I fear I would have been the kid telling my parents "this is boring" as we traveled through museums or listened to park rangers. I'd have been the one who fell asleep in my mom's lap during the twenty-minute films I now cannot wait to watch at each park. Reminded that I am a "late bloomer," as I call myself, I appreciate that *older* Joy finds joy in nearly everything she does.

It was not until I started traveling that I began embracing my name at a deeper level and appreciating my parents saving the name *Joy* for their last child. Mom told me many times they named me Joy because I brought joy to the family. I always liked my name, but the more I traveled, the more people I met, the more of God's creations I encountered, the more joyful I became. And the more joyful I became, the more Joy became not just my name but my identity. Joy is who I am. I am joy.

The next morning, I drove five miles to the visitor center at the entrance to the park. I watched the film at the visitor center twice because I had time, enjoyed it, and don't remember information after hearing it just once. The film featured the Dakotas, the park, and Theodore Roosevelt. I joined the guided tour of one of Roosevelt's cabins, the Maltese Cross Cabin. The traditional-looking log cabin was Teddy's home when he visited the Dakota Territory in the early 1880s. Now a small group of us were standing there immersed in history, gawking at the former president's humble abode, three rooms plus an attic. One room is a den, office, or sitting room, another is a kitchen, and the third is Roosevelt's bedroom, now furnished with a bed and trunk. Roosevelt's tour guides or other companions reportedly slept in the attic. The nostalgia drew me in.

Roosevelt sold his place of solitude after he took office in 1901, which was spurred by the assassination of his predecessor William McKinley. Historians moved the president's cabin five times to allow more people to appreciate its role in history. The first time was to the 1904 world's fair in Saint Louis, Missouri, and then to Portland, Oregon, the following year. I was without a notebook and couldn't jot down the other places it was moved to, but each move was for publicity and efforts to educate the public. The cabin now rests behind the visitor center at the TRNP South Unit, seven miles from its original location.

After the tour, I walked to the bank near the post office where I had mailed postcards the previous day. At the bank, a teller exchanged my crumpled bills for fresh ones to put in my seven-year-old nephew's birthday card. I asked the two tellers what they recommended I do while I was in town. They suggested the Medora musical, which played at night, and they thought tickets sold for $30 to $40. I asked them about a Theodore Roosevelt impersonator that Jan, my new friend from Custer State Park, had suggested I inquire about, but they knew nothing.

I walked to the nearby information/tickets building and could not have timed it better. My watch displayed 3:23, and two ladies at the information building told me the show with a Theodore Roosevelt impersonator (also called a reprisor) was to begin at 3:30, one block away. I bought an $18 ticket for the only show of the day and walked into the Old Town Hall Theater in time to hear his sixteen-year-old "son," Teddy, (also an impersonator or reprisor) sharing stories with the audience. The two-hundred-seat theater was brimming with tourists, and I was one of them!

I am living the life. How awesome is this?

After his son's introduction, TR spoke for an hour. He interacted with the audience, made several puns, and told lighthearted stories of his life before, during, and after his presidency. Roosevelt talked about how he took solace in the back country after his wife, Alice, and mother died—in the same house, on the same day—February 14, 1884. His beloved wife died of a kidney disease two days after their only child was born. She had named their daughter Alice. His mother died from typhoid fever. He told us he married Edith, a girl he knew from childhood, three years later.

The twenty-sixth president told stories about his six children: Alice, and the five children he had with Edith. He said his children, especially his four boys, were known for pulling off practical jokes and mischievous stunts. Though he did not profess to be a good writer, Roosevelt enjoyed writing and wrote over thirty books. When he walked off the stage, he greeted folks at the door, shaking hands, posing for pictures, and answering questions. I snapped two pictures of the president but failed to photograph Teddy Junior, who had so professionally portrayed the son of a president at the turn of the century.

Joe Wiegand, the man who impersonated President Theodore Roosevelt, had performed in fifty states, at the White House, and overseas too. He traveled the US performing at clubs, historical societies, and veterans' organizations. And in the summer of 2019, Joe lived in Medora where he performed at the Old Town Hall Theater nearly every day at 3:30.

Before returning to my campsite, I drove to the Medora Campground, next to the national park, to dump my rig's tanks. A wooden box mounted on a post asked campers for $5 to offset the cost of dumping. I liked the honor system. It gave me a good feeling about humanity. The dump station was outside the park, so I didn't need to bother the employees or even enter the campground. The donation box made dumping simple, and I like simple.

I returned to site #2 at 7:45, giving myself enough time to heat some food in the microwave before generator hours ended. Even though the mosquitoes were holding their annual convention at the South Unit, I ate outside because of the stifling summer heat inside my rig. The temperature was supposed to drop to 55 degrees during the night, but my weather app's update reported the low would be 70 degrees and that was not until four in the morning. Since comfortable sleeping weather for me is fifties to low sixties, I expected a restless night.

So far I had experienced a few days or nights when I was too hot or too cold, but not for days on end like now. I drifted off to sleep on top of my comforter after two hours of tossing and turning and counting the proverbial sheep, followed by a line of bison with a string of my beloved burros bringing up the rear.

Waking up tired and nauseated from the caffeine and sugar detox, I ate some oatmeal and downed a couple of ibuprofen. It took me half the day to muster the energy to get on my bike. A mile from my site, I stopped at a hiking trail at the Peaceful Valley Ranch. There were several distance options, the shortest being five miles. I was not feeling up to five miles, but I locked my hybrid to the trail sign anyway and followed the path minutes behind a young hiker. Three teenage girls returning from an eleven-mile day warned me to watch the signs because they had made a wrong turn. Yikes! Wrong turns had become my norm. I did not want to hike over five miles, as it was after four already.

Two middle-aged men finishing their hike said there was a creek to cross about one thousand yards from where we stood. One said he took his shoes off and the other said he left his on. Two hundred yards later, I passed three hikers, and one guy said the creek was rocky and deep, and I might want to keep my shoes on. I was wearing my newest white socks with my new HOKA running shoes. My feet are wimps when hard surfaces are involved, but something inside me wouldn't let me quit, so onward I trudged.

When I got to the water's edge, three children were playing and swimming in the water. It was called Jones Creek, but the latte-colored water was as wide and deep as a river. Gathering more opinions on the shoes on or off idea from the parents watching their children, I got both answers. After flipping a coin in my head, I sat and yanked off my new shoes and socks. With my shorts pulled up high, and my shoes and socks above my head, I walked barefoot into the muddy, painfully rocky water.

The water grazed my shorts for the 100-yard crossing, and the current tugged at my legs. The opposite bank welcomed me with black muck and did not offer a foot washing station. I wiped my feet with a paper towel I found in my pocket and returned my socks and shoes to their grateful owners. A narrow trail lined with prickly brush and tall grasses kept me on course for the first mile, leading me to an entertaining stroll through a prairie dog town for the second mile.

Mile three led me up and down, up and down, through rocky single-track terrain where I caught up to the young man who had set out ahead of me. Wes said he was a hiker and carried a GPS and an emergency signal device. As he talked about hiking, I recalled my encounter with Linda, the wild horse photographer, and realized that going for hikes no more makes me a hiker than taking pictures makes me a photographer.

He assured me the left fork of the trail would take me back to the creek, confirming what the eleven-mile-hike girls had told me. I soldiered on, noting my morning ibuprofen had taken effect. Over the three-mile stretch, I took a zillion—well, maybe thirty—pictures that seemed like a zillion. The trail was so unique, I could not help myself. I captured pictures of the prairie dogs, the mountains, the tiny wildflowers, the narrow, narrow path, bison chips, and anything else I deemed picture-worthy. As I hiked, I looked at my surroundings with childlike wonder—simply in awe and now understanding why the young Theodore had enjoyed the area. It was so peaceful. Of course, I realize June may be the best time of year to visit TRNP. I have zero interest in moving to or visiting the Dakotas in the winter months.

By mile four, Wes, the experienced young hiker, had caught up to me, and we hiked together. He walked in front and was doing most of the talking, so he kept turning around to add emphasis with his hands. Weeks earlier he had received his bachelor's degree in chemical engineering from Colorado State University. Wes was working in the area for a month and planned to do a three-week hiking trip in Denali, Alaska, with a friend two weeks later. In August, he would start working on his doctorate at the same university, which offered him tuition plus a $2,200 per month stipend for the next four years.

Boy, did Amy and I get it wrong. We *paid* $1,200 a month for three years to get our doctorate degrees and worked full time to boot.

Wait until I tell Amy.

Wes said he already had an idea for his dissertation project that involved 3D imaging. For the rest of our hike, he explained intricacies of 3D imaging that fascinated me but soared over my head. He told me that one day soon, engineers would have the technical knowledge to create and print a part for a car or for a person.

"So, if my L5 vertebrae gets crushed in a car accident, I can just have another one printed?" I asked.

"That's the idea we're working on. Current technology can already create things from plastic. What I want to work on is advancing technology to create 3D images from other materials, such as polymers or composites. It's a long way off, but it's cool to think about, isn't it?"

"It sure is. That's some amazing stuff." My new hiking friend and I came upon a small creek and got our shoes wet and muddy as we stepped gingerly from rock to rock. The creek was more like what I expected the first passing would be like before I saw the raging river with children's heads bobbing up and down. When we returned to the big Jones Creek crossing, I opted to leave my brand-new, muddy, wet shoes on, and Wes opted to take his Timberlands off.

Wes and I said goodbye at the creek bank. I forded the waters alone, mounted my bike, and rode to the campground. Thanks to Wes, I didn't get lost, and our conversation expanded my mind as I learned about up-and-coming technologies. Another win-win in my book.

Best wishes, Wes. I look forward to following your work. Perhaps our paths will cross again one day.

CHAPTER TWENTY-SIX

Too Close for Comfort

JUNE 30

Still at Theodore Roosevelt South Unit, I woke Sunday morning without a headache but took a couple of ibuprofen just in case. That afternoon, I intended to ride on the loop eighteen miles to the barricade and back—farther than I had ridden in quite some time—but figured I could turn around sooner if my feet started screaming. Because the roads were smooth and I hadn't ridden on skinny tires since Randall fixed the gears in Rapid City, I opted to take my road bike. A few miles into the ride, my bike and I were feeling good. The gears shifted like new.

Twelve miles into my ride, an older couple in a white Denali passed me going up a hill, then grinned and waved as I passed them on the way down. I descended at an exhilarating 30-plus mph pace in the 25-mph zone. Fun stuff! But as I neared the bottom of the hill, I noticed three bison grazing on my left. Cars stopped. People were taking pictures from their windows. I squeezed the brakes hard. In front of me stood a lone bull, grazing on the side of the road and facing me.

He was less than fifty yards away, and the rest of the herd ambled close behind. I stopped, pulled out my phone, took a picture, and then started a video. Two seconds into the video, the bull looked up and started walking toward me. I didn't figure he was approaching because he wanted to lick my face or join me for a selfie. My phone made its way back into my jersey pocket in a flash, and I whispered a sincere apology for having taken a photograph without his consent.

Now, I know there is a fine line between brave and stupid. A has-been amateur cyclist standing at the bottom of a hill in the wrong gear, facing a 2,000-pound beast of an animal, seemed much closer to stupid than brave. The bull let me know I had crossed the line when I pulled out my phone.

Monitoring his movements but not making direct eye contact, I did a one-eighty with my bike. No longer interested in the lush grass, the bison lumbered in my direction. After awkwardly shifting gears, I climbed the hill I had raced down at 30 mph seconds earlier, fully aware that bison can run faster than that if so inspired. I glanced back. Now on the pavement, the bull walked directly behind me and started closing the gap. Forty yards . . . thirty yards . . . twenty. I kept turning the pedals at a slow, labored pace, looking back every few seconds to watch him still lumbering toward me. He wasn't charging me, but was he walking faster? I couldn't tell, but he was tracking me. Of that, I was certain. As I pedaled, I inched past the three bison, now on my right.

Don't make eye contact. Don't look at them. Just keep pedaling.

After a minute, and what seemed like ten, he had cut my lead in half. I picked up my pace—as much as a retired girl with bad knees and aching feet can pick up the pace on a 10% grade without bison assuming she wanted to play tag. The beast continued at his same labored pace. My wobbly legs somehow gained a few yards on him, and then a few more. And then . . . a few more. As I crested the climb, the legs I thought had nothing left regained their power. I flew down the other side of the ridge.

What was I thinking? That was way too close for comfort.

Boy, was I fortunate the bull didn't charge me. I wished I could have gotten more pictures and videos. However, if I had, that might have been my last wish. My heart continued to race long after I topped that hill, but I was alive—and never more grateful to be so. Joyful to be among the living, I let my legs and heart relax for a minute as I replayed the encounter in my head.

While I had been playing chicken with a bison, Judy, the woman I met in Rapid City and then again in Spearfish, texted me. She said crummy weather had slowed her down, but she hoped to make it to Theodore Roosevelt South before dark. I hoped she would make it too. I looked forward to getting to know her. She had told me she worked six months as an airline attendant and traveled via her motorhome the other half of the year. That story alone drew me in.

My ride took two hours, and I returned around four, which gave me plenty of time to shower, fix dinner, clean up, and journal about my day before joining the ranger's program at nine. TRNP South had a show every night, like at Custer State Park.

Minutes before the ranger program, Judy honked her horn as she inched by my site. She yelled the site number she was heading to, and I said I would meet her there. Tim arrived on his mountain bike before me, and we watched Judy settle into her site, already having dropped off her little Hyundai. She unhooked her tow dolly and backed in like she drove a truck for a living.

"Impressive," Tim said.

"Yeah. She's good, all right. Sure wish I could do that. I couldn't even get my rig in the first time in broad daylight, and hers is way bigger."

Tim laughed.

"Welcome Judy! I'm going to the ranger program. Wanna go?"

"Nah, I'm exhausted. You go on. We can go for a hike or a bike ride or something in the morning."

"Okay," I said. "Call me in the morning. I'm glad you're here."

Tim and Judy talked at her site, and as I enjoyed the program devoted to the Native American tribes who had once lived in the area, I wished I had brought a notebook to the amphitheater. It wasn't the first time I wished this and certainly would not be the last, but I enjoyed the programs even if I couldn't remember much of the information the next day.

As I lay in bed that night, I replayed the bison encounter again and again. I was looking forward to an easy hike or bike ride with Judy.

CHAPTER TWENTY-SEVEN

Surviving the Little Missouri River

JULY 1

The next morning I was feeling good—as in no-need-for-ibuprofen-with-my-oatmeal—*good*. I finished writing up postcards and walked to Judy's new campsite. She had already moved to a site big enough to park her car beside her RV. It seemed like a lot of extra work to pull a vehicle, but Judy said she appreciated having a car.

Judy suggested we float down the Little Missouri River in a kayak and an inner tube. Her idea sounded fun. Never having floated down a river, I was up for doing something new, something adventurous. She got everything together, and we drove to the visitor center at TRNP South in her car. We asked about putting her kayak in the Little Missouri River, but none of the employees had any answers. Surely Judy was not the first person to inquire about kayaking on the Little Missouri. It seemed like a common question, but the staff looked as if we were asking where we could launch our houseboat.

As we roamed the gift shop, Judy showed me her National Parks Passport and encouraged me to buy one for myself. After purchasing the booklet at any national park gift shop, the goal is to visit national parks and fill the passport with stickers or stamps, ideally from each of the sixty-plus national parks and three hundred-plus national areas and monuments. Despite having explored a handful of national parks, I had not heard of the passport until Judy shared it with me. She convinced me to buy one of those little treasures, and she helped me put the first stamp in my book: Theodore Roosevelt National Park, South, July 1, 2019. Let the good times begin!

After stopping at the post office in Medora to mail postcards, Judy drove us to Sully Creek State Park, about five miles away. We asked a ranger mowing the lawn where we could launch. She told us we'd need to purchase a day-use state park pass for $7 and pointed to a place to put a boat in the river. We secured a pass and then pumped up Judy's inflatable kayak and inner tube with a foot pump. Judy gave me a waterproof bag for my phone so it would float if we tipped over.

Judy's six-year-old papillon, Harper, was a trooper. Without a leash, he stayed close by as we walked the quarter mile from her car to the boat launch, which was actually more of a tiny 18-inch clearing in the brush along the river. Through the clearing, we scaled our way down a steep, rocky embankment and waded into the river. Judy put Harper on the back of her kayak, stepped in, and pushed off with her paddle. Following suit, I pushed off and plopped myself into the center of the inner tube.

We floated downstream, admiring the perfect view of the buttes and the amazing blue sky splattered with pillowy white clouds. Harper, perched at the stern inches behind Judy, looked confident like he had done this a million times. Judy planned to float down the river to her campsite, but I wasn't clear on how we would get back to her car at the state park. Still, I trusted my tour guide to work out the details.

Two hours into our excursion, I thanked my new friend for taking me on such a fun trip, and she suggested I not thank her too early, noting we had not gotten back yet. We laughed. Several times we walked in the water because our crafts dragged on the river bottom, and occasionally the current became swift, but most of the time we just row, row, rowed our boat gently down the stream. At about the three-hour mark, we switched places so I could try her kayak. Thirty minutes later we switched crafts again. When we got out to walk over a shallow area, I held on to the tube, but I hadn't gotten back on it yet. In half a second, the water changed from too shallow to float to a rushing current too deep and strong for either of us to fight. Judy pulled over to the bank for safety. She called for me to come to the bank, but I was further downstream.

To get back to her, I tried walking and then swimming when the water rose above my waist. I felt as though I was in one of those resistance swim pools designed to give you just as much resistance as you can swim against—the swimming equivalent of a treadmill. My efforts got me nowhere. It was funny at first. But then, the water got deeper, and the current stronger. Though swimming as hard as I could (which was not that hard given I'm not much of a swimmer and I was still holding onto a tube I could not climb into), I was getting whooshed further and further from my friend.

Judy pushed off and steered her way through the turbulence. Thankful she was willing to push away from the safe spot she found on the bank, I held on to the tube and quit fighting the raging waters.

Once I quit battling the current, I gave one big kick with my legs and hoisted myself back on top of the tube, which now posed as my lifesaver ring. With Judy and Harper close behind, the current shot us downstream as though we were on a ride at a water park. Within 200-300 yards, the water returned to the peaceful flow we had experienced earlier, and on we sailed. Minutes later, as though our lives had never been in danger, we once again marveled at the charm of the river, the stunning buttes, and the soft blue sky with the wispy snow-white clouds.

As the afternoon waned, we were talking, laughing, and genuinely enjoying ourselves when Judy noticed we were floating downstream slowly, and it was getting late. She directed us to anchor at the bank to see how much farther we had to float. Performing a little GPS magic with her phone, she determined we were not yet halfway to the campground, our intended destination.

"I have never had to bail like this before, but Joy, we are clearly not going to make it to the campground before dark. The river is flowing too slowly. Do you see that bridge up there? That may be a good place to get out."

"Are you serious? I'm game for whatever you think we need to do. You're the captain of this ship."

"Okay. I say we stop at the bridge and look around. Maybe we could walk up to the road and hitch a ride back to my car. If we leave the tube and kayak under the bridge, we can come back once we get to my car. I hate to leave them, but I don't think anyone would bother them. Who would even see them? What do you think?"

I shrugged. "I'm with you."

When we eased onto the sand under the concrete overpass, we knew we couldn't be far from civilization. It was a big bridge with cars driving overhead, but neither of us had any idea where we were. We stowed the kayak and tube in the bridge's crux and trudged up the steep embankment through thick, thorny, leg-scratching brush. Concerned that Harper might get thorns in his paws and burrs in his coat, Judy carried him. We forged our way to a clearing and found ourselves at a picnic area called Chimney Park, a stone's throw from the Medora Campground, which was another stone's throw from the entrance to Theodore Roosevelt National Park. Relieved to recognize our surroundings, we felt confident we would figure out a way to get home from there. We were a good three miles from Judy's car, and I figured we could walk even if we were five miles away, provided I cleaned the pesky river rocks out of my shoes first. My feet were killing me.

Thrilled to find a working restroom with sinks and running water, I rinsed out my socks and shoes. Judy did the same, but it did not take her nearly as long since she wore rubber water shoes without socks. As I rinsed my shoes, I heard her talking outside. I wondered if a friend had called her. It turns out my adventuresome friend had called 911 and had somehow arranged for a police officer to come check on us. She hoped he would give us a ride or at least show us the shortest walking route to her car. I never would have thought to call 911. Never. We were in dire straits, but I did not deem our situation 911-worthy. Judy did. She called. And I was happy to be with a bold, resourceful woman.

A ranger pulled up next to us and said we were out of his jurisdiction, but a Medora police officer would be with us soon. In less than one minute, two officers in two vehicles availed themselves to help two water-logged, stranded women and a happy-go-lucky papillon. Both police officers said they would give us a ride to Judy's car.

Judy looked at me and said, "There's no way we can get back down that embankment we just climbed and carry the kayak and tube back up through all those thorns, even if we deflated them down there."

"You're right. It was hard enough climbing up empty-handed."

When Judy inquired about a better place to get the kayak and tube out of the water, the officers told us about a beach at the opposite end of Medora Campground.

Judy said, "How about you and Harper go with the officer in his police car? I'll walk back to the bridge, get the boats, float to the beach, and meet you there."

"What?"

She handed me her keys. "You take Harper and my keys. The officer will take you back to my car and then you and Harper drive back and meet me down by the beach."

Judy had way more confidence in me than I did, but I agreed to her plan because I believed in her. She exuded enough confidence for both of us. The police officers, Nicholas and Scott, decided Nicholas would take Harper and me to Sully Creek, and Scott would go on his way. That was the plan. Judy vanished. Nicholas opened the back door, and Harper and I climbed into the "cage" in the back seat. I never dreamed I would be excited to ride in a police car, but there I was, thankful for the opportunity.

Poor Harper danced around in my lap and looked at me as if to say, "Wait. What's going on here? Isn't Mom coming with us?"

Unfortunately for Harper, his momma was already en route to the bridge. He was stuck with me, and he realized it too late.

Nicholas handed me the seatbelt buckle and waited for the click before he closed the door. Harper settled into my lap with a sigh. Guns, piled precariously next to us on the other side of the cage, caught my eye. If Officer Nicholas had two criminals to transport, he'd need to move the guns to make room. However, as this was Medora, North Dakota, I'm guessing they do not have many occasions to transport hardened criminals.

As he settled into the driver's seat, Nicholas said a few undistinguishable words into his radio and off he drove to Sully Creek State Park. I hoped he would sound the siren, but I wasn't bold enough to ask him to humor me. As I might with a cab driver, I inquired about the weather, about his service, and how Medora fared in the wintertime without all the visitors around. Officer Nicholas had served on the force full time for six years after working seasonally for nine. He told me that 150 residents lived in Medora all year, and winters do not get as bad on the western side of the state (where we were) as they do on the eastern side where he grew up. Less than a mile down the road, I felt as comfortable talking with the officer as I had with Judy when we first met.

"Will I need to drive into the park to find my friend? And will I have to pay to get into the park? I didn't think about it until now, but I have no cash on me."

"If you follow me there, you won't have to pay. I can get you in. It's not like you are going to stay."

Officer Nicholas dropped me off at Judy's car, and Harper jumped into the driver's seat with me. I was driving a Hyundai I had never driven, with a scared dog in my lap, and Nicholas pulled out onto the gravel road like he was chasing a bank robber. I drove slowly and fell behind. When we got to the pavement, he paused for me to catch up and then picked up speed. He was going at least 50 mph in what I was certain was a 25-mph zone, so I drove 35 mph to split the difference. Speeding didn't feel right even though I was following a man in blue, or maybe I should say *especially* because I was following a man in blue. I lagged all the way to the campground, where a peek at Judy's odometer told me we'd driven seven miles. No way could Judy and I have walked that far before dark with my pitiful feet, especially with an eight-pound, four-legged pup along. Oh, my goodness was I grateful to Officer Nicholas.

Inside Medora Campground, Officer Nicholas eased to a stop. I was thinking he was going to tell me how to find the beach. No, he motioned to park behind him and walked out of sight. Harper and I jumped out of Judy's car and tried to follow. I spotted his uniformed back and kept trekking. We found Judy talking with people on the beach as she was washing off her kayak with river water. She was fine—acting as though this was an everyday occurrence—and Harper and I were delighted to know she was okay. Not only did Officer Nicholas give Harper and me a ride, he escorted us to the beach and then offered to help carry the watercrafts back to Judy's car. I was blown away by his servant spirit and then he went one step further.

"I should get a picture of this scene," I said.

Judy summoned a guy she was talking with to get a picture and video of us walking to her car with the river, buttes, and sun setting in the background. Officer Nicholas obliged, pausing with us for a picture and then, while on video he and Judy carried the kayak and tube to Judy's car as I followed suit with a paddle and a surprisingly calm puppy in tow. We said a final thank you and Nicholas drove off as though it was a typical day in Medora.

Boy, have I met some good people in my travels.

It didn't occur to me until later that Officer Nicholas could have dropped off Harper and me at Judy's car and gone on his way. If given a chance to explain our plight, I'm sure the folks at the gate would have let me drive to the beach to pick up Judy without paying to get into the park. He did not need to escort us to the campground, much less carry the kayak up the beach. The more I thought about the situation, the more appreciative I became. The officer definitely went the extra mile for us.

Judy and I deflated the rafts and wrestled them into her trunk. We agreed it would be best for me to drive her car while she held Harper for the five-mile drive back to our campground. Harper needed a little mommy-time. As if the day had not held enough adventure, on our scenic drive through the park, a lone bison grazed close to the road. One last picture and video completed our day's adventures.

We got back to Judy's place moments after darkness enveloped the campground. I thanked her for the grand voyage, walked to my tiny house, showered, ate, and journaled about our unbelievably exciting excursion.

In my journal I wrote: *I find it astounding how nature can change from serene to scary in a matter of seconds. For a few minutes I was in danger. I was scared. So many things could have happened. Judy and I were vulnerable—out there in the river with a dog and no life jackets. We never needed them or even thought about them, but it makes me think about how I have been living. It all ended well, but I cringe when I think about what might have happened. Everyone is going to hear this story. Never a dull moment with Judy, that's for sure. What will tomorrow bring?*

(Several months later I added some introspection to my journal: *God was like a life jacket. I was floating downstream by myself—acting like I didn't need him. And worse yet, believing I could grab him at the last minute if the "water rose over my head" so to speak. I don't just want God to be my lifesaver. I miss having the relationship that I had with him in high school and college. Like I told Julie, it really is time to get my life back on track.*)

CHAPTER TWENTY-EIGHT

Another Adventure with Judy and Harper

JULY 2 – 3

After a good night's sleep, Judy, Harper, and I drove twelve miles to the Painted Canyon Welcome Center at Theodore Roosevelt National Park South for a hike. We had just set off and were enjoying the cool breeze when not even a mile down the trail, storm clouds rolled in, let loose, and drenched us before we could get back to the car. Blindsided by the sudden change in weather, Judy then drove us through a torrential downpour mixed with hail. We could not see six feet in front of the headlights. Thankful to be the passenger, I held tight to Harper as Judy squinted through the thumping wipers, gripped the wheel, and focused on the white line of the interstate. How quickly the weather can change and how fast a pleasant afternoon can go south.

Still, the weather is part of the adventure—all part of finding joy. In addition, there was another kind of joy rising inside me. It was an underlying joy in the connection I felt with the early settlers of our American West. When I thought of all they had faced, all the hardships they had endured to settle in this breathtaking expanse, I got chills. Men and women I would never meet or even read about had laid the path, the foundation for me to enjoy the amazing west. For their hard work and sacrifice, I am truly grateful.

Before we left for the hike, *Dark Sky* had predicted zero chance of rain for the afternoon, so, of course, I'd left the windows open in my tiny house. For twelve miles, I imagined the worst. Beneath the open dining table window was my box of books and notecards on top of my laptop. The bedroom window spans the better part of my bed, and more importantly, beneath that window was my beloved T-shirt quilt, which was designed for my motorhome and given to me at retirement by my school staff members and my good friend Debbie. In front of a third window was my swivel writing chair, which was adorned with a treasured school-colors afghan, a one-of-a-kind retirement gift from my dear coworker Tanya. The window above the kitchen sink concerned me the least, but the open fans above my bed and bathroom invited copious amounts of rain. For sure, I would return to a mess, but I prayed the rain would not ruin my computer, books, cards, quilt, and throw.

The rain dropped in buckets the entire thirty-minute drive. Judy drove through one of the most treacherous rainstorms I have ever witnessed. Cars with flashers blinking lined the shoulder. Judy soldiered on, just like our early settlers would have done in their Conestoga wagons. Thanks to Judy, we arrived at Cottonwood Campground safely. I rushed inside my tiny house, expecting to find a disaster. Surprisingly, my books, cards, and computer were dry, my afghan and quilt were only damp, and one towel soaked up the rain at the kitchen sink and bathroom. What a relief!

The next morning came fast, and Judy and Harper and I said a reluctant goodbye. Tim, our campground host, rode up and offered to take a photo of the three of us by Judy's place. I had camped at the TRNP South Unit for a week—the longest I had camped in one place. On my way out, I stopped to say goodbye to Tim and Donna and thank them for their hospitality. A bit sad about leaving, I lingered, and Tim verified my directions to the North Unit. We hugged and off I drove. At almost every park, I had gotten attached to the campground hosts, park employees, and fellow campers. Relationships really are everything. And as I journeyed on, that became more and more clear to me.

At the intersection of 94 and 85, I stopped to visit my friend Lana, who had treated me to two coffee shakes for my birthday a week earlier. For a week, I had consumed no sugar and no caffeine and felt close to my normal self. I planned to stop only for a visit, but I had sent Lana a text, so two shots sat cooling for me. She greeted me with a smile and almond milk in hand. Lana and her sister Laurie agreed I should try their infamous cinnamon roll coffee shake. My resolve failed me, and I enjoyed the treat.

Laurie matched Lana in the friendliness department, so we talked a good while as I stood outside the drive-up window. I told the brew hut sisters about my adventures at the South Unit, and they told me more about their family and life in the Dakotas. In addition to her full-time job and the coffee hut, Lana helped her husband as much as she could with his cows on their ranch. She also enjoyed growing vegetables in their garden, but said it was a lot of work.

I love listening to people's stories, especially when they are so different from mine. That trait came from my mother, except Mom could have been a therapist. She asked more and better questions, and she listened intently when people answered. She never probed. Mom was just inquisitive and genuinely interested. I think of her often when I meet new people. She would learn more about one of my friends in five minutes than I might have learned in five months or five years. Everyone who was privileged to know her appreciated that about the most influential woman in my life.

As we talked, Lana and Laurie cleaned and organized their space. I leaned on the window ledge, setting my drink on their counter between sips.

"We're searching for a buyer for Java Gypsy, because Laurie wants to retire. We've had this place five years. It's been good for our mental health, but it's time to let it go."

"Bet it's fun meeting people. Do you have a lot of regular customers?"

"Yes. We have a steady stream in the mornings, people who live around here, but we get a lot of people passing through like you too."

"Speaking of that," I said, "I'll be back through here on Saturday or Sunday."

"Oh, we will miss you then," Lana said. "We're taking the holiday weekend off. We won't be open until Monday."

When I asked if they thought the Conoco convenience store/gas station down the street stocked almond or soy milk, they chuckled and said they didn't think so.

Lana handed me the soy milk from their fridge. "Happy birthday!"

"Thank you! Thank you so much. That's so nice of you."

After I left the sisters, I went to Conoco to top off the gas tank. Even though I had only driven sixty miles since the last fill-up, I needed fifteen gallons because I had been running the generator. The generator burns about a half-gallon of gas for each hour of power. I made a mental note to keep track of my generator use, knowing I probably wouldn't because I'm not good with those kinds of details. My backup plan is to not worry about minor details, but sometimes it's important to pay attention to them because small things can accumulate and become significant. For example, by saving a few dollars here, consuming fewer calories there, exceeding expectations, showing gratitude, or offering a helping hand, I can make a positive impact. *Yes, I will ponder the small stuff, but I won't linger in fear and negativity*, I thought as I tightened the gas cap. Just for fun, I went inside and checked the milk options. The barista sisters were right. There was no almond or soy milk to be found.

With a full tank of petrol, I drove back to verify directions and say another thank you for the soy milk. Lana gave me a bag of crushed ice (in case I wanted to make smoothies or my own little version of a coffee shake) because she was shutting down their ice maker for the weekend. We also exchanged phone numbers. My new friend probably thought soy milk and ice were insignificant gestures, but I was already thinking about how the small stuff makes a big difference. Her thoughtfulness that day and on my birthday affected me enough to include this story. The little things people do make a difference. It's people who matter. It's people who make a difference. It's people who bring me joy.

Long after I returned home from this trip, I read two books by Andy Andrews that discuss the concept of the small stuff and the idea that everything you do makes a difference in this world. One is called *The Little Things: Why You Really Should Sweat the Small Stuff*, and the other is *The Butterfly Effect: How Your Life Matters*. I did not know about those books when I was out there in North Dakota contemplating the small stuff, but God was preparing my heart to appreciate the importance of small stuff and the difference it can make.

CHAPTER TWENTY-NINE

Happy Birthday, America!

JULY 3 - 4

Thanks to directions from Lana, I made it to Theodore Roosevelt National Park North, a sixty-mile drive from the South Unit, without incident. I met the host, a friendly single guy about my age named Terry, settled into site #18 in the late afternoon and enjoyed an uneventful evening by myself. The North Unit greeted me with a chilly morning rain to celebrate our nation's day of independence. At the South Unit, it had been so hot I ran the air conditioning during the day and tossed and turned at night.

Not wanting to sit inside on one of our country's most celebrated holidays, I dressed in warm rain gear and took off on my hybrid. Because the central and mountain time zones come together in the North Unit, a weird thing kept happening. The hour on my sports watch, Garmin bike computer, and cell phone vacillated as I rode. I never knew what time it was, but it didn't matter one bit. I was on retirement time, and I was at Teddy Roosevelt National Park on the birthday of our great nation. When it occurred to me that I had been at TRNP South for my own birthday eight days earlier, I thought *it doesn't get any better than this*!

An hour into my ride, the sun pushed away the clouds and warmed the park fifteen degrees in a matter of minutes. I shed the rain pants and rain jacket and was thankful I had opted for the ride. The scenic byway was a straight fourteen-mile stretch. I planned to go to the furthest parking area and ride back to the campground. Though it troubles me that I might never again complete rides of fifty miles and more, I tried to wrap my head around the idea that twenty to thirty miles was an acceptable distance. Twenty-eight miles would allow me to enjoy the park and get a little exercise yet finish before my feet started screaming.

To give some background, foot pain had been an issue since my early twenties when I moved to Georgia and began riding faster and longer with more serious cyclist friends. The longer and harder I rode, the more my feet would hurt. In addition to the foot pain, I developed neck and shoulder pain that on long rides would get so painful I could not turn my head to see if cars were approaching from behind. Because my left leg does 60 to 70 percent of the work due to my right leg being weaker, my right knee usually only complained when I rode in the mountains on multiple days in a row. On the 2010 coast-to-coast ride—because I sat on a hard skinny saddle for six hours a day in sweaty shorts, day after day—my rear end sometimes took over as my first body part to complain.

As the years of cycling and running have taken their toll on my already not-so-strong body, the aches and pains have gradually forced me to ride fewer miles with less intensity. For some reason, though, I have never contemplated not riding. I quit running in 2015, but getting rid of the bikes has never been an option. Cycling is part of me. It is part of my identity that I don't want to give up. As long as I am able, I will ride and deal with the aches and pains as they come.

When I reached the River Bend Overlook, my water bottles were nearly empty. Having run dry so many times through the years, one of my biggest cycling concerns is running out of water. In the heat I typically drink a twenty-ounce bottle of water every thirty to forty minutes. When I suspect I will ride for two hours I bring four bottles, which is all I can comfortably carry on my road bike. Usually if I run out, I can refill at a water fountain or buy more at a convenience store along the way. Riding in areas without those options was new to me. So, as I had done at TRNP South Unit, I gratefully accepted eight ounces from the Nalgene bottle of Colorado newlyweds. Overhearing our conversation, a family confirmed my suspicions: water fountains and restrooms were only at the visitor center, several miles away. The generous young couple and I enjoyed the spectacular views while taking pictures and discussing the park, their wedding, and their honeymoon plans.

The overlook included a large parking area, trailheads, a platform viewing deck, and a short trail with steps down to a rock shelter the Civilian Conservation Corps (CCC) had built in the early 1930s. I ventured to the shelter for more pictures of the breathtaking grass and tree-covered buttes. The green buttes flanked by variegated rock buttes with their layered bands of oranges, yellows, browns, and grays, made for a spectacular panoramic backdrop of the now notorious (to me, anyway) Little Missouri River.

Along the scenic drive, I kept meeting up with a family who was excited about seeing the Badlands region—primarily the North and South Dakotas—and bison for the first time. Simultaneously, we arrived at the end of the byway, Oxbow Overlook. The odometer on my bike computer read exactly ten miles, fewer than I had expected. Sometimes I forget to turn my bike computer back on after stops, so I didn't know if the ten-mile reading was accurate. On our return, the family caught up to me as a herd of bison crossed the road. I snuck behind their truck and parked my bike so I could get pictures of the bison. I felt safe standing with the family beside their pickup. The father promised me if I got into trouble, they would throw my bike in the back of their truck and drive me past the bison. He understood the unpredictability of the amazing, yet potentially dangerous, animals.

I stood with the family, grateful that I so often crossed paths with good, kindhearted people. Was it because most people I met were in travel/vacation mode, hence in a relaxed and happy state, or was I just fortunate to meet great people? Either way, I felt blessed. The grandma of the family protecting me videoed the bison crossing from one side of the truck, and I videoed them from the other side. The two teen girls shared a pair of binoculars and an expensive-looking Cannon with a big lens. It was a spectacular do-over of my birthday except we were closer and safer, and we stayed until the entire herd crossed the road and no longer posed a threat.

Guess whose car I spotted parked at the entrance of the campground when I returned? Yep! It didn't take me long to find Judy and Harper talking to our host, Terry, at his site. Judy had driven from the South Unit and said in an hour she was going to see the Fourth of July fireworks in a nearby town called Arnegard, North Dakota. She agreed to me tagging along, so sixty minutes later I stood at her door, excited to see a fireworks display. I'd already had an amazing day and now fireworks? We made a stop at a grocery store in Watford City, North Dakota, and the couple in line behind us assured us Arnegard was the place to enjoy a fabulous display.

Once in Arnegard, we stumbled upon the firehouse.

"Let's pull in here. I'm sure the firefighters will know where the fireworks are going to be set off tonight."

"Great idea, Judy."

The firefighters welcomed us with open arms. Two showed us around the station and said they were all volunteer firefighters for the small town of Arnegard, population 198. The volunteers took pride in their work and enjoyed telling us about their station and their town as much as we enjoyed learning about them. One of the men showed us around the station and pointed out the oldest, vintage truck in the fleet. Leslie, one of the firefighters, took a picture of Judy, Harper, and me grinning ear to ear at the opened door of the newest fire truck, then gathered the gang for me to snap a photo of six of them. Around 9, we thanked the crew for the tour, and a firefighter named Richard gave us a personal escort via four-wheeler to the ball diamond, staged with fireworks ready to be lit. The show would begin at 11 p.m. and last forty-five minutes. That seemed late, but then we realized because we were at the convergence of two time zones, it didn't get dark enough for fireworks until 11 Central time.

Judy spotted a bar down the street from where we had parked. She suggested we walk down there to check it out since we were so early. As we sat at the bar to order, I realized I did not have my money, my credit card, or my driver's license. Because I didn't want to lug a purse around, I had wrapped a couple of twenties around a credit card and my driver's license and stuffed the wad into my pocket. Immediately, I fell into panic-mode and told Judy I needed to "retrace my steps" as my mom always taught. Judy gave me her keys. I rushed out, praying fervently as I hustled to her car.

I found my loot outside the passenger door in the street, untouched. What a relief! I thanked God and rushed back to the bar to find Judy had ordered me a Diet Coke to go. Filled with cigarette smoke and laughing patrons, the bar resembled a scene from a western. I expected the firefighters to rush in and put out the fire, but no such luck. Judy finished a piece of key lime pie, paid the bill, left a generous tip, and off we went. I was glad Judy didn't want to hang out in a smoky bar either. We pulled two chairs from her trunk and sat facing the baseball field, ready for a show that would not start for well over an hour. Harper sat on Judy's lap, perfectly content.

"How's he going to handle the fireworks?"

"Oh, he'll be fine. I've taken him to the fireworks every year since he was a puppy. I talk to him the whole time about how beautiful and loud they are, and he just watches, never even flinches."

"That is amazing. My sister doesn't go to fireworks displays anymore because the firecrackers and bottle rockets scare her dog to death. She stays home with her dog on the fourth now. Her dog freaks out during storms too. Poor baby."

"Maybe it's because her dog can't see what's making the noise. I don't know. I love fireworks, so I had to make sure he did too. Taking him to the fireworks when he was a pup, holding and talking to him works for us."

We had premier seats for the most dramatic fireworks spectacle I have seen, ever. The tiny town of fewer than two hundred residents puts on a show and a half. The display lasted over forty-five minutes, and they launched several fireworks at a time for the entire performance. Many times that night, we believed the finale was starting because they were that plentiful. Harper sat and watched with us while Judy talked to him, using words such as *pretty*, *loud*, and *wow*—just as Judy had said. What a great dog. The finale, fifteen minutes before midnight, was magnificent. Judy, Harper, and I returned to Juniper Campground, where we were staying, well after midnight. What a perfect celebration of our nation's independence.

Happy birthday, America!

CHAPTER THIRTY

More Adventures with Judy and Harper

JULY 5-8

At breakfast I thought it was time to figure out my next destination. As I looked at my atlas I realized it no longer made sense for me to visit Anamoose, North Dakota, where my maternal grandfather was born in 1902. It made me a little sad. My brother and his wife Pam had visited Anamoose recently. Tom said there were probably fewer than 250 people living there, so as my brother and his wife explored the small town, it was obvious they were visitors. Everyone stopped to talk to them. Tom and Pam enjoyed their visit, and I wanted to see the little community myself.

But now, because I had driven across Nebraska, rather than North Dakota, and was at TNRP on the west side of the state, I was 250 miles west of Anamoose. So many other places had taken my focus that Anamoose got lost in the shuffle. Now it made no sense to backtrack, so my grandfather's birthplace would need to be a destination for another excursion. I wonder if oversights like that occur to give me an incentive to return. There was no way I could fit every goal into my trip. Anamoose remains on the bucket list.

Before I figured out where I would go next, Judy and Harper picked me up in her car and we were off on another adventure. Judy drove us to Little Missouri State Park, an hour from TRNP North. At the entrance an employee told us that one extended family had filled the thirty-site campground for an annual weeklong family reunion. Horses, horse trailers, and happy relatives filled the park. After driving through the park and campground, we picked a hiking trail and set off for the unknown. Miles and miles of trails that were primarily designed for horses made some trail sections rough with a capital R. The last half-mile of the trail we hiked was super steep, like Mount Kilimanjaro-steep, and as narrow as a railroad tie. We could barely tell we were on the path, much less hike through without getting mauled by the brush. Our legs looked like a pack of felines had attacked.

If not for the heat, blue jeans would have made the hike much more enjoyable. The views of the Badlands from the trail were as spectacular as the views at River Bend Overlook on the Fourth of July, but the pain from the "cat scratches" distracted us from the beauty. A mile from the end of our trek, Harper hurt his foot. Although he had a pair of homemade hiking booties, he didn't have them on, and it appeared a thistle had burrowed its way into his right front paw between the pads and hid from view. Not able to extract the thistle, Judy carried him the rest of the way in his little pack that she strapped to her chest. As we emerged from the thickets into a clearing where we had parked, we met a park ranger on a horse. We chatted with her about the park, the trails, and the family reunion. We took pictures with her and her horse, Lakota, plus more pictures of the badland buttes we had just hiked before heading back to Juniper Campground.

Outside the state park, I took pictures and video of a pumpjack. Some might find that an oil well detracts from the magnificence of the hills, but I found it intriguing. At the entryway to TRNP North, we stopped again for another photo opportunity. Harper sat on the wall of the entrance sign by himself, happy to oblige, as Judy took a few glamor shots. Because I take pictures of the signs at every state and park I visit, we took several of ourselves on the wall of the stately Theodore Roosevelt National Park sign. A few minutes after we got back in the car, I took a video of a bison walking by himself in the grass only two feet from Judy's passenger side window. I could hardly contain my excitement.

"Harper should bark at him to get his attention," Judy said. "He's not looking at us."

"Oh, no!" I chuckled. "I'm glad Harper didn't hear you say that. I am perfectly fine with bison not acknowledging our presence."

When Judy pulled into the campground at 7 p.m., our campground host Terry reminded us about the ranger program at 8 p.m. We rushed back to our respective homes, cleaned up, ate, and met at the amphitheater an hour later. After the ranger program about cowboys, Judy drove us to the River Bend Overlook, where we could get a cell signal.

Judy and Harper were full of adventure. I wanted to keep traveling with them, so we pored over a map on Judy's phone for areas that would suit both of us. We found a private RV park that looked doable, but we would need to confirm availability in the morning. She dropped me off at my place and we agreed to meet up in the morning at the entrance of the campground.

That next morning, while I was dumping my tanks (admittedly the worst routine task for RVers), I thought of my friends back home who were poolside or preparing for a post-holiday get-together with family and friends. Don't misunderstand. I love getting together with family and friends, but on that particular Saturday, I could not have been any happier than I was right then, dumping my tanks by myself on a warm, sunny morning at a national park nearly two-thousand miles from home.

Of course, I had enjoyed a marvelous Fourth of July, and a nice hike the day after, but as I completed an unpleasant task, I realized that I am living my dream and finding joy even in the mundane, poopy jobs no one likes. *Yes, I am one happy camper.*

A short while later, Judy and I met up and parked our rigs near the entrance of Juniper Campground, then crossed the street to the Buckhorn Trailhead. The rock formations near the trailhead were like none I had ever seen. We watched two pre-teen girls scamper around their mother on the steep, round, slick, chestnut-colored rocks.

The smooth rocks resembled Goliath-sized bowling balls. The rocks and little cave-like hideaways made for fun pictures with Harper, who still limped if Judy didn't carry him. (She never found the thorn or whatever pierced his paw.) Beyond the bowling ball-shaped rocks, we found a play-ground of natural uneven terraces, ledges, and platforms all formed from the same rock that enticed Judy and me to join the girls and their mother for an hour of exploration.

After enjoying ourselves on the rocks, we opted to skip the trail hike. Judy and I settled into our motorhomes and drove 120 miles tandem style to the campground we'd located the night before, which was off I-94 in Glendive, Montana. We agreed to stay two nights because it was late in the afternoon, they only charged us $25 a night, we wanted to hike or bike, and we needed to do laundry. The campground owners were spry and friendly and looked to be in their late 80s. The grounds needed some TLC, but the campground offered hookups—a perk not available at TRNP or nearby Makoshika State Park.

As we registered and paid for our sites at the office I asked, "How do you pronounce the name of the state park?"

"Mack-oh-SHE-kuh," the owner said.

"Really?" her niece said. "I've always heard it pronounced Ma-KO-shi-kuh with the emphasis on the KO."

"So there you have it," the owner said. "Even we don't know how it's supposed to be pronounced, and we've lived here all our lives."

Judy and I chuckled. We tried to repeat the pronunciations, but the women laughed at our efforts. When Judy expressed an interest in having a fire, the owner said she would have her husband, Bill, bring us a fire ring once we got settled.

No sooner had Judy and I pulled into our side-by-side sites did we see Bill driving down the gravel lane with a fire ring hanging from his forklift. He asked us to pick a spot, and he dropped it where Judy pointed at the corner of her site. Perfect!

We then drove six miles in my RV to Makoshika State Park to search for a good place to hike or bike. When we returned, Judy unhitched her car while I turned my rig around. I pulled in backward, allowing our house doors to face each other—Judy's ingenious idea. The setup made it easier and safer for Harper to hobble back and forth from Judy's place to mine, which made all three of us happy. Another win-win.

Judy bought firewood and then cozied up her place by extending her slides and awning, spreading a tablecloth on the picnic table, setting up lawn chairs, hanging outdoor lights, connecting an extra water hose to the spigot, and more. (I appreciated her efforts and later bought tablecloths and lights for myself but never did get my place to look as homey as hers.)

After dinner, Judy split the wood with her axe and started a fire. We enjoyed each other's company and the fire until Judy retired at midnight. An hour later, exhausted, I doused the embers with water from the hose—a practice I learned from my brother when I was a kid.

Late the next morning we rode our bikes to Makoshika State Park and then hiked out to a natural phenomenon I had never seen. We crossed a bridge composed of one gigantic flat rock maybe the size of four tractor trailers, suspended between two rock mounds three stories high above a jagged rock crevasse. We took pictures of each other leaping on the amazing natural bridge. Judy is such a good photographer that in the photos I look like I'm leaping as high as Michael Jordan in his infamous drive to the basket from the foul line. Since the park was still in the Badlands area, the rock formations were as unique as those at Badlands National Park. The bridge made for a memorable Sunday morning hike.

On the bike ride back to the campground in Glendive where we were staying, we rode through a little water park. Judy played along with two preschool boys soaking each other with water guns and got soaked herself. I didn't join in but adored watching them play. The boys cried when Judy said she needed to leave. With Judy soaking wet, we rode on back to our campsites, got cleaned up, and ate an early dinner. My bike ride with Judy that day made Montana the twenty-first state on my list. With each new state I checked off, I felt more and more confident I would reach my fifty-state goal.

We topped off the day with a three-hour laundromat adventure. The owners of the laundromat had labeled half the machines "greasers." People who worked on the oil rigs used those machines to wash their work clothes. We returned to the campground after dark, and seconds after we got our clean clothes inside, a downpour ensued, keeping us inside our respective homes for the evening.

Judy and I agreed to keep traveling together. Over breakfast we looked at a map and decided on Billings, Montana. The city looked big enough to have a place to get our oil changed and maybe get new tires for Judy's tow dolly. We pulled out of the campground together shortly after noon that Monday. Both of our rigs needed propane, so we stopped at a station before hitting the highway. Propane was ninety cents a gallon. The guy who filled our tanks told us it was cheap because they had so much of it in Montana. He got no complaints from us. Propane had been costing me over $3 a gallon. We happily filled our tanks for $5.

"Too bad we can't come back to Glendive every time we need propane," I said to Judy.

We headed west and three hours later, Judy and I stocked up on much-needed supplies at the Billings Walmart. By the time we finished shopping it was getting dark. Since we didn't have reservations anywhere, we ended up spending the night side by side in the Billings Walmart parking lot. We didn't know where we would end up next, but as long as we were driving west, I was game for hanging with Judy as long as I could.

CHAPTER THIRTY-ONE

From Billings to Lovell

JULY 9 – 10

Tuesday morning in Billings, Judy and I managed to get oil changes for both rigs. Not ready to part ways, we looked at a map and picked a campground in the Bighorn Canyon National Recreation Area as our next destination. I followed Judy until we found ourselves a quarter mile down a rough, dirt road. She called and said her GPS showed we would be on that road for twenty miles. Twenty miles on gravel? No way!

Judy found an alternate paved route on Google maps and maneuvered a loop through a field of uneven, unknown terrain. The field was a precarious place to make a U-turn, but with no vehicles in sight, she faced the opposite direction in ninety seconds. I had no trouble making the U-turn on the road. As we were verifying the route, help arrived out of the blue—a blue Mercedes, that is. A British couple in a dark blue Mercedes stopped and asked us where we wanted to go. The man gave us the same directions Google Maps had, so we felt more confident about our alternate route.

"It will be a longer drive, but I assure you, you will not have to drive on a gravel road," he said. "Imagine a Brit giving you Americans directions in the middle of nowhere!"

We laughed. "Thank you so much," Judy and I said in unison.

When we drove into the town of Lovell, Wyoming (population 2,360), Judy pulled up beside a man watering the city flowers, one hanging basket at a time, from a four-wheeler with a water tank on the back. Not knowing why she had stopped to talk to him, I presumed she was asking him if we were still on the right track to the campground at Bighorn. Confused, I followed Judy, who followed the man on the four-wheeler. Were we getting our own personal escort? We had several miles left to go, yet he directed us only a few blocks. When he stopped, he guided us into side-by-side, level

157

campsites in a cozy little five-site campground, complete with restrooms and a dump station. Talk about small-town hospitality!

Our new friend, Garrett, told us we could stay at the semi-shaded Lovell City Camper Park for three days—with cell service—for free, or we could drive down the road to Horseshoe Bend Campground in Bighorn Canyon National Recreation Area, pay $30 a night, and have no cell coverage or shade. After almost two seconds of consideration, we made the tough decision to change our plans and stay at the city park in Lovell. When Garrett told us about a midnight kayak ride in the canyon on Saturday night, that sealed the deal for Judy.

"What? A group kayak ride at midnight in a canyon? Are you serious? I never know what's going to happen when I'm with you!" I said, laughing.

Judy shrugged and gave me one of her sweet little smiles. I knew right then we would be going on another kayak adventure.

Once Garrett left, Judy pulled her rig around, positioning her house backward in her site, so our house doors faced each other. We got ourselves settled, and Judy pulled her car off the dolly so we could go for a scenic drive. She drove down Highway 37 for about eighteen miles, stopping at every lookout, which allowed us to enjoy the short hikes to the best views of the mountains and the river that ran through the canyon. We took pictures of every sight near and far, knowing the pictures would not do the panoramic views justice, but we could not help ourselves. The sights were amazing. I hoped I would never take God's creations for granted.

The bighorn mountains in the distance were half exposed rock and half green trees, shrubs, weeds, and grass. Rocky terrain along the road resembled the Georgia red clay that I know, but plants and weeds of unusual textures filled much of the ground.

The views of the river winding through the canyon were spectacular, with striated walls of beige, gray, and orange. The Bighorn River appeared to be a one thousand-foot drop from where Judy and I were taking photos and flowed well beyond our visual field. The orange and red hues from the sunset, combined with the gray rock and orange clay, made for a breathtaking show of light and shadows.

We noticed the river was as calm as an empty swimming pool (but was an uninviting, dark, muddy green), and Judy mentioned that she had never kayaked in a canyon because the waters are usually too rough.

The next morning, we were unsure how the day would unfold. We thought Judy might drive me to the end of highway 37, so I could ride back to the campsite while she and Harper went for a hike. We strapped my hybrid bike onto Judy's bike rack and then Judy backed out of her site. CRUNCH! While we were sleeping, a tree had grown up behind her car.

"Yikes! My bike!"

We jumped out to discover the arms of the bike rack were bent so badly they nearly touched the trunk. My bike showed no signs of damage. Whew! That could have been bad. She wrestled the rack back into place, added a couple of heavy-duty straps, and we moved on. We stopped at the Cal S. Taggart Bighorn Canyon National Recreation Area Visitor Center to inquire about activities in the area and the midnight kayak trip. On a big fold-out map, an employee named Tedd showed us a few potential hikes and handed Judy the map. Then a ranger named Jasmine emerged from a back room and opened another map. She highlighted a few driving routes that would give us a good overview of the Bighorn area before folding the map and handing it to Judy.

"Can you tell us about the midnight kayak ride?" Judy asked.

"Well . . . I can tell you the tour is full. We already have four on the waiting list."

Judy's whole body went limp. "Are you serious? I have my own kayak. Can I just tag along? I won't be any trouble."

Jasmine explained that the guides were only allowed to take a certain number of participants. Judy persisted and Jasmine agreed to add us to the wait list but told us not to get our hopes up. After they let us watch the park film we set off to see the sights.

My friend and chauffeur drove to the end of the paved road and down to the boat ramp. A family coming out of the water shared highlights of their trip to Yellowstone National Park. Yellowstone was still on my bucket list, but I was getting nervous about not having enough time to do everything I wanted to do before meeting my cousin Linda in California.

"Oh, if you could go for even a day or two, it would be worth the drive. You have to at least drive through the park. You've got to see Old Faithful and the Grand Canyon of Yellowstone," said the dad.

"Okay. You're right. I've heard Old Faithful is amazing. I haven't heard of the Yellowstone Grand Canyon, though."

"Oh, it's just like a miniature Grand Canyon. You can hike down to the bottom. You gotta see it," said his teenaged daughter. "It's beautiful."

"You can't be this close and not go see at least part of Yellowstone. It's over two million acres, so you won't see the entire park in a day, but you need to at least get the T-shirt."

"Okay. Thanks for the tip. I'll try to fit it in even if it's just for a day or two."

Judy dropped my bike and me off in a parking area and insisted on dousing me with sunscreen. She sprayed me with SPF 30 and sent me on my way.

Four twenty-ounce water bottles for a 27-mile jaunt, I thought would be sufficient. Since the road looked mostly downhill, I figured I would have enough water and would not need to rely on sightseers to supplement my supply. If all went as planned, I'd be back to my rig in a couple of hours. However, only ten miles into my ride, I ran out of water—only yards before the Horseshoe Bend Campground turnoff. The highway wasn't all downhill as I had thought. I had stopped at overlooks too, which added more time to my ride. And it was blazing hot that day.

I didn't have the gumption to ride two miles in and two miles out to get water at the campground. My feet were already whimpering, and I still had seventeen miles to the Lovell City Camper Park. Seventeen miles in the heat with no water was going to be torturous. But adding another four miles in hopes of finding water at the Horseshoe Bend Campground seemed more difficult than riding with no water, so I trudged on ahead. Then, a quarter mile later, a ranger station appeared on my right.

A young ranger in the parking lot invited me inside and encouraged me to fill my bottles at the sink from a filter faucet. He took me to the back room and showed me how he had only days earlier hooked up two filter systems and a water softener. However, after being filtered twice and run through a water softener, the water still tasted like metallic vinegar. I cannot imagine what it must have tasted like before he put in the filters or what the unfiltered water at the campground must have tasted like. I thanked him for saving me and didn't say a word about the taste. He showed me the map of the park and verified I had fifteen miles to the welcome center and seventeen to the campground.

With my water bottles full, I rode on even though my left foot screamed at me to stop. It felt as if someone had tied tourniquets around my quadriceps and connected them to my pedals so that with each pedal stroke, the tourniquets tightened. My feet always hurt when I ride but not usually that bad on a short ride. The pain became excruciating. By the time I coasted into the welcome center parking lot, the lack of blood flow to my feet caused the pedals to quit turning.

A mere two miles from the Lovell campground, I collapsed on the grass and tossed both shoes aside. My feet hurt all the way to my hips. I couldn't move, much less pedal another two miles. I laid next to the park sign, hoping no one would see me crying. Five minutes, then ten minutes passed before I forced my shoes on my still-aching feet and rode home. Ten minutes after returning to my tiny house and taking off my shoes, the vice-grip pain subsided enough for me to shower and reflect on a wonderful ride through the Bighorn mountains.

I worked hard for state #22, but the struggle made marking off Wyoming all the sweeter.

CHAPTER THIRTY-TWO

More Fireworks?

JULY 11 - 13

Judy and Harper returned from their adventure after dark. She told me she had opted to kayak in the canyon rather than hike in the heat like she had originally planned. She said it was a most glorious trip, as she and Harper had the whole canyon to themselves! That sounded awesome and a little dangerous at the same time. I don't know anyone with a more adventurous spirit than my new friend Judy. She amazes me. We agreed to catch up in the morning.

After breakfast, we toured Montana and Wyoming in Judy's car—a twelve-hour day. Judy drove 220 miles along the roads that Jasmine at the visitor center had highlighted on a map for us. As we traversed the highlighted loop, we stopped at overlook after overlook to take short hikes and pictures.

At the farthest point of our intended drive, we discovered we were only eighteen miles from Yellowstone National Park. Judy thought we should drive on into the park. She said her tent was in the trunk. Knowing I didn't have a sweatshirt, my glasses, a sleeping bag, or food or water for the evening, much less another day, I cringed.

Before I had time to stress over my lack of preparedness, my tour guide thought better of her last-minute Yellowstone idea and turned onto the highlighted road toward Cody, Wyoming. Whew! I was never more thankful that a trip to Yellowstone got thwarted. Yellowstone remained on my bucket list and for that I was grateful.

In Cody, we were delighted to find an indoor/outdoor bar where an entertainer was singing and playing her guitar on the patio. The musician reminded me of my friend Dave's granddaughter, Chloe, who sings and plays at bars and other venues in Nashville and occasionally at a resort near my home. From our table, I snapped one close-up picture of the country singer and texted it to Dave and his wife, Sandra. Before we left, I let the promising young star know I appreciated her and enjoyed her songs as I dropped a tip in the already-full Stetson at her feet.

On Friday, Judy, Harper, and I followed another highlighted loop around Wyoming that Jasmine had suggested and had another fabulous day of driving, hiking, talking, and sightseeing. I appreciated Judy having a car and being willing to drive another 150 miles to see places we wouldn't be able to cover so easily in our motorhomes. For the price of a tank or two of gas, I got to enjoy being the passenger and assistant navigator.

When Judy and I first arrived in Lovell, Garrett had said we could stay three nights at the Lovell City Campground, but then he told Judy about the kayak ride on Saturday night, which would make our stay four nights. He told us it wouldn't be a problem if we wanted to stay an extra night to do the canyon ride, so we hung around in hopes we would hear from Jasmine. On Saturday, we stayed at the campground since we had not heard from her. Judy and I always had projects to do around our homes, and Harper was happy to run back and forth from Judy's rig to mine. At 3:30, Jasmine called Judy. Other kayakers had canceled, so we were in! I was looking forward to the experience, but Judy was ecstatic.

"Kayaking on the night of a full moon. How exciting! Can you believe it?" Judy said. "I've never done this before!"

"I haven't either. I've never heard of kayaking in a canyon in the daylight, much less at midnight, with a group and tour guide."

We scrambled to get ready. I didn't know what to wear, what to bring, or what to expect, but I knew it would be fun. Lots of fun! Everything with Judy is fun. I fired questions at my friend about what to bring and what to expect, like she was some expert midnight kayaker woman. She had done the exact number of midnight kayak trips as me. Zero. Yet she had clearly become the big sister of our relationship, so I looked to her for guidance.

We could barely contain our excitement. We were really going to get to kayak in a canyon under the light of the full moon. What a rush. However, minutes before we started loading our things to drive to the marina, Jasmine called Judy back and said they had canceled the trip because of high winds and heavy rain in the forecast. Our hearts sank. What an emotional roller coaster.

We didn't have time for a pity party because Judy remembered hearing about a fireworks display in Byron, Wyoming. Byron (population 589) is eight miles southwest of the "metropolis" of Lovell, which is the largest town in Big Horn County with a population of nearly 2,400. (In comparison, more than 2,400 students attended my high school in Indiana, and over 600 students were in my graduating class.) That second weekend in July was the annual Byron Days celebration and fireworks were part of the festivities.

"Hey, let's just go to the fireworks in Byron. It'll be fun," Judy said.

Sounded like a great plan B to me. So, one hour after we would have driven to the boat launch for a once-in-a-lifetime kayaking trip, we pulled into a clearing in Byron where we saw a dozen or so cars parked. We asked a local family there in the field if it was a good place to see the fireworks. They assured us it was better than going into the park. Judy shut off her engine, and we talked with Marla and Mary, sixty-five-year-old twins from Cheyenne, Wyoming, who were parked next to us. Marla talked extensively about the Cheyenne Frontier Days and Rodeo. She told us Cheyenne scheduled nine days of rodeos and big-name concerts and a carnival with rides and food and other events. This outdoor rodeo and western celebration is the world's largest of its kind and attracts people from all over the country.

When Judy found out the festival was in two weeks, she said it sounded like something she would like to do. The women talked about where Judy might park her motorhome during the festival. Marla told us to stay in touch and gave each of us a business card that her daughter had designed. Because her mom and aunt connected with everyone they talked to and made new friends everywhere they went, the daughter had given them the title of "relationship specialists" on their cards. Judy and I got a kick out of the twins and their unique business cards.

After an hour of waiting and talking, others started leaving the parking area. Judy asked a local family parked on the other side of us what was happening. They said friends had called from the park, and the organizers had decided not to set off the fireworks because of the strong winds. What a bummer. No fireworks. Disappointed, we drove back to Lovell Camper Park. We didn't kayak in the canyon, and we didn't see a fireworks display, but on the plus side, Judy and I sure enjoyed chatting with a couple of relationship specialists. And we were extremely thankful we found out about the bad weather before getting into a kayak. I could only imagine the terror of being in a storm, in a canyon, in the middle of the night, in a kayak. Thank God for blessings in disguise.

CHAPTER THIRTY-THREE

On the Road Again

JULY 14 – 16

Sunday morning, Judy and I enjoyed breakfast together at our picnic table. As we talked, we realized we had different routes in mind and agreed to go our separate ways. It seemed like only a few days, but we had traveled side by side for two weeks. Time does fly when you're having fun! I enjoyed being with her and Harper so much, I didn't want to say goodbye. Judy was so positive, so delightful, so resourceful, so knowledgeable, so spontaneous, and so fun. And Harper had gotten comfortable with me. I even kept dog treats in my RV, for goodness' sake. I loved having him around. Still, my plans were to keep traveling west, hopefully starting with Yellowstone, and Judy, now that she knew about the frontier days and rodeo, wanted to go east to Cheyenne, so it was time to part.

We packed up, dumped and filled our tanks, wrote Garrett a thank you note with a donation to help compensate for our stay, checked our routes, asked a neighbor to take pictures of us, and hugged goodbye. To make our departure a little easier, we agreed to meet up again down the road. A lump formed in my throat as we pulled out of Lovell Camper Park and headed in opposite directions.

Thanks for the good times, Judy and Harper. My family and friends will hear Judy and Harper stories for years to come. Happy trails!

I stopped for gas and mailed postcards at the Lovell post office and then happened upon a do-it-yourself truck wash a few miles out of town. I had devoted three days to washing and waxing my rig before leaving Georgia but had done no cleaning since the first of May, other than squeegeeing windows at gas stations. A good washing was long overdue. I plugged in $22 in quarters and spent a ridiculous amount of time rushing around with pink foam gushing from the brush as I scrubbed, only to find my rig wearing a pink coat even after a thorough rinsing. It was not only pink, but still dirty, so I followed up with another rinse cycle and wiped it down with a wet rag. After a third rinse cycle, I dried it once more and called the job "good enough."

From the truck wash, I drove fifty miles to Beck Lake Park in Cody, Wyoming, fifty miles from Yellowstone National Park East Gate and one hundred miles from Grant Village Campground in Yellowstone, where I hoped to get a site. An empty parking lot less than half a mile from the lake made for a perfect place to park my tiny house. On my hybrid, I tooled around the little lake and through the surrounding neighborhoods. I was taking pictures of a meandering doe in someone's yard when I looked up and saw gray clouds looming over my rig. Yikes! I raced back in time to get my bike on the rack and covered before a torrential downpour hit. Thankfully I made it into my tiny house without getting drenched. That was my silver lining in the gray clouds. The clouds moved on after five minutes, but boy, did it rain buckets.

This was my second ride in the cowboy state, and even though I had to cut it short, the loop around the lake in Cody made for a pleasant ten-mile ride in state #22. Yeehaw! It felt good to be approaching the halfway mark of my fifty-state goal. Three more states: Idaho, Washington, and Oregon, and I would be halfway there.

I looked at my *AllStays* app to find a place to park for the night. Happy to find a Walmart close by, I took a shower in my tiny house and then put Rig in drive and headed west.

After a pleasant night's stay at the Cody Walmart, I arrived at Yellowstone's east gate at 8 a.m. on Monday, July 15. I quickly jumped out of Rig and took a picture of the big brown Yellowstone sign. Another sign just past the gate said, "Grant Village Campground FULL." When I tried to call to reserve a site at another campground in Yellowstone, I had no cell reception, so I kept driving. Because Mom always taught us that "it never hurts to ask," at ten, I stopped at a gift shop and called Grant Village Campground. They had one site available.

The woman on the phone said, "This site was not there a few minutes ago. You must be living right."

"Thank you. I was hoping you would have a site. I really want to see Yellowstone and can't believe this worked out!"

A chuckle on the other end of the phone made me smile as the woman named Charlotte secured my reservation for site C98 at Grant Village in

Yellowstone National Park. This was it. I really was going to get to see Yellowstone—another dream come true.

Having secured a site, I took my time driving through the national park and taking in every morsel of beauty. I stopped at every overlook that would accommodate my 25-foot motorhome—and there were a lot of them. Several of the pictures I took on my phone were of calm, crystal-clear lakes surrounded by tall pines under a canopy of wispy white clouds and blue skies as far as my eyes could see. When I dreamed of visiting Yellowstone, I imagined mountains. The mountains were glorious, but the lakes were a pleasant bonus. The park contains over 200 lakes! I had no idea.

En route to my campsite, I stopped at the Yellowstone General Store at Fishing Bridge, pressed a stamp in my new National Parks Passport and bought a T-shirt. Too bad I couldn't tell the family Judy and I met at Bighorn that I made it to Yellowstone and "bought the T-shirt." I knew Judy would be proud that I got the passport stamp since she had introduced me to the idea when we were together at Theodore Roosevelt National Park.

At 3 p.m., a few of us waited in a short check-in line at the campground. Later that night, the line was four times as long. My advice to fellow RVers is to arrive EARLY. But like I learned at Badlands National Park, it's difficult to drive straight to a campsite and not stop at all the scenic overlooks.

After settling into my site, which did not take long because most national park campgrounds do not offer water or electric hookups, I pedaled around the campground on my hybrid, exploring my new neighborhood. It reminded me of the fun times my sister Cathy and I had as children, exploring every time our family went to a new campground. Our parents took us tent camping in Michigan state parks every summer. That had to be a lot of work to feed, entertain, bathe, and sleep six children for a weekend or a week, but without a doubt that is where my love of camping in the great outdoors got its roots.

Tooling around campgrounds never gets old. And, of course, I had to get a picture of my bike in front of the campground sign. While I was on my trip, I had no idea how much looking back at pictures with dates and times would help me piece together the details of my story. The journal I kept provided the foundation for this book, and my highlighted atlas reminds me of my route, but *oh*, the pictures—that's how I've kept the details straight.

Early Tuesday morning, after looking at my atlas and calculating that I was only thirty miles from the Grand Tetons, I opted to head south to try to get a campsite there for a couple of days. The more National Parks I could squeeze into my trip the better.

I drove out the south gate of Yellowstone on a highway creatively named South Entrance Road, also called the John D. Rockefeller Jr. Memorial Parkway, and highways 26, 89, 189, and 191. It took me directly into Grand Teton National Park. In awe of the surrounding beauty, I stopped at waterfalls and mountain views whenever possible. I entered the Tetons at 10:45 a.m. and drove on to Lizard Creek Campground, the second of six campgrounds from the north entrance, for my first attempt at securing a site. It was a first come, first served campground, so I followed the instructions on the sign to find a site and come back to the kiosk to register. Grateful for a spot again, I settled into site #50 by noon. Alyssa, the vibrant twenty-something park host, directed me to a clearing a quarter mile from my site where I could get a cell signal.

With my red canvas chair over my shoulder, I walked down a hill and settled into my office with a view of Jackson Lake and the Teton mountain range. John Muir is quoted as saying, "The mountains are calling, and I must go." Well, the Grand Tetons were definitely calling me. The Tetons, including the area called Jackson Hole, cover nearly five hundred square miles and certainly make a grand statement. I caught up with my sister Lynn on the phone and soaked in the splendor of the majestic snow-capped gray rocks as we talked.

At seven that evening, I rode my bike to the Grand Teton National Park sign to get a picture. I met a couple, Doug and Dana, who had enjoyed five days at Bighorn where I had just explored with Judy. We talked for a few minutes and exchanged photography services. I never have trouble finding someone at state or park signs to take my picture in front of the sign. Everyone stopped at a sign is there for the same reason, so I just have to offer to take a picture of them and they will offer to take one of me. Doug was a veterinarian who served in the Air Force and had inspected farms, slaughterhouses, and meat packaging plants for many years.

"Do you still eat meat after seeing what you've seen?"

"Yes, just not hot dogs. They're made from all the inedible parts of the animals."

"I could not imagine having a job like that and thinking *any* part of an animal was edible. I bet you have seen some horrible things."

"Yeah, it was bad sometimes. Especially when we had to give warnings or citations or shut a plant down because they couldn't clean up their act. Yeah, I saw some bad stuff. You wouldn't want to hear about most of it."

"I'm sure you are right."

We talked another minute or two and wished each other well as they pulled away in their car and I on my bike. As I rode around the park, I stopped several times and took more photos of the snow-capped mountains and pristine, blue-green Jackson Lake. Around eight I noticed the sky getting prematurely dark, so I rode back to my site at Lizard Creek. Not five minutes after I secured my bike and got inside my tiny house did it start pouring. I had escaped another downpour. Was that the third time or the fourth since Ambassador Park? I couldn't remember, but I was grateful each time I missed getting drenched, grateful for the little things. It only rained until bedtime, which made for a quiet first night in the Tetons.

CHAPTER THIRTY-FOUR

Touring the Tetons with a New Friend

July 17 - 18

Now that I was becoming somewhat of a pro at securing first come, first served sites, Wednesday morning I drove an hour south of Lizard Creek to Gros Ventre Campground, still in Grand Teton National Park, and settled into a new site by 9:30. Of course the fact that the campground offered two hundred sites was in my favor. One perk about the first come scenario is that once you get a site you can stay up to two weeks—that's the case in most state and national parks I've visited. I paid for two nights because packing up and finding a new place to live every day can be tiresome. That plan gave me the day to ride a little, explore the new campground, read, and catch up in my journal. I hoped to get in a good ride in the Tetons the next day.

The next afternoon I drove my RV to a large parking area where I had seen a smoothly paved bike trail on my drive in the day before. It was five miles from my site at the Gros Ventre Campground. I longed for the days gone by when I could have easily ridden from a campground, enjoyed 20-30 miles on a trail and then ridden back to the campground. Now, if I had ridden my bike to the trail, my knees and feet would have told me to turn around and ride back to the campground as soon as I got to the trail.

As I prepared for a ride, I noticed a man pulling his road bike out from the rear of his Honda CRV. I asked if he had ridden on the bike path. He said he had many times and that he lived in Jackson. He planned to do a 23-mile loop. We introduced ourselves, and I asked Greg if I could tag along.

"I'd love the company," he said.

I got myself and my bike ready and looked at my phone. *Dark Sky* told me that the wind was blowing steadily at 20 mph. We should expect 30 to 40 mph gusts, and the wind speed would increase as we rode. How encouraging. At Greg's suggestion, we began with the wind at our backs.

"There will be a slight downgrade when we come back. That will make it easier to ride into the wind when the grade is in our favor."

I love the camaraderie of cyclists. Casual riders are as easygoing and friendly as campers. I felt totally comfortable asking a stranger if I could ride with him.

"If I can't keep up with your pace, I'm fine with you going on without me."

"Well, same to you. My riding buddy did not want to tackle the wind," Greg said.

The bike path was narrow so we rode side by side on the road, changing to single file for the occasional car or motorhome to pass. It was easy to talk and hear each other with the wind at our backs. We talked about cycling, our careers, Jackson and the Tetons, Greg's current jobs driving a tour bus and captaining a boat on Jenny Lake, my travels, etc.

"I've lived in Jackson for forty-five years, but I was born in Michigan."

"I was born in Michigan too," I said.

We saw a sign for the Teton Science School, Kelly Campus.

"My son went to that school. There were about fifty children who attended when he was there."

"Can we ride down that road to see it? I kind of have a thing for schools."

"It's about a mile or two."

"Excellent."

We turned left and got nailed with 30 to 40 mph crosswinds that nearly knocked me over, but I persevered. The log-home buildings of the school campus fascinated me. One main building housed the classrooms and the dining room, and a smaller building hosted a museum of sorts. Students lived in tiny cabins.

"This is an elementary school and children *live* here?"

"Yeah, my son never did because we lived in town, but most of the children would have too far of a commute, so they stay here."

"I can't imagine."

My mind flashed to Jennifer, the owner of Paula's Gift and Coffee Shop in Valentine, Nebraska, whose high school was seventy-five miles from her home. At least she was in high school when she and her parents had to make the decision to move the family—and her family moved, not just her. Those cabins housed five- to ten-year-old children! It blew my mind to think about it. I took pictures, and Greg shared some facts about the school as we rode back into the crosswind.

The wind pushed us around. My new cycling pal and I experienced challenging moments, but we stayed upright. Thankfully, the wind played no role in the enjoyment level of our ride. As we talked, we discovered we had both ridden our bikes across the country. Greg's trip had been five years earlier, with a group of sixteen riders who carried everything, including their tents and cook stoves, on their bikes. They took turns cooking and washing dishes. In contrast, I had ridden coast-to-coast nine years earlier with a group of thirty-two riders. A truck carried our luggage. Five staff members provided a smorgasbord of snacks every thirty miles and offered bike repair services if necessary. We ate two meals a day at restaurants, got a rest day every ten days, and slept in a motel every night. I told him I never made my bed, much less my breakfast and dinner. Our tours were different, but we agreed our trips from the Pacific to the Atlantic marked the best summer of our lives.

Greg took me by an old Mormon community, where a few homes and barns remained in an open field. We were wearing cycling shoes, which have cleats to clip into our pedals, making it difficult to walk, especially through fields. It looked like everything was closed so we just looked at the buildings from the outside. The large number of visitors also made it difficult to explore or get pictures without people in them, so I took pictures of one home and had Greg take one of me in front of a barn and we moved on.

"A group of Michiganders restored the remaining five or six home-steads a few years ago to preserve their history," Greg said. "I don't think anyone has lived in them since I moved here to Jackson."

"I appreciate you stopping to show it to me. That barn is pretty cool."

I didn't understand the historic significance of the community until later. It is called the Mormon Row Historic District, and it was added to the national register of historic places in 1997. The barn is one of the most photographed barns in the country, probably as popular for the majestic mountain view as it is for the barn. The stately wood structure of vintage chestnut is surrounded by grass. Behind it, the smoky gray peaks and blue sky dotted with cirrus clouds make quite a postcard. Since that encounter, I have seen the barn in books and maps, but on that day with Greg as my tour guide, I was oblivious to its importance. Now that I have seen it in person, I can appreciate it for all its beauty and significance.

After leaving the Mormon community, we rode on the trail, heading toward the parking lot where we'd met. That stretch was well-paved and wide enough to allow us to ride next to each other. I was enjoying our ride and felt a smidge of sadness when Greg announced we had only six miles left. Despite the loud wind whooshing in our faces so that I often had to ask Greg to repeat himself, and the strong breeze nearly knocking me over twice, I do not recall ever having such a pleasant ride in the wind. Wind, elevation, and rain are cyclists' biggest challenges. Wyoming had treated me to all three. *Thanks, Greg, for making that historic ride in Jackson Hole so enjoyable, so memorable.*

When we got back to the parking lot, he helped me put my bike cover over my bikes. Given the wicked wind gusts, I would never have gotten it on by myself. I gave him a quick tour of my motorhome, and we exchanged phone numbers. He told me I was only ten miles from town, so I tentatively planned to drive into Jackson that evening. Greg offered to show me around if I did. I showered and sent him a text asking if Jackson had a grocery store. He said there was a Smith's across from his place, and we agreed to meet in the Smith's parking lot at 8 p.m. That was the soonest I could get there.

Since I knew it would be getting close to dark by eight, I also knew I was setting myself up for failure, but I didn't want to be so close to Jackson and not get to see a little of the town. I aimed to head back to my campsite by nine so I could drive and back into my site before total darkness settled across the Tetons. Anticipating an evening drive with large animals in the area, who do not always follow the rules of the road, made me nervous. Elk and deer run across roads any time they want, and they are especially prone to do it at dusk when drivers can't see them as well.

At 7:45, I parked my tiny house in a back corner of Smith's parking lot and zipped in and out of the store for a few groceries. When Greg pulled up beside me, I felt a twinge in my stomach. Riding my bike with a stranger probably ten years my senior felt perfectly safe. The idea of getting into a car with him to drive me to who-knows-where was a different story. This arrangement almost felt like a date. For years, dating experts have urged women to meet their date at the bar or restaurant for their safety. Women are told to not allow ourselves to be vulnerable. Smart women don't relinquish their control. And here I was, about to get in the car with a man I had met a mere five hours earlier.

I dismissed the negative thought and climbed in the car with Greg. My gut told me all would be fine. And it was. Greg drove into town and found a spot to park on the street. We got out and walked down the main street through a busy pedestrian district.

Greg took me into the Million Dollar Cowboy Bar to show me the bar stools. The place was packed, but there was one empty stool at the end of a long row of stools at the bar, right by the door.

"These are real horse saddles mounted on traditional bar stool posts," Greg said.

I rubbed the top of the vacant saddle. "How clever. How perfect for a bar in cowboy country."

We both smiled and turned to the door. What a great start to my tour of Jackson.

"I have another place in mind to get drinks. Just wanted you to see the unique bar stools," Greg said as he held the door for me. "This place is always busy."

Like Mormon Row, the Cowboy Bar is legendary too. Yeehaw! Touring Jackson on foot was fun. Greg made me feel like I was his guest.

We strolled down the street to the infamous Silver Dollar Bar & Grill. The bar, inlaid with over two thousand silver dollars, curved around the room in a soft S shape, making the largest and most intriguing counter I have seen—albeit I haven't seen many bars. We ordered drinks and talked at a regular table. Greg noticed one television was showing the Tour de France. Neither of us had seen much of the tour that summer, but we had kept up with it for the past thirty years. After all, it's the most popular cycling event in the world. It was fun and quite fitting to watch with a fellow cyclist as the pros raced to the finish line for the stage win.

"Yikes. Greg, it's 9:30!"

He paid for our drinks, and we hurried out. We walked a couple of blocks to the square, where he took a picture of me under an arch made of antlers (yet another famous Jackson tourist attraction).

Greg pointed to the area behind the antler arch and said, "In the winter, they make the park into a skating rink."

"Oh, I bet that's fun! Especially with all those trees." I laughed at the thought of me trying to ice skate without running into the trees that seemed to be all around the area I thought Greg was pointing to.

In the car on our way back to Smith's, a deer ran across the road.

I pointed and yelled. "Greg! A deer!"

Greg slammed on his brakes just in time for the deer to cross safely in front of us. My heart raced, but Greg acted like it was an everyday occurrence and drove on as usual. When he dropped me off at my motorhome, I thanked him for making it a great day, and he wished me safe travels.

As I drove along the John D. Rockefeller Jr. Memorial Parkway in the dark of the cloud-covered moon, I kept the speedometer ten miles under the speed limit. My headlights allowed me to see the road perfectly, except when oncoming headlights shone in my face every twelve seconds. When oncoming traffic blinded me, I prayed the deer would not try to cross at the same time. Fortunately, the deer must have crossed earlier. I did not see any of those little rascals the whole ten-mile stretch. Staying out later than I had planned turned out just fine. My worry was in vain.

When I returned to Gros Ventre Campground, my neighbors had their cars parked in the space I needed to back in safely, and the mirrors and backup camera were of no use in the dark campground. I opted to front in. Typically, sites are designed for people to back in so they can easily front out. The picnic tables are positioned so they would be by the house door. And the hookups, if available, are located on the opposite side of the site to be out of the way. Since there are no hookups in the park and I planned to leave in the morning, it didn't matter that I was "backward" for the night.

In hindsight, maybe I should not have met up with Greg at such a late hour. Had I hit a deer or had anything negative happen, I would be beating myself up for my poor judgment to this day. Looking back, it seems surreal. I knew at the time it was strange that we had met a few hours earlier and were acting like old friends, but like I said, cyclists have that camaraderie about them. He is a nice guy, and I enjoyed his company. Friends have told me I am too trusting for my own good, but it all worked out in the end. Greg is the gentleman I pegged him to be.

Because it all worked out in my favor, I have another friend and a good story to tell. Greg and I remain friends to this day, probably because of the enjoyable evening we spent together in Jackson as well as our afternoon bike ride in the wind. I was thankful to be home and so grateful for a fabulous day that I fell asleep two minutes after my head hit the pillow, despite having downed two diet sodas at the Silver Dollar Bar & Grill.

CHAPTER THIRTY-FIVE

Parking Fun

JULY 19 – 20

The cars in the campsite across from me were still there when I needed to back out of my site at Gros Ventre. There is no standard size for sites or roads in most campgrounds, and now that I had camped in a few national parks, I had noticed that most of them were on the small side when it comes to driving and maneuvering space.

National Park campgrounds were mostly designed before big trucks and motorhomes had even been thought of, much less become the norm for campers. Each site had plenty of space for a tent and a car, but many sites now have multiple vehicles even if the people are tent camping. With a lot of inching back, double-checking, and guidance from a neighboring camper, I backed out of my site without hitting my neighbor's cars. Because I was enjoying the Tetons so much, my plan was to stay one more night at another campground if I could manage to get another site. If not, I might drive through Yellowstone again.

Once I was free from the trappings of the campground, I drove forty miles north on the John D. Rockefeller Jr. Memorial Parkway to Colter Bay Campground, still in the Grand Teton National Park. Like Gros Ventre, Colter Bay had over two hundred sites. I snagged a site without a problem. Because I am a mediocre backer-inner, backing into my site was a challenge and once in, getting out looked impossible. The campers across the way had parked two vehicles half on their site and half on the road. Most campers are courteous and concerned enough about the safety of their vehicles that they do not park in the road. Cars parked in my way just happened to be the case for two days in a row. In addition, a hardwood tree towered close to my rig in the direction I would need to turn to exit. I'd have to figure it out in the morning. The chances of the eighty-year-old tree moving overnight were slim, so I hoped my neighbors would leave in their cars before I needed to pull out.

Once I got my rig settled, I sat reading and journaling in my recliner outside and blissfully lost track of time. Losing track of time is a common phenomenon with me, partly because I am retired and partly because I travel. I look at my watch a lot but promptly forget what time it was when I started or finished a task or departed or arrived or went to bed or woke up. Time doesn't seem to matter so much when I am traveling by myself. It's freeing. When I am traveling, seldom do I have critical time constraints, and I like it that way.

After a good long exploratory walk and return to my chair, I wrote this in my journal: *I have so many thoughts and observations to write about, yet when I have time to write, I only write about the events of my day. I cannot seem to remember those introspective thoughts and observations.* Depicting how the mountains stir my soul or describing the smell of the air or the sounds of the birds would add interest to my stories. Physical and emotional descriptions come to me easily, yet those eloquent words of reflection are harder to come by.

It was dusk when I returned from my walk around Colter Bay, and I smelled smoke from my neighbor's campfire. A newborn baby cried in the distance. Other than the crying, the campground remained quiet. Minutes later, another baby crying on the other side of me sounded older, louder, and in more distress than the first. Little ones in distress made me contemplate how difficult it would be to camp—especially tent camp—with babies or toddlers. It's got to be as tough on the older members of the family as it is on the babies. People do it, though. If you are one of those families, I take my helmet off to you and your little ones.

By midnight, either the babies quit crying or I fell asleep and didn't hear them anymore. In the morning, I thought about them and hoped they were okay, but that's the kind of situation where you never hear the story.

As I ate my breakfast, I noticed one of my neighbor's vehicles still obstructed my exit route. They had left in one car for the day, which forced me to develop an exit strategy with little turning radius. It seemed as though my site was the only one not perpendicular to the road. And trees planted on either side of my motorhome added to the challenge. As I surveyed the other sites, I realized why this one was available at the last minute. All but one site near mine were easy exit, pull-through sites. The one, catty corner from me offered plenty of room for two cars and a tent. Its lone tree hovered over the tent, nowhere near where the cars were parked.

No struggles there.

I walked down the road because I needed a new perspective, figuratively and literally. In those few minutes, I had worked myself into an uncharacteristic "why me" frenzy. To pull out in the correct direction, I'd have to inch close to the tree on my left toward the parked vehicle and then make a super sharp turn into a road no wider than my rig, rather than the traditional 90-degree turn. Without folding my RV in half, I didn't see that maneuver happening.

No way could I make that sharp turn with the trees and the car in my way. My only option, as I saw it, required some creative problem-solving. Maybe I could drive out the wrong direction on the one-way road. As I walked around the loop to survey the situation, another camper stepped out and said he figured it would be okay to drive the wrong direction. This fellow traveler said he would help me and stop traffic if necessary. I love how campers look out for each other. (*Thanks, John from Colorado.*) So, that's what I opted to do. But even going the wrong way, the turn was much tighter than I imagined. The maneuver made me nervous. I took it super slow and jumped out a couple of times to make sure I was clearing the trees.

Thankfully, I squeezed out of there before meeting anyone coming the other way. I marvel how people in bigger rigs than mine get around campgrounds, and I often wonder why park authorities don't prune trees here and there to make navigating through the parks easier for mediocre RV drivers like me. For now, I had escaped and was happy to have done so without even a scratch on my rig—or worse, a dent on the car across from me. Whew! I was officially free to head north.

Chapter Thirty-Six

A Return to Yellowstone

July 20

After I squeezed out of that last site in the Tetons, I abandoned the "poor me" attitude that had trapped me for a moment and focused my sights on returning to Yellowstone National Park. The weeds of doubt and negativity crept in sometimes, and I needed to pull them before they took root. I'm embarrassed that I had that moment of weakness, and I didn't want to say anything about it, but I have to admit that I'm not always as saintly as my mother. That woman always had a positive outlook on every situation. Mom had more faith than all six of her children combined. Her silver-lining-attitude, her it-will-all-work-out, and her how-can-we-make-it-work response to every life situation had rubbed off on her six children, but none of us can compare to our mother. She was the queen of positivity. Mom was our rock. While I was struggling with the frustration of getting out of the campsite, her teachings gave me the encouragement I needed to get through the stressful situation.

If all went as planned, I would be back in Yellowstone by noon to enjoy another day in one of the most cherished national parks in the country. What's more, the John D. Rockefeller Jr. Memorial Parkway that connects the two parks is spectacular. I stopped for pictures at overlooks and embraced the allure of the west. I thought of my mom again and how she would have loved touring and visiting the national parks. Mom was my biggest cheerleader. She offered nothing but encouragement any time I wanted to try something new. Though she's been gone from this life for over fifteen years, I feel her presence every day. She is a big part of why I'm doing what I'm doing.

Once back at Yellowstone, I followed the signs to Old Faithful. It surprised me to see the size of the viewing area. Yellowstone Park planners must have realized the geysers would attract sizable crowds before it became the first national park of the United States in 1872. A large, welcoming, and accommodating area for spectators surrounded the geyser, and I quietly joined the hundreds of people already seated in the courtyard.

Every adult, me included, held a cell phone or a camera ready to take pictures and videos of the most famous geyser in the world, Old Faithful. It got its name for being so predictable. It erupts day and night every 30 to 120 minutes, 365 days a year.

People around me whispered, almost reverent, as though waiting for a service to begin. When Old Faithful erupted, it started slowly with steam and squirts of water, like those from a super-soaker water gun. Over three-minutes' time, steam built up with bigger and bigger sprays to a crescendo of hot, almost boiling, water spewing twelve stories high for a full minute. What a spectacular display of nature. Chills ran up my spine. Again, my words and even my videos don't do it justice. Trust me. See Old Faithful in person to fully grasp the magnitude.

The Old Faithful encounter made me think of being at a fireworks display or the laser show on Stone Mountain in Georgia. For five minutes, people of all ages enjoyed the geyser—like family movie night except without the popcorn. Folks come from all over the world to see the geysers at Yellowstone. I couldn't decipher many languages of the surrounding families, but when it came to the oohs and aahs and smiles and sighs at the finale, we all understood. And peace reigned. We knew we had seen something spectacular, something unique. I found it exhilarating to be a part of such a diverse crowd, experiencing a show of nature so amazing that again, words alone cannot describe.

Old Faithful calmed down and went back to steaming and spitting little bursts of water, and one thousand smiling people parted ways. I expected a rush to the parking lot, but some people watched the steam dwindle, some walked the pathways around Old Faithful and other geysers, some went to the restaurant and gift shop, and a few chatted softly as they strolled to the parking lot. Visitors spread out before, during, and after the show, so one thousand people in the area seemed like the crowd at a Tuesday night Little League game.

Following many onlookers, I walked the boardwalks surrounding other not-so-famous geysers and stepped inside the historic Old Faithful Inn for a look at the gigantic logs inside. Jaw-dropping, eye-popping, amazing! The massive stone fireplace and mile-high ceiling in the lobby would challenge any builder today. How construction workers put those massive logs together over one hundred years ago, I can only imagine. I marveled at the workmanship, impressed that builders constructed such fine structures with no computers, or sophisticated equipment. A woman behind the desk told me the inn was built at the turn of the twentieth century and at nearly 200,000 square feet, is said to be the largest log structure in the world.

Thankful to the man and his daughter at Bighorn who urged me to see the park even if I could not stay long, I followed the signs and drove to the Grand Canyon of Yellowstone, stopping often at overlooks and waterfalls. They were right. It is a must-see park. I wish I could paint better pictures with words, but describing the views from the overlooks with words on paper is more difficult than recreating the sounds a turtle makes. One day I will get better at descriptions, but for now, let's lean on the adage that "You have to see it for yourself."

At the canyon, I spoke with a family who had walked down to the viewing area, and despite the late hour, they encouraged me to go and to bring my hiking poles. I didn't think I'd need my poles, but it was a good time to try them out. The view at the bottom of the trail was worth the time and effort. The canyon was breathtaking. I took snapshots of the Yellowstone River Falls in the canyon and videoed the waterfall from the top. The views from top to bottom were worth every effort, but I didn't get on the road again until 7:45 p.m.

Darkness was coming fast and I was far from the north gate, with no reservation for the night. What was I thinking? Well, I wasn't. The day had been all about seeing Old Faithful and the Grand Canyon. I never took a minute to think about what I would do come nightfall. Maybe I thought I would drive through the two-million-acre park and end up at a Walmart on the other side. Calling during the day to make a reservation at one of the Yellowstone campgrounds never crossed my mind.

The roads were narrow and steep, and with nightfall setting in, the cliffs and the possible presence of large roaming wildlife made driving more challenging than I was prepared for. I stopped at every campground since I left Old Faithful, only to find them full. No other plan came to mind other than to keep driving.

Before I left Grand Teton that morning, I had figured I would either find a campsite before it got too late, or I would be out of the park and find a camping area or a Flying J-type place to park for the night. Nothing like that seemed to come to fruition. Sometimes my lack of planning stressed me out. This was one of those times. On the flip side, however, there is something to be said for the spontaneity of life, especially when traveling. I never know what adventures I might stumble upon when I leave a little wiggle room in my schedule.

At 9:30 p.m., I pulled into the last campground before the Mammoth north entrance and ignored the *No Vacancy* sign. No one sat at the host site, so I searched the campground, hoping to find a spot and ask forgiveness in the morning. No such luck. I left the campground and drove around the area called Mammoth Hot Springs, which is like a miniature town within the park. Now dark, I spotted a visitor center, a post office, an inn, a tiny gas station, a few municipal buildings, and what looked like several cabins or duplexes for rent. Exhausted and out of daylight, I concluded I would park at the edge of the visitor center lot and pray that no one, meaning no park ranger, would knock during the night and tell me to leave. I was frustrated with myself and extremely nervous. There were no signs posted that said, "no parking," but neither were there any motorhomes in any of the lots. Of course, that's because the motorhomes were all parked where they were supposed to—in one of the dozen campgrounds throughout the park.

CHAPTER THIRTY-SEVEN

Mammoth Hot Springs

JULY 21

After a restless night, I woke at 5:23. No one had knocked on my door. Thank goodness! It was still dark, so I drove to the post office across the parking lot, figuring it might help if I didn't stay parked in the same place for long. On Sunday morning, there would be no issue with me parking by the post office.

Since it was only 5:30 in the morning I decided to catch up on some cleaning in my tiny house. After that, I ate breakfast, wrote out postcards and birthday cards, and got ready for the day. By the time I was ready to drop the cards in the convenient blue box, the sun was up, and the Albright Visitor Center was open. I left my rig parked at the post office and walked to the visitor center.

While at the visitor center, I learned that before the turn of the century, the barracks and its surrounding area served as an army base. The park took over the base and turned the barracks into ranger housing in 1916. Now the duplex-type buildings form a neighborhood for the park rangers and the Chief of Yellowstone National Park. I surmised that I had slept in front of four park rangers' homes. In the dark, their homes looked like rental cottages. My saving grace had to be that I arrived after dark and left before first light.

Big lesson learned. I made a mental note to not make that mistake again. Sleeping in a parking lot was far from the ideal Yellowstone experience, but it certainly was memorable. It gave me one more story to tell, and one more reason to thank God for looking out for me. It all worked out in the end. And for that I am grateful.

I continued driving around in my RV to explore the area I had traveled in the dark of night hours earlier. I had spotted elk feeding on the lush grassy lawn last night, but they had moved on by morning. As I drove, I found the area Mammoth Hot Springs was named for and pulled into a parking lot. Walkways surrounded the springs. A stairway to the peak, with boardwalks stretching over the hot rocks, lets visitors easily explore.

My sister Sandi called me, so I walked and rambled about the natural beauty for an hour.

"Oh, Sandi, there's trash in the springs. There's a pacifier and a bucket hat. I'm guessing they got dropped or blown into the spring by accident, but the candy wrappers, straws, and water bottles? That's just carelessness."

"So sad. I don't understand why people do stuff like that."

"Me either. These hot springs are like little puddles of steaming water, and there are tons of them all around me. Oh my gosh, this sign is interesting. It says, 'DANGER, Hot Water, Will Scald.' There's a red line through a pointed finger touching the water. Makes you wonder how many people have stuck their fingers in these things."

"Yeah, guess people just have to see for themselves sometimes."

"Okay, now past the sign and the railing where I'm standing, there's a little lake with steam rising as high as the trees, a miniature geyser. I know you've been here before, but thanks for listening to me. This place is just incredible."

"Isn't it, though?"

"Yes. I just walked up some wooden stairs. What a view from up here. Sure wish you could see the hot springs with the mountains in the distance. The mountains are covered with green trees, and some kind of moss or grass."

"Yes! I remember those colors and those trees. Just so vibrant."

"Pictures don't do it justice, but I just took one, and it turned out pretty good. It looks like rainbows over multiple layers of naturally terraced, striated, jagged rock the size of a few football fields with mountains in the background. I'll send you a few of these after we hang up."

"Okay."

"Hey, if the water wasn't over 150 degrees, the rocks under these stairs would be fun to climb. It'd be almost like hiking the dunes at Lake Michigan."

As I walked around marveling at the hot springs, I told Sandi about my night parked in front of the rangers' housing. She always seems to hear about the times I lack good judgment. To this day, I'm still as uneasy about that night as I am about my bike ride past the barricaded, washed-out loop road at Theodore Roosevelt National Park.

When Sandi and I hung up, I took a couple dozen pictures of the hot springs and sent her a few. Before I walked back to my rig, I sat on some steps and stared at the trees in the distance, taking it all in. What a trip to remember. Yellowstone and the Tetons had exceeded my expectations.

From the springs it took me only five minutes to drive to the north entrance of the park. The dark brown national park sign was more grandiose than the one I had seen upon entering a few days earlier. Of course I had to stop for pictures. A young couple pulled up in a black sedan, and we immediately smiled and handed each other our phones. The friendliness of tourists always makes me feel good. After exchanging pictures in front of the "Leaving Yellowstone National Park" sign, I headed north toward Montana. From the Yellowstone north gate, I was still four hundred miles away, but Glacier National Park was finally within my reach.

CHAPTER THIRTY-EIGHT

A Day in My Life

JULY 21 – 22

Twenty-five miles beyond Yellowstone's north gate, a rest area by a river lured me in. I stopped for a quick gaze and a few deep breaths of fresh Montana air. Out came the phone when I saw the Montana state sign outside the building. I had already taken a picture of the gigantic Montana sign when Judy and I explored the region in her car, but this sign was unique, and it marked my re-entry into the state known for its big sky. This sign resembled three side-by-side billboards. In the middle was a painting of the United States of America flag. It was flanked, a little lower, by the Montana state flag on the left and a POW-MIA (prisoner of war, missing in action) flag painted on its right. After I took a picture of the sign, I walked a few feet away to take one of the river and discovered it was the Yellowstone River. Sandwiched between trees and foothills, the water looked as calm and clean as the lakes at Yellowstone. What a view. It made me think of the welcome center in Chamberlain, South Dakota, where visitors could see the Missouri River below.

My next stop was for gas in Three Forks, Montana, where I waited fourteen minutes for the woman in the car in front of me to go inside and pay for her gas so I could pull up to the pump. A family in an SUV pulled in behind, trapping me. The station was super busy. I could not believe she left her car by the pump for that long. She came out with a handful of drinks and snacks and drove off. Eventually, I was able to get gas. From there I drove a couple of hours to Helena, the state capital of Montana, where I worked out at a Planet Fitness until closing time. Advised that I couldn't park there overnight, I moved on to the adjacent grocery store lot.

I parked close to some trucks and left the windows and blinds open, as I always do. Seeing what's outside makes me feel safer, especially when it's dark. I heard a crash and looked out a window. Under the security lights, there was a guy sitting by the dumpster on the backside of Planet Fitness. Our eyes met, but I couldn't figure out what caused the clang, so I watched the area for another ten seconds. He didn't move. It seemed creepy—him sitting by himself with his back against the building next to a dumpster. I double-checked my doors. They were locked. Thirty minutes later, I texted my friend Tony. He suggested closing the windows and blinds. As I closed the windows, I noticed the creepy guy was gone.

I looked out periodically during the night and early morning and never saw him again. When you see a guy you've never met working out in a Planet Fitness, he is "workout guy." When you hear a crash late at night and then see a guy sitting next to a dumpster in the dark, leaning against the back wall of a Planet Fitness and staring at an occupied motorhome, he's "creepy guy." A wave of peace fell over me when I realized I would never see him again.

Who knows what that was about? All in "a day in my life."

By mid-morning, I slipped into Planet Fitness to catch up on emails and update my phone because every Planet Fitness offers Wi-Fi and a table or a lounge area for members. After that I wanted to drive north to Great Falls, Montana, and hoped to find a bike trail and squeeze in a gym workout there too. A phone call with a friend held me up, and I didn't arrive at the Great Falls Planet Fitness until 5 p.m. That left me with no time to ride. The tiny Planet Fitness parking lot forced me to park at a business down the street. As I packed my gym bag, I allowed another friend to keep me on the phone for over two hours. I always have difficulty finding that balance of being there for a friend and allowing someone to keep me from doing what I need to do. Nervous about walking back in the dark, I lifted for thirty minutes, showered, and hustled back at dusk.

I had planned to stay in that parking lot for the night, but it was off a busy street with excessive and loud traffic. Even though two men at the convenience store across the street had assured me it would be safe, my gut told me otherwise. Early in my travels, I made an agreement with myself that if I didn't feel right about a place, I would move on. This was one of those moments I followed my gut. With help from *AllStays*, I found a Walmart three miles away. Tony texted me as I contemplated my options, and he noted that Walmart parking lots have security cameras. Point taken. Janette, at the Walmart customer service desk, assured me I could join the other overnighters.

Walmart: home sweet home.

When I called Tony to thank him for encouraging me to find a more peaceful place, we picked up the conversation about our motorhomes from the night we met at the Walmart in Rapid City, South Dakota.

Tony and I talked about the problems with his motorhome. We'd bought our RVs the same year, but his was new and mine was three years old. Tony's new rig experience was a disaster. The generator didn't work. Screws popped out through the outside walls. The roof leaked above his bed and above the bed in the front. He found mold under the flooring, and the list went on. Two dealerships would not help him, so he took it to the factory in Elkhart, Indiana, in the middle of winter to have the flooring, the back wall, the section over the cab, and the roof replaced. To add to the frustration, Tony had to return to the factory multiple times and fought with the warranty company to get them to pay for the repairs. Standard practice is for new RVs to come with a one-year manufacturer's warranty, but some manufacturers make it difficult for new owners to cash in on the agreement.

After Tony provided detailed explanations of his fiasco, he said, "And every time I had to go back to the factory, I found their camping area packed with people from all over the country. They had all been sold RVs with structural problems like mine. My RV is mostly good now, but I'm kinda bitter about it."

"After hearing your story, I am so happy I bought a used camper."

"Yeah, I'm not sure I would buy a new one again," Tony said. "No matter who I bought it from."

"Totally understandable. When I started looking for a motorhome, I wanted new and I wanted used. I wanted gas and I wanted diesel. I wanted slide outs and I wanted no slide outs. I wanted to buy one from a private owner, and I wanted the assurance of buying from a reputable dealer. And you bought a new rig from a "reputable" dealer and you got burned on both counts. I hate that for you. What a mess."

Tony and I changed the subject. He told me he was in Colorado, and I told him I was excited about being 150 miles from Glacier National Park. Talking about our travels, both of us being the youngest of large, loving families, and our love of music ended our day on a more positive note.

CHAPTER THIRTY-NINE

So Close

JULY 23 – 24

Glacier National Park had been calling my name long before Amy and Glenn and I planned to meet there. So, after a morning run through the Great Falls Walmart, I drove 150 miles to answer Glacier's call. Anxious to get a site, I stopped at Glacier National Park's huge wood and rock sign for a quick photo and didn't linger to bask in the moment like I did at Mount Rushmore. Then the last eight miles of the road became so rutted that I bounced like a rag doll on a trampoline with children jumping around it. I thought my motorhome was going to fall apart and my bladder would burst. I arrived just in time to see a ranger hang the "FULL" sign at Two Medicine Campground.

"Oh, bummer. Is the campground really full?"

"Number twenty may be open," she said, "but it's a handicapped site, so you could only stay one night."

"I'm fine with that. I'd be happy to move in the morning."

"Okay then, go on ahead."

As I drove to the last open site, I thought about how things were always working out. *How 'bout that? I got the last site! Here we go, 23, 22, 21—oh, no! It looks like those people are backing into my site.*

Sure enough. As I got to #20, a couple in a luxury charcoal-colored class B backed into my site, and I sat there, dumbfounded. I'm usually the one to get the last site. I guess things can't go right for me every time. Maybe, as the reservation lady at Grant Village in Yellowstone said, this time *they* were the ones who "must be living right."

Oh well. Nothing I can do about it now.

I dumped the tanks and asked a ranger where I could stay for one night. I was not a happy camper when he told me my only option was a private campground outside the park, and I would need to drive eight miles back down that horribly rutted gravel road. He was nice enough and gave me good directions but not getting that last site was quite a blow—maybe more so because I had gotten my hopes up and then had them dashed in a matter of seconds.

After a thirty-second pity party, I drove to Red Eagle Campground on Native American Reservation land. The bumps on that eight-mile stretch taxed my kidneys, that's for sure! Not wanting my motorhome to lose any parts, I drove slowly and methodically, dodging the biggest ruts and hitting as few of the craters as possible. Fifty-five minutes later, I arrived and was glad to find plenty of sites available. The Red Eagle Campground acted as an overflow to Glacier National Park. It hadn't occurred to me on my drive to Glacier that I might need a plan B. I was ever so grateful for the Red Eagle option.

Leaving my rig on a level site, I walked to the office to pay. Two young men ran the park office and wrapped firewood into sellable bundles at the same time. The roads were the same treacherous, rutted gravel as the road I'd survived to get there, and there were no facilities, but my secluded site only set me back $25. And once I discovered the nearby and enchanting Two Medicine River that I could see from my site, I got over the disappointment of not staying inside Glacier National Park. Traveling the way I do, I'm bound to have setbacks. It's all part of the journey.

That evening, I rode my knobby-tired bike to the Glacier National Park sign and found a couple willing to exchange glamour shots—and some park tips—in front of the nostalgic brown-and-white sign enveloped in stately stacked rock.

"You absolutely need to drive on the Going-to-the-Sun Road. The views are spectacular," the woman said.

"I heard I couldn't drive on that road because my rig is too big."

"How big is your motorhome?" the man asked. "People do it, but maybe they have a size limit."

"Well, they have shuttles. You could find out about the shuttle once you get there," the woman said.

"Oh, a shuttle? That would be nice. Then I could appreciate the mountains while someone else did the driving. I'll check into the shuttle idea. Thanks so much."

When I returned to the main park gate, Ranger Rita offered to help me make sense of the park's layout. She laid out two options to ride the shuttle through the park and then told me about a nearby waterfall I could see that evening. A hike to a waterfall sounded like a splendid plan. I thanked Rita and rode to the path that led to the falls.

A ten-minute effortless hike brought me to a bridge with a most spectacular view. A young family from Alabama and I walked across the bridge together and chatted, admiring the aqua-colored water flowing under our feet and gushing over the rocky face before our eyes. Water didn't flow from the peak like other falls but spewed from a gigantic hole in the middle of the mountain. Dry rocks beside the falls allowed the ambitious to climb almost to the top. The tween boys in the family kept walking and climbing while their parents and I took pictures and videos from the best viewing area beyond the bridge. Thunder rumbling in the distance encouraged me to cut my visit short. I waved goodbye to the family because a ten-minute hike and a thirty-minute bike ride stood between me and safety.

I returned to see that Ranger Rita was lowering and folding the gate-house flag, and we talked as she did so. We talked about how huge Glacier is and how big some of the other parks are in comparison. When I heard a clap of thunder, I realized I'd better wrap it up.

"Thank you for telling me about that waterfall. I've never seen one like it. It's so unique, how the water comes out of the middle."

"Oh, yes. It's also interesting to track the falls over time. In the spring, when the snow melts, there's so much water it gushes over the top and through the lower crevasse. Now that most of the snow is melted, the water only flows through the bottom section. It still fascinates me, and I have seen it for several years now."

"How cool. I'm glad you told me that. I can't imagine how thunderous that waterfall would be if it had water rushing down from the top, too. Thanks so much, Rita. Have a great night."

"Yes, you too. Stay dry."

"Yeah, I'd better hurry back."

My evening turned out to be special. I got to ride, hike, observe a unique waterfall, learn from a ranger, and meet a pleasant family from Alabama. It drizzled on my return trek, but I got home before dark. I wasn't back inside my tiny house five minutes before the thunder clapped above my head and a massive downpour hit Red Eagle Campground. A last-minute bike and hike plan had turned into a memorable encounter, and I had narrowly escaped riding in a thunderstorm . . . again!

Seventy miles separated Two Medicine Campground at East Glacier and Apgar Campground at West Glacier. Even though I had been through Yellowstone, which is vast, I still found it difficult to comprehend driving seventy miles and still being in the same park, all the while knowing Glacier isn't even one of the largest national parks.

During our conversation at the flagpole the night before, Ranger Rita told me Glacier encompassed more than a million acres. Glacier is ranked the twelfth largest national park in terms of acres, nestled just behind the Grand Canyon at eleven and the Everglades at ten, which spans half again as many acres at 1.5 million, albeit a large percentage of those acres are wetlands. She said that Yellowstone, the eighth largest national park, measured twice the size of Glacier, yet as big as it is, Yellowstone measures only one-quarter the size of the largest and most northern of all national parks, Wrangell-Saint Elias, which covers over eight million acres of Alaskan tundra. What Rita and some of the other park rangers know about the national parks and the animals that live in them astounded me. I had this overwhelming feeling that the whole National Park System existed just to bring us joy.

Rita shared that the Apgar Campground in West Glacier had filled up by 10:30 the previous morning, so I should plan to get there by 9 or 9:30. I knew I would need to allow time to stop at overlooks and appreciate the views, so I got an early start. At 8:50 a.m., I drove through loop A at Apgar Campground. Although I couldn't find an open site, a ranger assured me there were available spots and encouraged me to drive through the other loops.

"If you see a site without a tag, ask the people if they're leaving. If they are, ask them if you can have their site."

In the fourth loop, the third person I asked, a young father of four, said I could take his site.

"If you leave a lawn chair or something on the picnic table here with your name on it, it will kind of hold the site for you. We won't be packed up for another hour but go back and tell the rangers you want site B91. It's mostly level, and we liked the location."

"Okay. Thanks so much. It seems like there's got to be a better system. This is kind of hairy."

"Yeah, we thought so too—guess it's the way they've always done it. Enjoy your stay," he called to me.

As I returned to fill out a registration form, I heard a ranger call to Ranger Paula, saying, "I just drove through. We are full. It's 9:31."

Whew, I made it just in time. That seemed way too hectic, but I got in. I had a site at Glacier! Glacier National Park! Ranger Paula suggested I park at the Apgar Visitor Center until the family at B91 cleared out, so I drove a mile to the nearly full parking lot and ate breakfast in my tiny house, grateful I had done what it took to secure a site. For a moment, I sighed with relief and reveled in the realization that I was really at Glacier National Park—a dream come true.

At the Apgar Visitor Center, I added a stamp to my national parks passport and bought a couple of gifts for friends. I asked the employee who rang up my sale about the Going-to-the-Sun Road. She confirmed that I would not be allowed to drive my motorhome, nor would I want to anyway.

"The road is super narrow, and the park offers the shuttle service for free to reduce the traffic on the Going-to-the-Sun Road. It gets busy out there."

"That is nice. I will definitely take advantage of that little perk. So, can you tell me how it works? Are there hop on and hop off spots along the route?"

"Yes. If you want to see everything, it will take you a whole day. Take a look at that big map outside this door." She pointed to the door I had just come in. "You can see on the map where the stops are. There's one here and one at the campground and then at all the big attractions or hiking trails in the park."

"Oh, looks like I will need to stay two days, then. Thanks so much for your help."

I walked out to review the huge map, and another tourist told me that smaller van-type shuttles moved people through the east side of the park, while larger shuttles drove them through the west side. He pointed to a spot in the middle of the map and told me that Logan Pass was the hub where people had to get off one shuttle and get on another. On my walk to my motorhome, I developed a plan. I would drive back to the campground and get settled, make next week's plans, ride my bike and maybe do a short hike, and then catch the first shuttle ride in the morning to see the rest of the park.

Once I got settled into my campsite, I rode my bike to Apgar Village, next to the visitor center, and ordered a vanilla latte (back to my sugar and caffeine habit). With the latte in hand, I sat on a rock overlooking Lake

McDonald, the largest lake in the park. My adventuresome friend Judy had given me the phone number of her friend Debbie, who owned a vacation home on Flathead Lake in Montana, sixty miles from West Glacier. On a whim a week earlier, I called Debbie, and she told me she would be at her cottage most of the summer. We had a delightful conversation, and she said I was welcome to visit anytime.

As I enjoyed the view of the lake, I called Debbie, and we worked out the logistics of a visit to her place on Flathead Lake. Before we hung up, Debbie suggested I try a rails-to-trails ride in the Idaho panhandle after I left her place. She said from there it wouldn't be far to my cousins' home in Spokane, Washington.

If all went smoothly, I would get to Seattle by August third, in time to see my cyclist friend Anthony, who had ridden his bike there. He had texted me a couple of days earlier and said that he'd made it to his friend's house and that he would be there until August ninth. I chuckled to myself when I recalled saying in Nebraska that Anthony would probably beat me to Seattle. He had really done it! In Seattle, I'd also visit with Jenny, my sister Cathy's childhood friend, for a few days.

All the pieces of the puzzle were fitting together. I could not have been happier with the way things were playing out. After I hung up with Debbie, my sister Lynn called. Since I had left her house in Indiana at the end of May, she had shown a sincere interest in my trip. I shared my plans for the next several days.

"I enjoy following you on Instagram and getting pictures and texts, but I like to hear your voice," she said.

"How touching, Lynn. You don't know how good it makes me feel to know you care about where I am and what I'm doing. You are so sweet. So, what's happening in your world?"

"Oh, working. Nothing too exciting. I'm not sitting by a lake at Glacier National Park, that's for sure."

At 3 p.m., my sister got back to work, and I took off on my road bike. Earlier, my intent was to get a route suggestion from a ranger or campground host, but since I'd left from the Apgar Village a mile away, that didn't pan out. From the village, I turned onto the Going-to-the-Sun Road. Not far from the visitor center, I stopped at a beach area on Lake McDonald and saw a sign for a hiking trail. I wished I had tossed a towel and a pair of sneakers in a backpack before I left my campsite. If I had, I could have parked my bike, hiked, sat on the beach for a bit, and then finished my ride. Or, if I had ridden my hybrid, I would have worn running shoes rather than cycling cleats.

Still, it was a wonderful ride. I can't always be prepared for every scenario that might arise, and I can't stress over the small stuff.

Let it go, Joy. Let it go.

After watching two little girls frolic in the water at Lake McDonald, I turned my bike toward the campground and saw a sign that said, "No bikes 11 a.m. to 4 p.m." My watch showed it was 4:12. Oops! I had ridden for forty-five minutes on a road I was not supposed to ride on at midday. Fortunately, I hadn't ridden the steep or super narrow part of the mountain. After I read the sign, I rode to an area called Fish Creek and then back through Apgar Village before returning to site B91. Oddly, I never saw another "no bikes" sign.

I showered and started the generator to dry my hair and recharge the house batteries. Most campgrounds allow generators from 8 a.m. to 8 p.m. As I was looking at my atlas, I heard a knock on the door. I assumed it was the neighbor I had been talking to when I put my bike back on the rack. It was not. At my window stood a stern-faced, uniformed, park ranger.

"You're thirty minutes past generator hours."

"Oh, no! Okay, officer, I will turn it off right away. I'm sorry."

Cutting off the generator, I glanced at the clock. It was 7:35 p.m. Or was it 6:35? Or 8:35? Had I crossed a time zone without realizing it? Well, if I had that would make it 6:30. Right? Six p.m. is early to shut down. My mind spun. I am not a rebel. I try to follow rules that make sense, yet twice in one day I had inadvertently broken time-related park rules. I felt like a horrible camper. They say "no harm, no foul," but I still felt bad about being a rule breaker.

It was not until I read the information posted at the registration kiosk the next morning that I saw the generator hours: 8 to10 a.m., 12 to 2 p.m., and 5 to 7 p.m. Never had I seen such strict hours. Exploring from 7 a.m. until 7 p.m. left no time to fire up the generator. Days earlier, I had concluded that I needed to run the generator for a couple of hours every day to keep the batteries charged. How was I supposed to do that if I was out enjoying the park?

Maybe I would benefit from solar panels. Solar power isn't perfect but would installing a couple of panels keep my batteries from getting too low when I found myself in situations like this? This was the first time I had considered venturing into solar, but I had no interest in researching solar options while I was traveling. Like Scarlett, I said to myself, "I can't think about that now. I'll go crazy if I do. I'll . . . I'll think about it tomorrow."

CHAPTER FORTY

Glacier National Park

JULY 25

Given all the information about the shuttle the day before, I walked to the entrance of the campground well before the scheduled 7 a.m. pickup time. As I waited for the shuttle, I talked with Alecia, a fellow camper my age, about what hikes we might tackle. She was leaning toward doing a hike on a trail near Logan Pass and then going to the final shuttle stop at St. Mary Village right outside the park's east gate later in the day. She said she had heard the village had a big lodge with a coffeeshop, café, and gift shop. That sounded like a good plan. I had hoped to sit next to her on the shuttle, but she got the last seat, and I had no alternative except to stand in the aisle toward the front. My feet were already crying. For no apparent reason, this morning they were hurting more than usual.

Standing on the bus escalated their crying to screaming, which forced me to give them my undivided attention. I contemplated whether I could keep up with Alecia or if I would have to send her on ahead as I did with my friend Amy at Ambassador Park. When the shuttle stopped at Avalanche Creek, passengers disembarked to either hike the highly recommended Avalanche Creek Trail or wait for a smaller shuttle to transport them through the narrow section of the Going-to-the-Sun Road.

Alecia and I waited in line to catch a shuttle to Logan Pass, which was about the halfway point to St. Mary at the eastern end of the park. When a van arrived, the next thirteen people in line got on and the driver called back and asked for a single rider to jump on board. Alecia raced forward and off she went. I never saw her again.

So much for hiking with my new friend. Well. . . at least I got to meet her.

With my feet aching, I stood in line for another thirty minutes, watching two more shuttles load before a third took me to Logan Pass.

Logan Pass is the hub where everyone transfers from a small shuttle to a big one or vice versa. The visitor center there bulged with tourists and offered breathtaking mountainous views. I had presumed the Going-to-the-Sun Road would take me to warmer temperatures as the shuttles drove me closer to the sun, but Logan Pass is the highest drivable elevation in the park at over 6,600 feet—and the temperature had dropped. I was not prepared for colder weather.

Temperatures in the mid-fifties and wind blowing at 20 to 30 mph made it feel more like 50 below. Other tourists touted the Hidden Lake Trail as the hike to tackle if I only had time and stamina for one. A sign said the trail was closed 1.5 miles in because of bear activity. Fish spawning in the outlet invited the bears to go fishing, and the "Do Not Disturb" sign was for us spectators who might not want to find out what would happen if we interrupted their feast.

Although three miles was my limit anyway, a man next to me said, "There's not much to see on the first mile and a half. The best views of the trail are beyond the barricade and lake. I recommend you try another trail if you can't walk far."

I boarded the first St. Mary shuttle with a lively, informative, thirty-something driver of Native American descent, who introduced himself as Jonathan. He said he loved his job, and it showed. Enthusiasm flowed from his body as he shared novel information about the road, the park, the animals, himself, and his family. The narrow and busy Going-to-the-Sun Road surprised me, and how close Jonathan drove to the edge of a mile-long drop-off unnerved me. Oncoming traffic drove inches from a natural mountain wall, leaving no room for error for either lane.

Going-to-the-Sun Road resembled the Needles Highway, SD 87, in Custer State Park. Tunnels and switchbacks were too narrow for any vehicle bigger than a van. Personally, I would be too nervous to drive a van on that narrow road, much less a van full of chatty tourists, even if the van was going to the sun.

Jonathan told us that unskilled drivers often left their driver-side mirrors on the road. He also told us three accidents had occurred within the week. One car went down the mountain. Rangers closed the road for hours while they sent emergency crews to the rescue. Miraculously, the driver survived. Happy to have the opportunity to ride on Jonathan's shuttle rather than my vehicle, my eyes stayed glued to the mountainous and cavernous landscape where the mountains touched the sky. The views from the shuttle exceeded all others. Seeing the lush mountains and valleys from my window seat filled my heart with awe. I was thankful for Jonathan and the other drivers. What joy! I was in heaven.

At St. Mary, I explored the shopping area and the lodge, which was designed as a rustic mountain lodge built with wooden pillars and beams and wood walls and flooring. Glass display cases in the lobby showcased bears and other taxidermy whose lives were sacrificed for the "viewing pleasure" of guests. I asked a few questions of the women at the desk, then walked by the restaurant and out the front doors.

From the lodge, I was fortunate to get on Jonathan's shuttle again. He dropped several of us off to hike the amazing St. Mary Falls Trail, where I stopped multiple times for pictures of the cascading aqua waters. I followed the trail to a rock beneath a torrent whose cold mist made me shiver. The overhanging rock created the sense of a cool, dark, damp cave. So much water flowed over the cliff with such force, that the unrelenting roar was deafening. The trail led hikers to walk behind the flow of water from above. I stood underneath in awe for a moment, taking in the beauty, then suddenly felt the need to emerge from the depths of the earth and climb to the crest.

When I reached the top I took pictures and short videos of the raging waters flowing into a basin below. The water was so blue it looked as though it had food coloring in it. Just fascinating. Although the trail stretched for three miles and led to another waterfall, I turned back. On my hike down the ridge, a young couple caught up with me. Hiking and talking with them took my mind off my ailing feet for a bit. When we got to the shuttle stop at the end of the trail, I sat down on a rock to give my feet a break. Thankfully, the next shuttle came in less than five minutes. When the young couple and I arrived at Logan Pass, we thought we would have to transfer, but because of the late hour, our driver got the okay from a dispatcher to take me to the Apgar Campground and the couple to the Apgar Visitor Center, where they had parked.

I enjoyed hearing about Glacier National Park from the four shuttle drivers I rode with that day. Jonathan and another driver drove school buses, one driver was a school nurse, and another called driving her retirement job. Each of them loved the park and spoke highly of their work, stating they felt privileged to get paid for driving people around such a special park.

Some of the best views were from the shuttle, and in places where there were no pull-offs or parking lots. If I were driving, I would not have been able to look down at the cliffs and valleys and across to other peaks. The snow-capped mountain range was as breathtaking a scene as one could imagine. Other spectacular views within the park reward those who are willing and able to hike. My feet ached, but the views of the trees and rocks and waterfalls made every agonizing step worth the effort. And it is in those moments that the true joy of traveling reveals itself. Each step, though challenging at times, becomes a testament to the beauty awaiting those who dare to dream, to explore, to "go to the sun."

CHAPTER FORTY-ONE

A New Friend

JULY 26

Friday morning I woke with a bit of sadness that I could not stay another day at the Apgar Campground. Yet I was grateful to have had the opportunity to get a feel for the incredible Glacier National Park with its indescribable mountains, valleys, lakes, and waterfalls, and of course, the infamous Going-to-the-Sun Road. It was time for me to move on. The day before I had made plans with Judy's friend Debbie, and I hoped to make it to my cousins' home in Spokane by Sunday. Also, my motorhome needed its house batteries recharged after dry camping with no hookups for three days. The only way to recharge them is to drive, run the generator, or plug in to electricity. Though it was only sixty miles, I hoped driving to Debbie's would give them a full charge.

A family claimed site B91 before I pulled out at 9:30 a.m., similar to the way I had secured the site two days earlier. It seemed like a ridiculous system to me, but if it worked for others, who am I to say anything negative about the inner workings of a national park campground? (However, as I revised this chapter I learned they no longer use the first come, first served method of securing campsites at Glacier. They now take reservations only.)

On the way out I stopped at the Apgar Visitor Center and bought postcards and reusable bags. My friend Sue had given me the suggestion to give shopping bags from national parks as gifts or use them as gift bags. I love the idea of a gift that keeps on giving. Because they were never more than $5, and they don't take up much room, I bought bags at every national park.

Knowing I might not have cell coverage as I traveled through Montana, I wrote down the directions to Debbie's place and took off toward Flathead Lake. The drive along the lake exhilarated me. Flathead is the largest fresh-water lake in the region, and I got glimpses of the sparkling cobalt-blue water through the trees at several points along the twenty-seven-mile stretch. Thankfully, I never lost cell service and the map on my phone gave perfect directions. When I got close, I called Debbie. She met me at the end of her road. I was so grateful she met me there because the road zigged and zagged with many forks and driveways—a perfect place for me to get lost. Debbie directed me to back in alongside her detached garage.

We spent the afternoon talking as Debbie gave me a tour of her second home, her brother's cabin, and their lakefront property, which had been in the family for years. As the two of us sat outside overlooking the lake and getting to know each other, I thought about how blessed I was to have met so many great people. Debbie is a longtime friend of Judy, and Debbie welcomed me as though I were also a longtime friend. She didn't know me. She only knew that Judy and I had become friends, and she invited me to stay overnight at her home.

Debbie also invited friends and family for dinner. We relished the relaxed atmosphere of lake life. I enjoyed getting to know everyone and hearing their stories. She and her brother and her other guests told me details of the Hiawatha Trail in Idaho, and they all said I would enjoy the experience. The trail was on my way to Spokane, so it would be the perfect Idaho panhandle ride.

After the others left, Debbie and I finished cleaning up the kitchen, and she and her black standard poodle walked me out to my tiny house in the dark. Debbie's family was coming the next day for a reunion. That Friday in July was probably the only day I could have come to her lake house and not felt I was in her way. I love it when the timing turns out so well. I was thankful for a nice evening with great people, a gorgeous "campsite" on the lake, and the prospect of a fabulous ride in Idaho. Life was working out for me.

The next morning, Debbie and I talked for two hours over breakfast, which included about half a bowl of cherries. Debbie told me Flathead was known for its delicious, sweet, dark cherries. And oh, were they good. Eating them brought back fond memories of my family buying buckets of cherries from roadside stands when we visited Michigan. We would eat them in the car and spit the pits out the windows, which were always down in the summer. Dad joked about having "4 x 70" air conditioning, which meant he drove with four windows down at 70 miles per hour.

When it was time to leave, her brother Zack and his dog walked over and took pictures of Debbie and me before she gave me directions to get out of her neighborhood. I couldn't get those delicious cherries out of my mind and was determined to find a roadside stand on my way out of town. My mission turned into a "wild cherry chase" as I turned down half a dozen side roads looking for Flathead cherries. I could not find a stand anywhere. For some reason I thought they would be everywhere like they were in Michigan when I was a kid. Fifty miles from Debbie's lake house, I paid $4 for a snack bag of cherries at a tiny store, but they paled in comparison. As I drove and spit the pits out the window, I made a mental note to ask Debbie where to buy cherries on my next visit. Despite the disappointment of not finding the elusive roadside stand, the memories of eating Michigan cherries with my family were as sweet as the cherries themselves, reminding me of the joy in the simplest of moments.

CHAPTER FORTY-TWO

The Route of the Hiawatha

JULY 27

After accounting for my failed attempts to find Flathead cherries, it took me three hours to drive one hundred miles from Debbie's home on Flathead Lake to the Idaho state line. I got to the Hiawatha trailhead one mile into the state at 1 p.m. and drove three miles on gravel before locating a place to parallel park. My usual perfect timing didn't seem so perfect when I arrived at an overcrowded, well-known trail on a sunny Saturday afternoon in July. But weekends are busy no matter where I might go. Enjoying Glacier during the week, visiting Debbie on Friday, and meeting up with my cousins in Spokane on Sunday made Saturday the only day for the trail. I paused for a moment and took joy in realizing Saturday would be the ideal day for a trail ride. Riding with others would make the Route of the Hiawatha Trail even more special. In addition to the perfect weather, that Saturday was also my sister Cathy's fifty-ninth birthday, and I would celebrate her by doing what I love most. It would make Cathy happy too, because she has always been one of my biggest cheerleaders.

The Route of the Hiawatha follows fifteen miles of the Bitterroot Mountains along an old train route at the state lines of Idaho and Montana. Cyclists who are fortunate enough to ride the trail enjoy ten old train tunnels and seven trestle bridges so high above the valleys that they are eyeball-to-eyeball with the peaks of the spruce-covered mountains. The views from the trestles are stunning—the main reason the trail is so popular.

Most trails are free, but the Hiawatha cost twelve bucks. Because of the long, dark tunnels, the first and last being 1.6 miles, they required headlights. I always use my DiNotte headlight (and taillight), so I did not need to rent one. Peter, the clerk who took my trail payment, suggested I decide at the other end whether I would ride the $10 shuttle to the start.

He guessed I would choose to bike back once I got to the end, where the shuttles picked up exhausted riders. I appreciated him giving me that option because I thought they required everyone to ride the shuttle back. So, $12 for the privilege of riding fifteen miles on a trail, then $10 for a shuttle ride back? That sounded like a lot of money for one person, much less for a family. The expense alone made the trail a bucket list event.

To follow so many young children riding the trail on tiny bikes, some with training wheels, astounded me. The trail attracts and caters to young families, but I found it to be quite challenging. The Hiawatha, composed of large white gravel chunks and a plethora of potholes, made for a washboard ride quite different from the typical asphalt or loose aggregate of most bike trails. My arms and hands ached as much as my legs and feet.

Although the trail offered a gradual 2% downhill grade, I could not ride fast because of the surface and also because of the massive number of children and adults who didn't understand trail etiquette. I witnessed no "slower riders keep to the right" kind of effort from ninety percent of the families. Children and adults seemed oblivious to other riders who might want to go faster than them. Many groups rode three and four abreast, never looking back, never acknowledging overtaking riders. Some stopped in front of me mid-pedal—with no warning. The Hiawatha on a summer weekend would clearly not be the ride for hard core mountain bikers.

Though too crowded for serious bikers, it was still quite the adventurous ride. The scenic trail sported interpretive signs and pull-offs conducive to group riding, and the mountains, tunnels, and trestles contributed to the trail's charm and popularity, though not the rough gravel surface. It was one of the roughest rails-to-trails I have ever encountered. The tunnels stayed wet, rutty, slick, and cold, as in refrigerator-cold. They felt more cave-like than other trail tunnels. Outside the tunnels, the wind blew with such force that I struggled to stay upright, as I did the day I rode in the Tetons with Greg. I marveled at how those little children rode in that wind. The wind also blew dust in my eyes, and some children were not wearing sunglasses. How they coped, I will never know. Yet in all that wind, I found myself thanking God for making such a beautiful landscape and allowing me to enjoy it so completely on that blissful Saturday afternoon.

About halfway down the trail, the adventure increased when creative bike racks emerged. Several little ones tuckered out, so moms and dads strapped little bicycles to their own bikes and put the children in wagons or on handlebars or wherever. One man strapped two training-wheeled bicycles to the back of his bike with a cord. I didn't stick around long enough to catch how that solution played out. The children who rode the trail that day—the majority aged twelve and under, were tough. Families talked, smiled, cheered, and laughed. There was no whining, crying, or arguing from the parents or the children. I applauded those children and their parents who dared to take on such a challenging ride.

At the end of the trail, a line of people waited over an hour to put their bikes on trucks. The scene reminded me of riding the PALM (Pedal Across Lower Michigan) with my Uncle Wil where we waited in an hours-long line to put our bikes on a truck before we boarded a bus to trek across Lower Michigan. However, my uncle and I stood in line one time for a 250-mile weeklong bike ride, not a fifteen-mile afternoon adventure. I rode back up the trail to avoid waiting in that line. When I returned to the starting point, I merged with people I'd seen waiting for the shuttle. In other words, boarding and riding the shuttle took as long as riding the fifteen miles uphill. As I rode uphill, I noticed I was the exception rather than the rule. As I often do, I chose the road less traveled.

I paid a visit to a tent kiosk where employees sold snacks, shirts, and stickers. A supervisor told me they had sold one thousand tickets that day, which made July 27 one of the busiest days of the summer. Peter, the employee I met at the start, his supervisor, and I chatted about cycling and the trail. After hearing about my cross-country bike trip and my mission to ride in all fifty states, the supervisor seemed touched that I chose her trail to be my only Idaho ride. When I told her Idaho was my twenty-third state and that Washington (state twenty-four) and Oregon (state twenty-five) would mark my halfway point, she gave me a Hiawatha sticker and mag-net for my motorhome. How fortunate that the Route of the Hiawatha stretched between Debbie's place on Flathead Lake and my cousins' home in Spokane. Like so many other attractions I had visited, I had never heard of the Hiawatha until Debbie mentioned it. Now I was a proud Hiawatha Trail finisher. So it goes with the unforeseen joys of my travels.

I returned to my tiny house a muddy, white-gravel-grime disaster. My black bike was now a speckled gray. The trail ride proved to be as amazing as Debbie and her friends had told me, but it felt good to be home. I don't take that perk for granted, as I appreciate having the option to shower and eat before getting behind the wheel. I was parked a mile from the ticket booth, and no one had parked close by, which gave me plenty of privacy. After a shower and dinner, I pulled out with the intent to drive west toward my cousins' home in Spokane. I drove past a lot of cars along the driveway and in the designated parking areas, which showed many riders were still on the Hiawatha Trail as the sun hovered over the horizon. I would not want to ride that trail in the dark or even at dusk. Everyone used headlights, but I found the trail challenging enough in the midday sun. I was thankful I had finished well before dark.

AllStays gave me directions to a Walmart thirty miles west of the Hiawatha on I 90. I talked to the birthday girl, my sister Cathy, for thirty miles, did my usual shopping, and got permission to stay overnight. After I put my groceries away, I called Cathy's friend Jenny to make plans for the next weekend. I planned to stay with my cousins Ivan and Erin in Spokane for three days and then drive toward Seattle to get to Jenny's by Friday. Jenny said a Seattle festival would provide plenty of entertainment, and she would ask friends about a place to park my motorhome while I stayed with her.

I looked forward to getting together with my cousins and with a friend I hadn't seen in decades, plus tag up with my cycling friend Anthony who would be in Seattle for another week after my arrival. After I got to Jenny's, I would make plans to connect with my cousin Linda (Erin's mom) and my friend Cindy in California.

By the end of the weekend, we'd set dates for Linda to join me in Yosemite National Park. At that point I would also determine when I might meet up with my friend Kim, who planned to meet me at a Utah national park, and my friend Pam, who lived in Arizona. All my ducks were lining up. By the time I hit the golden state, I would be on the home stretch of my trip and my fifty-state dream. Life on the road is good. It may not be for everyone, but it sure was working out for me.

CHAPTER FORTY-THREE

The Accident

JULY 28 – 29

Sunday morning, I drove from Walmart to the Planet Fitness in Spokane Valley, worked out, showered, and then drove ten miles to my cousins' home in Spokane, arriving a little after noon as planned. I parked my rig by their behemoth garage, and Ivan drove me up their rutted quarter-mile driveway in his big, black four-wheel drive Ford Expedition.

"Pavers are coming next Monday to pave our whole driveway," Ivan said. "The ruts got bad this spring, but we've had so much rain, they haven't been able to get to us."

"Oh, that will be nice," I said as we four-wheeled along. "Concrete or asphalt?"

"Asphalt."

After dinner, Ivan and Erin were discussing bike routes for me to try in Spokane on Monday when we noticed the sun dropping below the horizon. Erin drove me down the hill to my tiny house to get clothes and toiletries so I could stay in their upstairs guest room. She and I talked as we walked toward Rig. Distracted by our conversation, I didn't notice the drop-off from the concrete of the garage to the gravel drive. As my right foot stepped into the gravel, it was as though I was on the second to the bottom step of a flight of stairs, yet thinking I was on the bottom step. PHOOM! Out went my right knee and down I went, screaming in pain.

Splayed out in the gravel, I experienced the same debilitating pain as when I had fallen off the bench at a gym six years earlier. And when I stepped in a sinkhole on the playground at my school ten years before that. And when racing a dog across a field the summer before graduate school. And when playing a pickup game of basketball my junior year in college. And when attempting a back handspring in gymnastics class my freshman year. And when my knee blew out for the first time my senior year in high school as I warmed up for practice at a basket by myself. In every situation, my right knee dislocated first, and the absence of stability caused me to fall.

Never have I hurt my knee in a blaze of glory. The dislocation never happened sliding into home for the game-winning run or getting fouled as I made a shot at the buzzer to win the championship or even in a bicycle crash. Yet of all the times I had injured my knee, this one ranked as the most anticlimactic. My legs were not as strong as they were three years earlier when I competed in time trials, where cyclists race one at a time against the clock, but they were still strong. Yet after one misstep, one moment of carelessness, the rest of my trip was now in jeopardy.

I writhed in the gravel, screaming in pain, as Erin, the only physical therapist on my dad's side of the family, rushed to my aid. What a way to begin a visit with cousins I barely knew. I rocked back and forth on her gravel driveway for several minutes. Erin let me cry. She gave me time to catch my breath and gain composure while she called Ivan for backup. Then, somehow, we got inside Rig to get clothes, food, and toiletries, and Erin and Ivan got me back to their house. I inched up the stairs on my butt and climbed into their guest bed in excruciating pain.

Although the pain had brought back the memory of every other time I'd hurt the same knee, this time was different. My knee just needed some rest. By the next afternoon, I would be ready to ride that trail Erin and Ivan had told me about.

Later, I would recognize this eternal optimism as that fine line between positive thinking and denial. Every single time I'd hurt my knee, I thought I would be okay in a few minutes or a few hours or a few days. Why I thought this time would be different, I still can't explain.

Around midnight I woke up to go to the bathroom and found a grapefruit in the middle of my right leg where my knee had been. I stood with my weight on my left leg. The intense pain kept me from hopping. Not knowing what to do, I stood motionless and cried. No crutches. No pain killers. Nothing to lean on. No one to help me. I refrained from sitting and scooting across the floor for fear I might not possess the strength to stand again. The pain was indescribable. It took my breath away—and it still does every time I think about it. Equally painful, though, was the gut-wrenching realization that I would not be riding in Washington, my twenty-fourth state, the next day. Life had punched me in the gut and that hurt as much as my knee.

After a thirty-minute round trip to the bathroom and back, I leaned against the bed, hoisted my leg to the top of the mattress, laid my head on the pillow, and let out an audible, exhausted sigh. At 2:30 and 5 a.m., my bladder forced me to repeat the process, with a slightly better success rate after the discovery of a doable back and forth twisting maneuver with my left foot—heel, toe, heel, toe. I pray you never need to use that trick but try moving the equivalent of ten steps on only one leg without hopping, sitting, or jerking. The task is not easy, even when pain is not a factor. That proved to be one long night of sleepless agony. Come daybreak, rather than dropping me off at a trailhead as we had planned, I would need Ivan to take me to an urgent care or emergency room.

After phone calls with my sister Sandi and brother Tom and much debate with Erin and Ivan over where I would get the fastest and best care, we opted for the emergency room rather than an urgent care or an orthopedic specialist. Thankful that my cousins are bodybuilders and power lifters, Ivan carried me effortlessly from his couch to his truck and drove me to Providence Hospital in Spokane. A young, dark-haired guy greeted us with a wheelchair and rolled me inside to the check-in desk. Ivan said to call him when I finished, and he'd come back to pick me up.

I didn't wait long before a young tech took me for X-rays, after first slipping me some kind of painkiller. She wanted to manipulate my leg without the rest of the patients hearing me scream. She didn't give me enough or she didn't wait long enough for it to take effect. Either way, when she tried to straighten my right knee on the table, my scream convinced her to let go of my leg and give me another pill. The tech left me alone for what seemed like forever. When she returned to contort my leg into six unnatural positions, the pain was bearable. Thank God for modern-day pain medication. I cannot imagine the pain early travelers going west had to bear when they had such mishaps. Finally, X-rays completed, I dozed in another room, waiting for the doctor.

The doctor eased into the room, slid the X-rays in front of the lighted box and quietly introduced herself as Dr. Armstrong. After a long pause, she informed me she saw two significant vertical fractures on my kneecap. Yes. The fall broke my knee. She said I had only strained, not torn, my lateral collateral ligament (LCL) on the outside of my knee.

The pain had subsided with the drugs, but the news that I had broken my knee brought tears. With sympathy in her voice, she said she could give me a prescription for pain medication and fit me with an immobilizer and crutches. Before she walked out, the doctor told me not to put any weight on my right leg and to follow up with an orthopedic specialist by the end of the week. The news devastated me. I wasn't ready for my trip to be over. Alone, the tears flowed again. Tears of heart-crushing disappointment.

Six years earlier, almost to the day, I had received an eerily similar report from the emergency room doctor at home in Georgia. After an embarrassing slip off a bench at the gym before I was to teach an indoor cycling class, the doctor told me he had identified three horizontal fractures on my right kneecap and explained I would need surgery to fuse my patella back together.

Everyone at the hospital in Spokane spoke to me with kindness and sympathy. Dr. Armstrong treated me like a friend, yet I found myself as stunned by her report as I was by the report in 2013. I didn't fall that hard. In fact, as I watched the replay in my mind, I'd hit the gravel in slow motion. How could my kneecap break if I floated to the rocks like a feather? The vertical fractures sounded more serious than the three horizontal fractures I incurred when my knee slammed into the rubber floor at the gym. With one injury upon another, my patella now resembled a tic-tac-toe board with an extra line for good measure. Until these last two accidents, however, fractures had never accompanied the knee dislocation. Tearing ligaments wasn't enough? Did I need to add multiple fractures? This was not a case where I wanted to be an overachiever.

The possibility of a looming surgery unnerved me. Would I need an operation in Washington? In Georgia? Now? Later . . . or not at all? I posed plenty of questions, but no one provided answers. "Follow up with an orthopedic specialist in three or four days" was all the doctor said. One thing I knew for sure, my trip west was over. I could not walk, much less drive my motorhome and hike in Yosemite or the Grand Canyon. It was clear I would have to go home. But when? And how?

Three hours later, when Ivan parked under the awning at the emergency room door, the same young man wheeled me to the passenger side of my cousin's Expedition. My right leg was wrapped and strapped into an ankle-to-hip immobilizer. It stuck out straight, and crutches nestled between the armrest and my torso. A prescription for pain medicine lay on my lap, and a small smile danced across my face.

A smile?

Yes, a smile. Partly because the drugs had kicked in and partly because that's what I do. People ask me if I always smile or why I smile so much.

Well, the alternative doesn't seem appealing or fitting. A smile matches a joyful spirit. Who wants to be around someone who is frowning and complaining? Mom, who loved me more than anyone on this earth, taught me to find the good in every situation. Maintaining a positive outlook on life was a skill she practiced every day for seventy-nine years and encouraged her children and grandchildren to do the same. If a secret to a successful life exists, my mother, Helen Walker, would have said success is how you view the world—success is about your perspective. The woman I most admire lived her life as a "glass is half-full" kind of woman and, for that example, I am forever grateful.

My six-month trip west got cut in half. People say "things happen for a reason." I've said it myself, but I'm not sure it is always true. Either way, I try to accept the bad with the good. Like my mother taught me, I am learning to be content whatever the circumstances. Joy comes from within, but it is also a process. I didn't inherit dominant "positive attitude genes" from my parents, but through the years I am becoming more like those people I spend time with and admire. My hope is that my parents would be proud of the Joy I am becoming.

My trip would not have been the same without my family and friends in the Midwest, and Bonnie, Rita and Ellen, the man in the black truck, Anthony, Judy, Tony, Glenn and Amy, Lana and Laurie, Greg, Debbie, Ivan and Erin, and so many others. Was it God who put those people in my path? On this trip I learned to lean on God from the first storm in Indiana to the storm and detours in Minnesota. Now I would have to lean on him to help me through this situation with my knee and other challenges that are bound to come my way.

As that one little misstep pushed the pause button on my trip west, I made a choice to focus on my relationship with him. For years I hadn't made time for God. Slowly I drifted away. I knew he was always there, and I never quit believing in him, but we hadn't been close in a long time. God had become like a childhood friend who lived on the other side of the country, and I had deemed it too much trouble to visit. It's not like I didn't know it was happening, but I don't remember any lines of demarcation either. There wasn't a crack-in-the-earth moment when I felt like I jumped from living for God to living for myself. One thing just led to another and to another.

I wanted to have the faith my mother had. She trusted God with every aspect of her life, and it was time for me to do the same. I missed having a close relationship with God. Trusting him would certainly bring more joy, and my life, not just my trip west, had become all about *finding joy*.

As you travel down the road of life, I implore you to embrace life. Don't wait. Do it now. Squeeze every bit of joy you can out of every day. Choose joy despite your circumstances. Finding joy in life is about the choices we make, and *joy is a choice*. My parents named me Joy, but it is my choice to live up to the name they gave me. And I want you to know you have the same option. My wish is that you, too, will choose joy.

Epilogue

July 29 – August 9, 2019

Words cannot express how grateful I am that my knee injury happened in the presence of my cousins Ivan and Erin, who were there to help me. Imagine if I'd had the accident alone in a national park, miles from family. Sure, I would have worked something out. I always do, but being with Erin and Ivan made the situation much easier. Not only did Ivan take me and pick me up from the hospital, but he washed, folded, and sorted my laundry while I hung out in the emergency room. He and Erin traded bedrooms with me, giving me their master bedroom on the ground floor. They said I could stay as long as I needed and recommended two of Spokane's finest knee surgeons, should I choose to seek their expertise.

My week filled with injury-related conversations with family, friends, insurance representatives, and an orthopedic doctor's office staff. Ivan and Erin's dog, Mr. Scott, kept me company during the day while they worked. Siblings, cousins, and friends discussed every plausible scenario to get me and my rig home before or after recovering. My sister Sherrie offered to fly to Spokane and fly home with me. And my friend Lisa went so far as saying she would quit her job, fly to Spokane, and drive my rig and me home. After weighing the pros and cons of every possibility, we opted for Lisa to keep her job and my brother Tom to fly from Asheville Regional to Spokane International and drive my motorhome and me across the country to my home in Georgia. Oh, how good my family and friends are to me!

Thursday night, four days after my accident, my cousins drove me around Spokane, pointing out the bike trail I didn't get to ride, a house they rented out, two of the four GNCs they owned, a revitalized neighborhood, and the downtown district. Friday night, the day I would have been joining Jenny in Seattle, Erin and Ivan invited friends for dinner, and the five of us talked by their firepit on the cozy back patio. Tom arrived Saturday afternoon, and we ate and talked by the fire until midnight again. I thanked God for my supportive family.

It took me three months to get to Spokane, and Tom intended to get me home in five to seven days. Tom would not be taking "the scenic route," as my dad would say. The scenic route from my home in Georgia to my cousins' home in Washington clocked in at 4,600 miles. The "straight home" route Tom and I would take would be closer to 2,400 miles.

We left Ivan and Erin's on Sunday, one week after I had arrived, and Tom drove four hundred miles to a Walmart in Bozeman, Montana, where we stayed overnight. The next day, he drove from Bozeman to The Little Bighorn National Battlefield in Montana. Before I left Georgia, my friend Tanya had suggested visiting Little Bighorn. The battlefield had remained on my radar since she told me how much her family enjoyed the historical park.

Even though Tom's goal was to get me home as quickly as possible, he still took the time to push me in a wheelchair around the grounds and up a steep hill to view the battlefield and the mass grave of the soldiers of the 7th Cavalry Regiment who died with Custer. With heavy hearts, my brother and I stood on the ground where Lieutenant Colonel George A. Custer made his famous last stand in the battle against the Northern Cheyenne, the Arapaho, and the Lakota Sioux Tribes. What looked like millions of snow-white tombstones in domino-style rows brought tears to my eyes. What a somber landmark.

The story behind that battle and so many others made little sense to me, but I thanked my brother for allowing me to experience such a big piece of the history of our country. Gravesites, especially war- and military-related gravesites, always make me emotional. Little Bighorn would be our only touristy stop on our eastern trek home. From the battlefield, we drove to a private campground in Casper, Wyoming, rounding out our second day on the road with 436 miles.

After Tom and I checked in and found our site at the Casper Campground—a run-down gravel parking lot—we drove to a five-star Thai restaurant for the best meal of our trip. When Tom and I returned to the campground, a couple in a truck and trailer occupied our site. The woman told Tom they had made a mistake, but she wasn't going to move. She called the owner who told—not asked—Tom to pull into a neighboring site. Tom backed into the smaller site but didn't appreciate the odd way the owner handled the mix-up. Though the spot sufficed for the night, the campground did not receive five stars from the Walker duo.

From Casper, my brother drove 484 miles to a state recreation area called Mormon Island in Grand Island, Nebraska. After circling the grounds, we picked site #3 for the view of the lake. Tom built a fire while I fixed a simple spaghetti dinner. The campground host told Tom to take all the firewood he wanted, no charge, and we enjoyed a peaceful evening by the fire with a view of the lake. Then at 3:30 in the morning, Tom and I woke to the sound of light rain. As he closed the bathroom vent, a whoosh of wind almost pushed my motorhome onto its side. Huge bolts of lightning flashed across the sky. Trees fell as though passed out, drunk. Two lay in the middle of the road next to my motorhome. A THUD on Rig's roof made my heart jump.

"That must have been a branch. Do you think I should drive away from these trees?" Tom said.

"How could you see to drive? Where would we go? You'd have to unplug us first. You know we're plugged in."

We waited. We watched tree branches brushing the ground next to us, water whooshing across the roads, and tents being tossed about like balloons. Then came another THUMP overhead.

"We are sitting ducks, Tom. What should we do?"

I prayed. Neither of us had checked the weather forecast since Spokane. I kicked myself for not checking the weather and *still* not having a plan for inclement weather.

"Nothing serious," Tom said. "My app says wind gusts are only going to be 60 to 90 mph. Says there will be trees down and damaging winds around all the surrounding counties. According to the radar, we're in the eye of the storm for another hour."

"We've got an hour of this? Seriously, Tom? What are we going to do?"

More branches and trees fell. More thunder. More lightning. More heart palpitations. Tent campers rushed to their cars. Tom and I did nothing. FOOMP! A third, much larger, branch hit the roof. Thankfully, the roof held against the branches as they tried to make their way into my dining room. I was grateful my motorhome held up under the storm. Tom inspected the ceiling, running his hand across the length of the living area. Nothing. Tom paced, looking out one window and then the other. We talked and I prayed some more.

"You sure there's no rain coming in? That last one sounded huge. I'm so thankful you're with me, Tom. The only reason I'm not freaking out is because you're here. Did I tell you about the storm I drove through in Minnesota?"

Tom and I diverted our attention with a conversation about storm survival. Maybe we should have done something like lie on the floor and pull a mattress over our heads, but no strategies or safety tips like that came to mind. After forty-five minutes, the storm calmed down, as did the Walker siblings. According to the radar, another round of storms would hit thirty minutes later. Tom climbed back into his bed and both of us read until we fell asleep. We were so exhausted, the second round didn't wake either of us. At daybreak, we woke to serious damage in the park. Tom walked to the shower house and talked with people assessing the damage. Limbs and downed trees covered the park. Tom climbed up and inspected my rig's roof and threw the branches and logs off.

"I didn't see any damage."

"Seriously? No damage? Nothing? Rigdon is tougher than I thought. Wow! I can't believe that. Well, okay then. Let's get out of here."

Tom unplugged my rig and inched out of our site.

Twenty seconds later, he eased on the brake and pointed to a fallen tree. "Look, Joy. We considered that site last night. That oak must have been a hundred years old."

"That's eerie, Tom. If we had picked that site . . ." I stopped myself. "Look at that blue tent. It's totally flat. Where do you think all those tent campers went? Oh, Tom, they must have been so scared."

"I'm sure most of them drove away before it got too bad. We will never know, though. It's like when you get stopped by an accident on the interstate. You never find out what happened."

"Yes. You're right. I always hate that."

Trees blocked all but one road in the park. What a nightmare. Since daybreak the rangers had been methodically cutting pathways for campers to drive out. We noticed the entrance gate was closed and blocked off with cones and signs that said: "Park closed until further notice." What a scary night. Still, I felt protected in yet another storm. Surviving the storm reaffirmed my recent resolve to trust in God, whether in storms or sunny skies.

We left Grand Island thankful we didn't get trapped there—or worse. Tom wanted to beat his record of 484 miles, hoping to hit five hundred on our fourth day on the road. We got to Kansas City in time for rush hour, which unfortunately added three hours to our drive time, thus resulting in Tom missing his five-hundred-mile goal by nearly fifty miles.

Finding a decent place to camp close to the highway each night challenged my brother and me. We could not wake up and determine where we would camp that night. Tom wanted to drive four to five hundred miles each day, but we had no guarantee that would happen. So, each day we drove until late afternoon, guesstimated how much farther we could drive before nightfall, and searched *AllStays* for a campground close to that distance. We both preferred state parks but weren't willing to drive out of our way to get to one. A bonus would be to find a restaurant nearby, but the night in Casper was the only time that worked out.

After a respectable 456-mile day, we pulled into Graham Cave State Park in Montgomery City, Missouri, seventy-five miles west of Saint Louis, at dusk. What a hidden gem. The park encompassed 369 acres. I wanted to explore the cave, but I could not walk across a campsite, much less down a trail or into a cave. We picked a level site and Tom walked to the host to pay. After I plugged my rig into shore power, I dumped the stormwater that had puddled in my bike cover, drenching my legs and feet in the process. Tom had driven twelve to fourteen hours a day for four days. The long days and short nights taxed us mentally and physically.

After dinner I thought it might be a good time to check in with my cousins in Spokane.

I called Erin and she invited us back.

"The pavers left an hour ago. The driveway's finished. It looks good. It's all nice and smooth now."

"Oh, that's awesome. I wish we could see it. Let me ask Tom if he'll turn around. We are only about 1,800 miles from you now."

We chuckled.

Erin said, "How 'bout I send you a couple of pictures?"

"Yeah, that'd probably be better. I'm happy for you guys."

Leaving Graham Cave made me sad. Gigantic, deciduous trees surrounded the campground, and the newly paved, curvy road enticed the cyclist in me. We didn't even see the entrance of the cave I longed to check out. It is easy to say I will go back to places, but I know that may never happen. The states offer so many spectacular places to explore. I cannot possibly see every park even once, yet there are many places I want to visit again. To be honest, I have left almost every state park, and certainly every national park, hoping to return, yet knowing the odds of returning to most of them are slim. If I wanted to stay focused on my goal of riding my bike in all fifty states, I would not have time to return to the states I had checked off on this trip for quite a while.

Our mission on day five was to overnight as close to my home as possible, so that on day six, Tom could visit with our sister Sandi, pick up some chairs she had for him, get me settled into my home, and still allow time to rent a car and drive to his home in Asheville, two hundred miles from my house. On top of driving me 2,400 miles across the country, Tom found out mid-week he would be making a seven-hundred-mile trek to New Orleans on Sunday to help his son, Zach, move out of his apartment and drive him back to Asheville on Tuesday. I am certain that during our trek across the country, Tom scratched "truck driver" off his potential retirement job list.

Thursday evening, Tom and I arrived at a family-owned pitiful excuse for a campground. We chose that one because it checked the most important boxes: close to the highway, a hundred miles from my home, and full hookups. Tom said if we found a campground with full hookups, he would flush my tanks well on Friday morning, and we could pull into my driveway with that task completed. I loved his plan because I did not wish to deal with flushing my tanks at home, knowing I wouldn't be able to drive for at least six weeks.

When I called the number for the campground to make a reservation and tell them we would arrive a little after 7:30 p.m., the owner told us to call again upon arrival. We arrived at 7:41, exhausted, and waited nineteen minutes for a miserably sick girl in a bathrobe to walk out and tell us she didn't know how to check us in, but that her brother should arrive soon to help us. At 8:10, her scruffy, thirty-something brother directed us to an open site. I noted many vintage trailers surrounded by more clutter than a vintage resale shop and junk yard combined. Tom paid cash, got a receipt, and thanked the guy for allowing us to stay for the night. We were thankful the site contained full hookups, as the owner had promised us on the phone.

My amazing brother got the electric hooked up as darkness enveloped us. We reminisced and marveled at our accomplishments for the past five days. Now, just over a hundred miles from my home, Tom walked with a spring in his step and contentment on his face. However, I became melancholy. I looked forward to being home, yet I had planned to get back home in

November or December, not the beginning of August. Not only was I returning home earlier than I had expected, but I wouldn't drive, frequent the gym, mow my grass, ride, or do anything physical for a long, long time. I was also unsure if knee surgery was in my future.

The next morning, I sensed that Tom was awake and moving, but I stayed in bed, half asleep. He asked me at 7:30 if I would like to stay in bed while he drove for a while. Before we left Spokane, I had envisioned doing that every day of the trip home, but the idea felt too prima donna-ish. Instead, I made the cross-country trip sitting on my swivel chair behind the passenger seat with my legs propped up on Tom's suitcase and a couple of pillows so we could talk.

"That sounds like a great idea but let me go to the restroom one more time before you dump the tanks."

My brother grinned at me and slowly shook his head.

"You've already flushed out the tanks?"

"Drained and refilled both tanks twice."

"Oh, my word! I guess I was really sleeping."

"Yeah . . . took me over an hour to get everything ready to go. Your tanks are clean."

"What an awesome brother I have!"

Tom drove me to the bathhouse, and we began the last leg of our trip. He drove the final 120 miles to our sister Sandi's house, just eight miles from my own, without stopping. We arrived at 11 a.m. Friday, as Tom had planned before he flew to Spokane. Sandi and her husband, Mark, greeted us in their driveway. They had made improvements to their home, so I hobbled around for an hour, marveling at the upgrades.

Tom hugged Sandi. "Tag. You're it. I'm going to drop Joy off at her house, but I'm going home."

When we pulled into my driveway, Tom wasted no time plugging my motorhome into the 30-amp outdoor outlet that my electrician friend, Steve, had installed when I bought Rig almost a year earlier. Tom brought items inside that I thought I might need over the next day or two, when Sandi could come help me. A man from Enterprise picked Tom up. Then Tom drove back to my house and packed the rental car. He hugged his baby sister, now in tears, and was prepared to get home to Asheville by 5 p.m.

"I can't thank you enough. You are the best. You are my favorite brother. I love you. Call me when you get home."

What a bittersweet moment. Goodbyes like that are always difficult for me. The cross-country time with my brother was priceless. Some nights, my belly ached from laughter as he told me stories of our childhood, some for the first time, like the one about how he taught his friend Brent to drive, or how he tried to squeeze his car through two trees—twice, but they are Tom's stories to share. I was happy to have the 2,400 miles behind us and grateful to be home, yet I didn't know why my journey west had to take such a quick U-turn. Having run out of pain medication halfway across the country, I was hurting and had no idea what my future held in terms of recovery. Lots of emotions.

Still, I had much to be thankful for, and I needed time to process it all. And time? I had plenty of that now. And I decided to spend more of it learning and growing in my relationship with God. He has given me the gift of life and the ability to find joy in every circumstance. God is the source of my joy, and for that, I am grateful. I thank God for sparing my life so many times on this trip and for returning me to my home in Georgia.

Upon reflection, I realize I cannot go through life without having faith in God. From those conversations at my friend Julie's kitchen table in Indiana to my cousins' home in Washington, I had come a long way in what I called my spiritual crawl. Now, I was moving toward God, but I was in more of a reflective, contemplative state. I didn't make any big decision to pray more or read my Bible or go to church. I didn't talk to anyone about my spiritual journey—not even my friend Julie who unknowingly had sparked this journey with her simple question, "How are you doing spiritually?" But I decided to keep walking toward him—whatever that might look like—and I determined to quit doing things I knew would disappoint him. I resolved to live my life with integrity and purpose. It was a step—a step in the right direction, and it made me feel good.

I had not traveled 7,000 miles by myself. True, my brother was with me for the last 2,400, but I realized that God was with me for *every* mile. He was there as I took in the breathtaking views of the Mississippi River, Badlands, Mount Rushmore, Crazy Horse, Old Faithful, Mammoth Hot Springs, the Grand Canyon of Yellowstone, the mountains and valleys along the Going-to-the-Sun Road in Glacier National Park, and the panoramic views at the overlooks on the Hiawatha trail.

Sometimes it's the journey and the inevitable storms along the way that enrich our souls and make us stronger if we just persist. I may not reach my dream of riding in all fifty states, but I know now that the growth, the "finding myself" part of the journey is the point of the pursuit. There will be obstacles, but I will not quit. For it is in the journey that I grow. Perhaps it is time for you to get out there and find what brings *you* joy.

I may be on crutches, but I'm behind you every step of the way.

One More Thing

Thank you for reading *Finding Joy in the West*. If you enjoyed it, I hope you will share it with others and leave a review on Amazon or Goodreads or similar sites. But really, I want you to know how amazing our country is, and I want you to go out and experience it yourself (if you haven't done so already). Create your own *joy*.

If traveling or cycling is not your deal, figure out what is and do it. What is on your bucket list? Do you want to paint, learn to play the guitar, learn another language, run a marathon, spend time with your children or grandchildren, write poetry or lyrics? Find your passion and pursue it with all your heart. Life is short. Life doesn't promise us tomorrow, so get out there and live your best life today. If you wake up tomorrow, do it all over again. If you can work out a way to get paid for your passion, all the better, but get out there and do it. Find your dream and live it. Find *your* joy!

Acknowledgements

This book would not have happened without the support of my family and friends. To my siblings, you mean more to me than you will ever know. To complete this project, I relied on the support of Janice, Nancy, Linda, Tom, and Mari Ann to read and offer feedback on the early drafts. Dan chipped in on a later draft, and Nancy, and Mari Ann stuck with me as we tweaked the final drafts. Also forthcoming with valuable writing advice were Beverly, Amber, Rona, and Millicent. Patti offered both encouragement and suggestions on everything related to the project. When it came to the final drafts and publishing and marketing, Chip, Melinda, Rebecca, Garrett, and Jane gave me more information and resources than I knew what to do with. Thanks to all of you. And oh, what a blessing to have Ardie and Vickie step in and help me get it all put together.

The Lord only knows what I would have done without Amy and Kathy. Amy held my hand through each stage and offered her support when the number of drafts exceeded my stamina. And I appreciate Kathy not only for her expertise in building my website, and helping me build an email list, but also for her patience with me in sending the first twenty-five emails, each of which required her last-minute help.

To all who have read my blog posts and offered your support in other ways, thank you for your encouragement. Thank you to those who have written the books about traveling, writing, publishing, marketing, and reaching goals that I have devoured. And this story would not have been worth reading if not for the kind souls I met along the way, many of whom have become friends. There is no way I can list everyone who lent a hand with *Finding Joy in the West*, so if I have left your name off this page, please know I appreciate you and thank you for helping me on this journey.

Finding Joy in the West has truly been a group effort. I am closer to all of you because of the struggles portrayed in this book and in the completion of it.

And finally, thank you to God for helping me realize that you are the source of my joy.

About Finding Joy in the West

Ride along with Joy, a retired elementary physical education teacher, on an inspiring quest to ride her bike in all fifty states. Anticipating scenic state and national parks, Joy discovers much more along her journey west. This adventure offers a rich array of experiences—highs and lows, floods and storms, sunshine and serendipity.

If you're a cyclist, an avid traveler, an RV enthusiast, or simply someone who likes to read about adventures, travel with Joy as she navigates challenges, embraces new and old relationships, marvels at God's creations, and deepens her faith. Her story is a testament to resilience and the pursuit of dreams.

Whether your aspiration is to embark on a biking adventure, explore new horizons, start a new career, or simply find more joy, *Finding Joy in the West* will inspire your journey.

Coming Soon

Finding Joy in the East: The Lighthouse Tour
by Joy M. Walker

Follow Joy as she continues her
journey traveling in her motorhome and
riding her bike on the east coast.

About the Author

Photo by Camera Works.

After a thirty-year career teaching elementary physical education, Joy M. Walker bought a motorhome and embarked on a quest to ride her bike in all fifty states. *Finding Joy in the West* fulfills her lifelong dream of publishing and encouraging others to find joy.

Learn more about Joy by following her:

Blog at www.joymwalker.com
Instagram.com/findingjoy626
Facebook.com/joy.m.walker.author
or contact her at joy@joymwalker.com.